CASH MANAGEMENT FOR THE DESIGN FIRM

CASH MANAGEMENT FOR THE DESIGN FIRM

FRANK A. STASIOWSKI

JOHN WILEY & SONS, INC.
New York / Chichester / Brisbane / Toronto / Singapore

Library of Congress Cataloging in Publication Data:

Stasiowski, Frank, 1948–
    Cash management for the design firm / Frank A. Stasiowksi.
      p. cm.
    Includes index.
    ISBN 0-471-59711-2 (alk. paper)
     1. Architectural firms—United States—Management. 2. Engineering
firms—United States—Management. 3. Small business—United
States—Cash position. I. Title.
NA1996.S72 1993
720'.68'1—dc20   93-14656

Printed in the United States of America

10 9 8 7 6 5 4 3 2 1

To my mother, Kathleen (Stasiowski) Worthington, who taught me to balance my first checking account, who helped me with my first paper route, and who has always stood behind me in every decision I have made.

PREFACE

Cash flow is so vital to the existence of a firm that it must be constantly monitored, and requires careful planning. A design firm lives or dies on its ability to manage cash above all else. For this reason, Chapter 1 provides an overview of cash management techniques.

Project budgeting is an immediate outgrowth of cash management because, ultimately, projects bring in cash. Chapter 2 provides a budgeting system to apply to projects, and suggests corrective measures to prevent costly overruns. Quite naturally, the price you charge the client directly affects cash flow as well, and Chapter 3 explains how the project manager and financial director develop profitable project pricing structures.

The next step after budgeting and pricing is controlling costs. Two full chapters are devoted to controlling project and overhead costs—Chapters 4 and 5. Recognizing the danger signals of potential cost overruns is perhaps the biggest challenge of a firm's financial leader.

Receiving an influx of sufficient capital to maintain operations depends greatly on the structuring of a firm's invoicing and billing process. Chapter 6—Getting Paid provides guidance on ways to improve collections and reiterates the significance of healthy cash flow.

The firm cannot rely on individual project plans alone; design firms must have an overall company planning and monitoring system, such as that outlined in Chapter 7—Planning and Monitoring Performance. A standardized contract format is equally important in providing an overall consistent approach to project budgets, prices, and cash management. Chapter 8—Contract Negotiations explains the most profitable contract types, and the principles of negotiating.

Financial controls are implemented to ensure that cash

flow is directed through the proper channels—and financial controls include financial reporting systems, the purchasing process, capital equipment acquisitions, and internal financial controls. These subjects are addressed in Chapters 9, 10, 11, and 12, respectively.

The final chapter looks at who the financial manager is within the structure of the design firm. Whether the financial manager is an employee charged specifically with the sole task of managing a firm's finances or a managing principal controlling finances along with myriad other responsibilities, the role remains the same. The "financial manager," as such, doesn't have to perform each and every task, but rather is the individual who weaves the intricate elements of finance together into a coherent force driving the firm's financial stability and profits forever upward.

FRANK STASIOWSKI

Newton Massachusetts
May 1993

AUTHOR'S NOTE

For seventeen years, Practice Management Associates has been leading workshops on finance for principals of architectural, engineering, and planning firms. As these workshops evolved, it became apparent that there exists a strong need to disseminate even more knowledge on financial techniques to managers with nonfinancial backgrounds. The principals of smaller firms in particular need this information in a format they can readily absorb and utilize immediately. This text was designed to meet that need.

Before beginning, please note that the term "financial manager" is used frequently throughout the book. While many firms have a specific individual assigned to the role of financial manager, this term is meant to denote anyone within the firm who handles the financial management duties—be it managing principal, partner, or chief executive operator.

Exercises appear at the end of most sections within the chapters, helpful checklists appear throughout, and final examinations at the end of each chapter. These exercises and examinations can and should be used to reinforce the text. These exercises are in the format of multiple choice questions, true or false statements, fill-in-the-blanks or discussion problems. For multiple choice questions, it is necessary to choose the most correct answer from the choices provided, based on information given in the text. For true/false questions, determine whether the statements given are true or false, and circle either "T" or "F." Fill-in-the-blanks are self-explanatory. There are also some instances where you will be asked to examine your own firm's financial management systems. While most of the quiz and test material is presented for reinforcement of the principles presented, be sure to fully research and complete all of the questions and challenges we offer. This will allow you to piece together a thorough overview of your firm and its cash management needs.

When you complete this text, you will not only have learned how to manage cash flow of your firm, but you will, if you fill out all of the questions, exercises, and examinations, gain a clearer picture of where your firm is at today and where it is headed for the future. Avenues for improvement will become evident as well, and you'll know where to turn to initiate those changes, based on the information offered here.

Successful firms have one common trait: they know where they have been, where they are going, and how they are going to get there. Their principals understand that design and engineering excellence alone do not create profits. Project profits are generated by tough project management that fits into an integrated firmwide cash management system. When regularly and systematically applied, the tactics outlined in this book on financial management will result in increased profitability at minimal cost.

Some of the techniques described in this book will appear overwhelming to those not familiar with them, yet they are relatively straightforward when worked through once or twice. By religiously practicing each step of financial planning outlined here, firms that previously operated on a reactive basis will find new ways of increasing profits by being able to track what is really happening with the firm's finances.

I trust you will examine the concepts presented here and begin to incorporate them into your daily practice. They are basic, easily used, and they work. The rewards are there if you take the time to plan.

FRANK A. STASIOWSKI

President, Practice Management Associates, Ltd.
Publisher, Professional Services Management Journal

ACKNOWLEDGEMENTS

The author would like to acknowledge the following sources for information for this text: *Financial Management for the Design Professional* by Lowell Goetz and Frank Stasiowski, *Distance Education Course on Financial Management for Australian Architects* by Frank Stasiowski, and Bill Fanning, Director of Research, whose financial input as an accountant has helped shape our financial research for over a decade.

In addition, the author would like to thank Julia Willard and Lisa Geiger for their work in organizing the text and figures for this book. Many thanks also to Judy Vulker, former Director of Training for the Royal Australian Institute of Architects for her input into the organization and development of the book.

CONTENTS

1
MANAGING CASH

Chapter Summary

- Suggestions for obtaining a line of credit
- What to do if you are rejected by a bank
- Other financing sources available for equipment loans
- How to obtain additional financing with employee stock ownership plans (ESOPs)
- How to prepare a forecast of cash receipts and disbursements
- Bank services available to improve cash management

Cash Flow and Success

Proper management of a design firm's cash reserves is extremely important, and keeping a positive cash flow in good times and bad is essential for continued existence. Cash flow is so vital to the existence of a firm that it must be constantly monitored. While the person in charge of finance is closest to the cash situation on a daily basis, the proper management of cash requires more than merely reacting to situations as they occur. It requires careful planning to ensure the necessary cash available when needed, while minimizing bank borrowings or disturbing of short-term investments.

1.1 CASH FROM CLIENTS

As a result of the banking crises of the early 1990s, there is increasing need to recognize that the primary source of cash in design practice is your clients. It is impossible to place too much emphasis on improving the negotiating and contracting skills of each design professional in your office through constant training and attention to these two vital areas of practice. A few rules are in order to set the stage for the balance of this text:

1. *Check Credit on All New Clients.* In today's world this simple act is a cash preserving strategy protecting you from investing in a future bad debt. It is bad business not to do a routine credit check. Even you are checked when you purchase more than $50 worth of merchandise at a store.

2. *Get Money Up Front.* No design firm can afford to finance its clients. Thus, every client should be asked for a two to three month advance payment to be credited to the final invoice on a project. If a client won't give you money in advance, you may be receiving a "telegraphed message" about that client's intentions once you start working.

3. *Learn How to Negotiate.* Study, study, study, study, study, study, study, and when you are done, study more. Then practice negotiating tactics everywhere. And if you don't like the heat, get out of the kitchen and put someone in who really enjoys negotiating and does it well.

4. *Stop Work Early.* When clients don't pay, they are not good clients. Stop work.

Remember, in the ultimate scheme of things, all cash comes from doing work. Put your mind in gear, and put as much creativity into up front cash generation techniques as you put into your design effort. And remember, lack of cash is the primary cause in 92% of all bankruptcies.

1.2 SOURCES OF CASH FLOW ADVICE

When cash is tight there are several outside sources that a firm can use to help with its cash management problems. The principal source is the firm's banker. The banker is usually well experienced in cash management procedures, and sometimes banks will have a specialist on staff to assist customers in improving cash management. If this expertise is to be truly useful, the banker must be thoroughly familiar with the firm and its operations. Most of a banker's clients are probably manufacturing and retailing businesses, which means that the banker may have relatively little familiarity with firms engaged in providing services. Therefore it will take an effort to familiarize the banker with a professional service firm.

Additionally, because of the savings and loan crisis, banks are exceedingly cautious about lending to firms without marketable inventory as collateral. This means it is even more important today to keep in touch with your banker regularly.

A good practice for the design professional is to keep the banker advised of operations by meeting at least once or twice a year to go over the firm's financial statements and prospects. Quarterly meetings are even better. One thing to keep in mind is that these meetings can be beneficial to both parties. The banker is a good source of marketing information because of membership in the Chamber of Commerce and other organizations as well as associations with many businesses. Often a banker is the first to know about firms moving into and out of the area and has an indication about new facilities being planned in the region.

The firm's outside accountant is another source of assistance in cash management. The CPA sees many types of businesses and is in a good position to make suggestions for improving cash management. During the course of an audit of financial review, the accountant studies cash flow procedures and can draw on his or her background serving other clients to make good suggestions. One thing to remember is that if you ever want to make any significant changes in your accounting procedures, talk them over first with your accountant. The accountant is also a good general business adviser because, through audit and tax work, he or she knows more about your firm than possibly anyone else. The accountant can often make good suggestions from the vantage point of an independent outside resource.

See Exhibit 1.1 for a checklist on utilizing your consultants.

EXERCISE 1.2 ▨

Your Use of Consultants

True or False

T   F   The principal source for cash management decisions is a firm's banker.

CHECKLIST FOR UTILIZING CONSULTANTS

YES	NO	
☐	☐	Is your banker adept at cash management procedures?
☐	☐	Does your bank have a cash management specialist?
☐	☐	Does your bank understand how design firm cash flow differs from that of manufacturing firms?
☐	☐	Do you sit down with your banker at least twice a year?
☐	☐	Have you thoroughly utilized your banker as a source for information about upcoming work?
☐	☐	Has your firm ever used an outside auditor?
☐	☐	How closely involved is your accountant in the firm's cash flow procedures?

Exhibit 1.1   There are several outside sources that you can use to help with cash management problems.

T	F	Bankers are generally familiar with cash flow operations in service firms.
T	F	A design firm should meet with its banker once every two years to go over cash flow.
T	F	An outside auditor is another source of assistance in cash management.
T	F	The only real source of cash in design practice is a firm's clients.
T	F	A CPA cannot assist in cash management.
T	F	Clients never pay cash in advance to a design firm.
T	F	It is only important that one person in a firm understand how to negotiate contracts.
T	F	Any changes in accounting procedures need not be discussed with your accountant.
T	F	Your accountant knows more about your firm than possibly anyone else.
T	F	Quarterly meetings with your banker are highly unnecessary.

1.3   OBTAINING A CREDIT LINE

In spite of the banking crisis and a shortage of funds "loan-able" by banks, most firms still need a line of credit to support their working capital needs and to help expand operations. Generally, the best time to arrange for a line of credit is when the firm does not have an immediate financial need or when banks are eager to loan money. Unfortunately, you cannot always time your requirements to fit the banker's needs and that means you will be competing for funds along with everyone else.

It is important to sell the banker like any other client when preparing a loan request. That means the banker should understand the objectives of the loan and have confidence in your firm. The banker must understand how design firms operate and your firm's position in the marketplace. He or she must learn your firm's strategy and its strengths and must have full and complete financial information, both current and projected. Most importantly, you need to document how the loan will be repaid. The firm should ask for a revolving line of credit, which means that as portions of the loan are repaid, they are available to be re-borrowed up to the limits of the credit line.

Bankers will generally want security for the loan, which means a pledge of accounts receivable. Usually, the amount of the loan will be determined by the amount of accounts receivable on the books that the banker considers current, that is, less than 90 days old. In that connection, it is important for the banker to understand the difference between a 90-day-old account and a retainer. A retainer is money withheld from the design professional's invoices to assure compliance with the terms of the contract. Since only a portion of the accounts receivable are paid, the balance remains on the books and should be identified as a retainer rather than as a partially paid invoice that grows older each month. If the firm does not distinguish between the two on its accounts receivable aging report and if the difference is not explained to the banker, he or she cannot be expected to make the distinction. Furthermore, many bankers do not understand the nature of the design profession and the fact that all receivables past 90 days are not potential bad debts. The banker should be made to understand that often a design professional working for a developer, for instance, will not be paid until the developer obtains his financing. The more you can get the banker to understand how your firm operates, the better your chances are for a loan.

Banks will lend a percentage against the accounts receivable, and the interest rate is generally related to the prime lending rate, or the rate that is available to the bank's largest and best customers. In many instances, particularly with smaller or newer firms, banks will request a personal guarantee of the loan by the principals in the firm. The principals should expect to be confronted with this request and must be prepared to deal with it.

In most cases the bank loan officer assembles the information presented, adds whatever analysis he or she makes and/or that of a credit analyst who reviews the application, and submits it to the bank's loan committee, made up of senior officials in the bank. The loan committee makes the final determination, after asking the loan officer for any additional information it may require.

If your application is ever rejected, you should meet with the loan officer to find out why. Possibly, the loan committee may feel it has enough of a particular type of loan and may not want to accept any more of this type in order to diversify its risks. In that case, you might be able to take the application directly to another bank with better results. On the other hand, if there is a weakness in the firm's finances, it will have to be corrected before submitting the application to another bank.

Exhibit 1.2 (on facing page) shows a cover letter for a loan application. Note in particular the kinds of information provided and the explanation of the purpose of the loan.

EXERCISE 1.3 ■■■■■■■■■■■■■■■■■■■■■■■■■■■■■■■■■

Credit Lines

Multiple Choice

1. The best time to arrange for a line of credit is
    a. when you do not have sufficient work.
    b. when you have an immediate cash need.
    c. when you do not have an immediate cash need.
    d. none of the above.

**EXAMPLE OF TRANSMITTAL LETTER
FOR LOAN APPLICATION**

**The Williams Design Collaborative
Interior Architecture/Facilities Planning/Project Coordination**

First National Bank of Bigtown, USA

Dear Banker:

Enclosed are financial statements and data on our firm. Specifically included in this package are

1. End of year and current financial statements on both cash and accrual basis
2. Accounts receivable aging schedule
3. Cash flow projection showing the effects of borrowing and repayment
4. A listing of major clients and prospective new projects showing our backlog of work
5. Personal financial statements for the principals
6. Corporate brochure including resumes of the principals

Our desire for bank financing is threefold: (1) We require working capital in order to continue our growth and to anticipate the requirements of upcoming projects. The nature of an interior architecture firm such as ours necessitates heavy expenditures prior to the start-up as well as during the performance of a project. This is because a portion of our interior design work is performed for building developers at a reduced rate until tenants are located and signed. Our role as consultant to larger architectural firms also delays our receipt of payments because the prime professional is paid before the consultant is paid. (2) We would like to convert our existing short-term loans to a more stable line of credit so that we do not have to keep renewing the loans on an individual basis. (3) Although our current banking relationship is in New Orleans, our office is in Houston. We recognize the importance of developing a strong banking relationship in Houston.

Initially, we are requesting $250,000—which is approximately 5% of our annual cash revenue. This would be in the form of a revolving line of credit. We would expect to pay not more than two points over the current prime lending rate. We anticipate the length of the loan to be one year (renewable terms) with interest payments on a quarterly basis.

After establishing a good relationship with your bank, we would seek to enlarge our revolving line of credit based on our firm's continuing needs and its ability to secure new and larger projects.

If you require any additional information, please do not hesitate to call me.

Yours very truly,

John L. Smith, Managing Principal
JLS:jc

Exhibit 1.2   This letter should go to a specific individual at the bank, either someone you know or someone to whom you have explained your requirements in advance.

2. In order to request a line of credit you must
   a. be sure the banker understands how design firm cash flow operates.
   b. explain to your banker your strengths and weaknesses.
   c. document how the loan will be repaid.
   d. all of the above.

3. In a design firm, a 90-day-old account is
   a. not healthy for the firm.
   b. a bad debt.
   c. a concern.
   d. not a potential bad debt.

4. Banks usually request
   a. no loan guarantee.
   b. a personal guarantee of a loan.
   c. you to negotiate the lending rate.
   d. none of the above.

5. Your application may be rejected because
   a. the bank has too many loans of the type you requested.
   b. you haven't prepared your proposal properly.
   c. your debt ratio is too high.
   d. all of the above.
   e. none of the above.

1.4 INTERNAL SOURCES OF FUNDS

Sources of funds within the firm can come from additional equity sold to new or existing stockholders or additional partners in the case of a partnership. Employee stock ownership plans (ESOPs) are an excellent source of internally generated funds that appear to fit the requirements of many firms, though they are still not widely used. An ESOP consists of a trust made up of all the employees and formed for the primary purpose of buying shares in the firm. Instead of a regular profit-sharing plan that places its funds in outside investments, the profits declared by the firm are placed with the ESOP, which then buys shares of the firm's stock, and thereby returns the funds to the firm. In effect, there is no cash outflow when profit-sharing funds are turned over to an ESOP as there is when they are placed with a regular profit-sharing plan.

A major stockholder can also divest holdings over time by

selling shares to the ESOP, which can borrow from a bank to finance the purchase. ESOP borrowings are backed by the financial strength of the firm and the firm's pledge to pay off the note through periodic contributions to the plan. An alternative is for the ESOP to hold a life insurance policy on the major stockholder and premiums paid through contributions. The policy enables the ESOP to buy the major stockholder's holdings from his or her estate.

A prime advantage of the ESOP is that it expands the owernership of the firm to all employees, which improves morale and productivity. At the same time an ESOP can maintain the closely held nature of the firm by a provision that requires departing employees to offer to sell their shares back to the plan upon termination. While there is dilution of equity as more shares are created, it should be offset by the growth in the firm sparked by the owner-employees. Control of the ESOP rests with the trustees appointed by the board of directors. Since the trustees are usually the major stockholders, control of the firm does not pass from their hands.

Another advantage of the ESOP is that it is able to finance equipment purchases with pretax dollars. For example, if the firm needs $100,000 for capital equipment, the ESOP borrows the funds (backed by the firm as a guarantor of the note) and buys stock in the firm. The firm uses the money to buy the equipment and makes periodic tax deductible contributions of profit-sharing funds to the ESOP to repay the note. Assuming for simplicity that the firm was in a 50% tax bracket, it would require $200,000 in earnings to pay off a note plus interest at a bank, whereas it would only require $100,000 in earnings to finance the purchase through the ESOP. When depreciation on the equipment is considered, a significant portion of the equipment cost can be paid for through tax deductions; exactly how much depends on the firm's tax bracket.

If interested, a firm should explore the formation of an ESOP with its accountant and attorney. Generally, the firm must be of sufficient size for the ESOP to support the costs involved. In addition to accountant and attorney fees involved in the setup and operation of the plan, an annual valuation of the stock must be made by an independent appraiser to guarantee a realistic price for the transactions, and there are government filing requirements each year, adding accounting cost to a firm.

EXERCISE 1.4 ▬▬▬▬▬▬▬▬▬▬▬▬▬▬▬▬▬▬▬▬

Exploring Alternative Sources of Funding

Multiple Choice

1. An ESOP is
   a. a complex insurance policy.
   b. an alternative to a profit plan.
   c. an easy retirement plan.
   d. a trust made up of all employees for the purpose of buying shares in the firm.
   e. none of the above.

2. The ESOP is mainly controlled
   a. by all the shareholders.
   b. by the trustees.
   c. by the CEO
   d. none of the above.

3. You may use an ESOP to
   a. finance equipment purchases with pretax dollars.
   b. renovate your office.
   c. share profits.
   d. none of the above.

4. In order to set up an ESOP you must
   a. consult your attorney.
   b. consult your accountant.
   c. be of sufficient size to support the costs involved.
   d. all of the above.
   e. none of the above.

5. Could your firm benefit from an ESOP plan?

   _____

6. If yes, what timetable would you set for planning an ESOP?

   _____

   _____

   _____

   _____

1.5   RAISING CAPITAL IN SMALL DESIGN FIRMS

Small firms are limited in the ways they can raise equity funds to support the firm and expand operations. A partnership must provide an opportunity for new partners to be admitted. In the case of a corporation, outside of being acquired by a larger firm, the best way to raise capital is through a stock purchase plan that is made available to key employees. The plan should be prepared by an attorney knowledgeable in the design industry and provide for periodic purchases over an established length of time. Generally, the purchase price is fixed at net book value or an adjustment to net book value at the end of the year, since that figure is easy to calculate. Net book value is the difference between assets and liabilities, and adjustments may sometimes be necessary to make the figure more realistic.

Obviously, the money for employees to purchase stock must come out of salaries and bonuses. Therefore the firm must be growing and successful to make the plan worthwhile. Pricing the shares at net book value tends to understate their value because no credit is given to backlog or the reputation of the firm. However, this is an important incentive for employees because it gives them an opportunity to see their shares grow. Since the shares do not usually pay dividends, the ability to share financially in growth is what ties these employees to the firm.

EXERCISE 1.5 ■

Sharing in Responsibility

1. What percentage of employees own part of your firm?

_____

2. Do you feel that ownership motivates employees to do their best?

_____

_____

_____

_____

3. What kind of programs do you have within your firm to raise capital?

_____

_____

4. Is there an organized effort/plan to improve the cash flow/ influx of work for your firm? If so, describe it.

_____

_____

_____

5. List five ways in which you could encourage your staff to raise capital:

1. _____

2. _____

3. _____

4. _____

5. _____

6. List five leadership criteria you would use to pick a new leader in your firm before selling stock to him or her.

1. _____

2. _____

3. _____

4. _____

5. _____

1.6 SIMPLE CASH FLOW REPORTS

The cash flow report is a key report necessary for cash management. It first shows historical information and then projects cash requirements over at least a three month period. It is well to start with a simple cash flow report, as shown in Exhibit 1.3, and examine trends such as the number of days lag between invoicing and collecting, major seasonal or one-time cash requirements, and growth patterns that will affect cash needs. After some experience, cash forecasting will become easier, and more detailed reports can be prepared, as shown in Exhibit 1.4. Gen-

SAMPLE CASH FLOW REPORT

Month, Year _4/94_

	Current Month		Forecast		
	Actual	Forecast	Month 1	Month 2	Month 3
Beginning cash balance	$2,000	$10,000	$10,000	$10,000	$5,000
Operating cash receipts:					
From: Projects	+80,000	100,000	90,000	120,000	125,000
Other income	+10,000	10,000	10,000	10,000	10,000
Project advances	+ 0	0	0	0	0
Subtotal	92,000	120,000	110,000	140,000	140,000
Operating cash disbursements:					
Net cash flow from operations	−109,000	105,000	100,000	110,000	120,000
Other cash receipts:					
Bank loan	+20,000	0	0	0	0
Other cash disbursements					
Payment of bank loans	− 0	0	0	25,000	10,000
Ending cash balance:	3,000	15,000	10,000	5,000	10,000
Bank loan outstanding	$100,000	$80,000	$80,000	$55,000	$45,000

Exhibit 1.3 The report summarizes cash status in an easy-to-read format. Receipts from clients and disbursements from operations must be estimated in detail on separate work-sheets similar to Exhibits 1.5 and 1.6.

erally, it is easier to forecast cash expenses because they do not vary much by month unless there are significant changes in operation. Exhibit 1.5 is a form that can be used to forecast expenses. Cash receipts are more difficult to predict because of the uncertainty of when clients will pay. Exhibit 1.6 shows a form used to forecast cash receipts by project. Exhibit 1.7 is an example of a cash flow analysis for a typical project.

One method used to forecast revenue is to take the various elements that make up a revenue forecast and estimate them separately as follows:

1. *Backlog (Work Under Contract That Is Not Yet Com-*

FINANCIAL PROJECTION AND CASH FORECAST

ABC ARCHITECTS, INC.
FINANCIAL PROJECTION AND CASH FORECAST
JUNE TO DECEMBER

Financial Projection	June	July	August	September	October	November	December
Estimated revenue	$10,000	$10,000	$20,000	$30,000	$40,000	$20,000	$20,000
Collections							
Previous month (30%)	3,000	3,000	3,000	6,000	9,000	12,000	6,000
2nd previous month (30%)	3,000	3,000	3,000	3,000	6,000	9,000	12,000
3rd previous month (30%)	3,000	3,000	3,000	3,000	3,000	6,000	9,000
Total collections	9,000	9,000	9,000	12,000	18,000	27,000	27,000
Expenses (est. at 80% of revenue)	7,200	7,200	7,200	9,600	14,400	21,600	21,600
Payment of expenses (one month lag)	7,200	7,200	7,200	7,200	9,600	14,400	21,600
Cash Forecast							
Cash receipts							
Collections	$9,000	$9,000	$9,000	$12,000	$18,000	$27,000	$27,000
Cash disbursements							
Salaries	3,200	3,200	3,200	3,200	5,000	7,000	9,000
Direct expenses	1,000	1,000	1,000	1,000	2,000	2,400	3,600
Office rent	2,000	2,000	2,000	2,000	2,000	3,000	4,000
Other expenses	1,000	1,000	1,000	1,000	600	2,000	5,000
Taxes	—	—	—	—	—	—	10,000
Computer purchase	—	—	—	—	20,000	—	—
Total cash disb.	7,200	7,200	7,200	7,200	29,600	14,400	31,600
Net cash gain (loss)	1,800	1,800	1,800	4,800	<11,600>	12,600	<4,600>
Cash balance (beg. of month)	5,000	6,800	8,600	10,400	15,200	3,600	16,600
Cumulative cash	6,800	8,600	10,400	15,200	3,600	16,600	12,000
Desired level of cash	5,000	5,000	5,000	5,000	5,000	5,000	5,000
Surplus/(deficit) cash	$1,800	$3,600	$5,400	$10,200	<$1,400>	$11,600	$7,000

Exhibit 1.4 Factors used to develop the financial projection are based on experience and then translated into the cash forecast.

pleted). This revenue will be earned over the forecast period and the amount and rate at which it will be earned should be fairly easy to predict.

2. *Current Proposals Outstanding.* The estimated fees for currently outstanding proposals are multiplied by a percentage that represents the likelihood of obtaining the project. This figure is then used in the projection.

FORECAST OF CASH FLOW FROM OPERATIONS

FISCAL YEAR *1994*

Month	Gross Payroll	Payroll-Related Costs	Facil. and Rent	Other Operating Expenses	Bonuses and Profit-Sharing	Income Taxes, City & State	Federal Income Taxes	Capital Items	Debt Repay.	Total Cash Disb.
Jan.	$62,000	$8,000	$15,000	$12,000	0	$1,000	$7,000	0	0	$105,000
Feb.	60,000	6,000	15,000	14,000	0	0	0	$5,000	0	100,000
Mar.	64,000	7,000	16,000	13,000	0	0	5,000	0	$5,000	110,000
Apr.	70,000	10,000	16,000	12,000	0	1,000	0	9,000	2,000	120,000
May	70,000	10,000	16,000	12,000	0	1,000	0	9,000	2,000	120,000
Total	$800,000	$80,000	$190,000	$160,000	$40,000	$4,000	$20,000	$30,000	$20,000	1,344,000

Exhibit 1.5 Cash disbursements are estimated on this work-sheet and the totals transferred to the "net cash flow from operations" column in Exhibit 1.3.

For example, if the firm has a proposal outstanding for $100,000 and there are two other firms in competition, then this proposal is weighted by one-third, or $33,000. An estimated start date is determined and the $33,000 is projected by month at a certain level of earnings.

3. *New Business Development.* An estimate is made of the number of new proposals expected to be written in the forecast period multiplied by the percent probability of success multiplied by the average contract size. This calculation gives the balance of the revenue estimate. For example, if the firm expects to write 40 additional proposals in the forecast year beyond those that are currently outstanding, and their probability of

FORECAST OF CASH RECEIPTS FROM PROJECTS

FISCAL YEAR _____

Project	Contract Type	Construction Cost Est.	Contract Amount	Amount Paid to Date	Balance Owed	Estimated Payments Schedule					
						Jan.	Feb.	Mar.	Apr.	May	June
123 Proj. X	Lump Sum	$2,000,000	$100,000	$26,000	$74,000		$18,000	$20,000	$16,000	$20,000	
142 Proj. Q	Lump Sum	4,000,000	240,000	0	240,000			10,000	10,000	20,000	20,000
248 Proj. U	% Const.	1,000,000	70,000	60,000	10,000		10,000				
542 Proj. S	Hourly	Study	15,000	2,000	13,000	6,000	6,000	1,000			
014 Proj. T	Hourly	Study	35,000	20,000	15,000	10,000	5,000				
Total Cash Receipts						$100,000	$90,000	$120,000	125,000	125,000	125,000

Exhibit 1.6 Cash receipts are estimated on this work-sheet and the totals transferred to the "operating cash receipts from projects" column in Exhibit 1.3.

success on each is one out of three (33%), and the average size of each proposal is $50,000, then this represents an additional $660,000 in revenue that is added to items 1 and 2 above. The $660,000 is projected to be earned at an estimated monthly level during the forecast period.

It is important that the total revenue estimated be reviewed by the marketing director, who is charged with obtaining the new work, and by the operations director, who is responsible for seeing that it gets done. They must both agree that the estimated revenue can be reasonably attained. Furthermore, the marketing and operations directors must analyze the revenue projection to see that it is balanced with the disciplines

EXAMPLE OF A CASH FLOW ANALYSIS FOR TYPICAL PROJECT

	Total	July	August	September	October
Project Y					
Collections	$40,000	0	$10,000	$10,000	$20,000
Disbursements					
Labor & overhead	27,000	14,000	10,000	3,000	
Reimbursable expenses	2,000	1,000	1,000		
Consultants' costs	7,000			3,000	4,000
TOTAL DISBURSEMENTS	36,000	15,000	11,000	6,000	4,000
Diff. between collect./disb.	4,000	⟨15,000⟩	⟨1,000⟩	4,000	16,000

Exhibit 1.7 The start-up costs incurred on a new project must be financed out of working capital.

and capabilities of the people on staff. Finally, the financial manager must review it and convert it to a cash receipts estimate by applying the above factors to determine when payments can be expected.

Another area of difficulty in preparing a cash forecast is in determining when consultants can be expected to submit their invoices. The best way to estimate a cash forecast is to use the terms of the contract, coupled with any past experience working with the consultant.

EXERCISE 1.6 ■■■■■■■■■■■■■■■■■■■■■■■■■

Reports

Multiple Choice

1. A cash flow report is used to
   a. measure lag time.
   b. measure lags between invoicing and collecting.
   c. measure the number of invoices coming in.
   d. none of the above.

2. Other uses for cash flow reports include
   a. seasonal cash requirements.
   b. major cash requirements.
   c. growth patterns that affect cash needs.
   d. all of the above.
   e. none of the above.

3. Backlog is
   a. work expected to be contracted.
   b. work under contract but not yet completed.
   c. work issued under contract.
   d. none of the above.

4. A value for new business is calculated by
   a. dividing proposals by their net worth.
   b. dividing proposals by one third.
   c. dividing the average size of the proposals by the probability of success.
   d. dividing the average size of the proposals by the probability of success and then multiplying by the number of outstanding proposals.

5. The person(s) charged with obtaining new work is (are)
   a. the board of directors.
   b. the CEO.
   c. the operations director.
   d. the marketing director.

6. One area of difficulty in preparing a cost forecast is
   a. in determining when clients will pay.
   b. in determining when consultants will submit invoices.
   c. in projecting future work.
   d. all of the above.

1.7 MORE CASH MANAGEMENT TECHNIQUES

There are several methods available to speed the flow of cash receipts into a central depository account and then to manage the outflow of funds so that excess cash is not sitting idle and not earning interest. Most of these techniques are applicable to larger firms or to those that may receive cash at several different locations. However, each firm should discuss its cash management needs with its banker to determine if there is a more efficient way to handle the receipt of funds.

1. *Zero Balance Accounts.* This is a method of disbursing funds from several bank accounts without allowing any idle funds to remain in these accounts. Zero balance accounts have no balance, but when a check is drawn against them and presented for payment, the bank automatically draws from a central depository account just enough money to cover the check. Likewise, any receipts into these accounts go directly to the central depository account. To keep track of these transactions, the bank's customer receives a daily cash balance report, generally by Telex, describing all the transactions that have occurred that day.

2. *Lock Boxes.* This is a special post office box that appears on the firm's invoices and to which clients are directed to send their checks. Only the bank has access to the box and it collects the checks several times during the day and deposits them directly into the firm's account. This procedure saves at least a day in getting checks deposited and is particularly useful if the firm does work in several cities. The bank will study the various locations where cash is received and can recommend the most efficient locations for lock boxes.

3. *Depository Transfer Checks* These checks are really drafts that one bank writes on another to authorize the transfer of funds to the writing bank. They are a useful device for moving funds quickly to a central depository account from regional bank accounts, because they move through the Federal Reserve system rather than through the mails.

4. *Wire Transfers.* This is a method of transferring funds even more quickly than by means of depository transfer checks. Funds are transferred the same day and often in a matter of hours. The cost of wire transfers is higher than that for depository transfer checks.

5. *Faxed Credit Cards.* For smaller payments encourage clients to pay you using a fax transmission of their corporate American Express, Visa, or Mastercard credit card. With Visa/Mastercard, you get almost immediate credit, while American Express may take 30–45 days to issue payment.

All these cash management techniques cost the bank money, the same as every transaction that occurs within any bank customer's account, such as receiving of deposits and payment of checks. The bank earns revenue by investing any excess funds held in customers' accounts and through loans, trust services, safe deposits, and all the other services a bank provides. When determining the charges for cash management services, the bank will look at the firm's entire banking relationship, including services provided to the principals of the firm as well. Sometimes the cash management service can be accommodated as "no charge" if the bank receives sufficient revenue from other business with the firm.

EXERCISE 1.7 ■■■■■■■■■■■■■■■■■■■■■■■■

Discussion Problem

Background. For many years Harlem Marine Engineers concentrated on work for the private sector, designing facilities for several shipbuilders on the East Coast. Several years ago they opened an office on the Gulf Coast in response to increased projects in that part of the country. Last year they acquired a large government project, working for the Navy Department at an installation on the West Coast.

The firm had a line of credit with a bank on the East Coast and for years had a $50,000 limit on the line, which was adequate in the past. Borrowings averaged around $20,000 for many years. There were a few bad debts, but the firm was free of borrowing for about 30 days a year. The bank renewed the line annually without question.

When the firm obtained work from the federal government, it found itself in a position where it had to begin work on a project before a contract was awarded, based on a notice to proceed. However, because of its inexperience in government work, there were often problems with the pre-award audits, problems that frequently were not resolved until months after the work was started. Very often it was as much as six months before problems were resolved and a contract was signed. At that time the firm would send its first invoice for services to date.

Project managers were paid bonuses on the volume of work they produced so there was considerable pressure to obtain as much work as possible. One project manager recently obtained a large assignment from a developer of marinas on the West Coast. After the project had been underway for three months, the developer unexpectedly went bankrupt, and the firm will probably have to write off $25,000 in losses.

Another project manager obtained most of his work as a consultant to architects or other engineering firms. He had many acquaintances in these firms. However, because his clients did not pay him until they were paid, he generally had an average of 90 days outstanding on accounts receivable.

Harlem Marine Engineers prospered as volume and manpower steadily increased over the years. Profits consistently averaged about 5% before taxes. Early last year borrowings exceeded the credit line limit and did not show any signs of declining. At this point, the financial manager became concerned and both he and the managing principal visited the bank and were told that, based on the firm's previous performance, the bank would increase their credit line to $75,000, but the interest rate was also raised from 2% to 2½% over the prime rate. The increase proved satisfactory for six months, but after another government contract was acquired, the $75,000 credit limit was reached and the financial manager went back to the bank for another increase. At that point the banker had to reluctantly tell him that, because of tight money conditions, the bank could not increase the line any further.

Assignment. List the various mistakes the firm was making from a cash flow standpoint. What options are available to the financial manager at this point? How can he bring the situation under control?

What kinds of cash flow reports are necessary and how often should they be prepared?

_____

_____

_____

_____

_____

_____

_____

_____

FINAL EXAMINATION—CHAPTER 1

Multiple Choice

1. The best source for cash flow assistance is
   a. your CEO.
   b. your banker.
   c. your attorney.
   d. your accountant.

2. A bank must understand that design firms
   a. may have longer payment periods.
   b. may have 90-day-old accounts.
   c. may have to wait until contractors get paid before they do.
   d. all of the above.
   e. none of the above.

3. Bankers request security for a loan, usually in the form of
   a. collateral.
   b. personal possessions.
   c. a pledge of accounts receivable.
   d. none of the above.

4. You would consider an ESOP as an option if you
   a. are looking for quick funding.
   b. seek to allow employees to buy stock in the firm.
   c. are thinking about ownership transition.
   d. none of the above.

5. The prime advantage of an ESOP is that
   a. it improves morale and productivity.
   b. it increases debt ratio.
   c. it decreases morale.
   d. none of the above.

6. The money for employees to buy stock comes from
   a. salaries.
   b. bonuses.
   c. personal assets.
   d. all of the above.

7. Cash forecasts are prepared to
   a. examine trends.
   b. determine cash needs.
   c. assess seasonal cash flow.
   d. all of the above.
   e. a and c only.

8. Work under contract but not yet completed is known as
   a. accounts receivables.
   b. backlog.
   c. new business value.
   d. assets.

9. A lock box is used for
   a. one-time cash deposits.
   b. bank access to checks.
   c. post office access.
   d. none of the above.

10. A bank draft one bank writes on another to authorize the transfer of funds to the writing bank is known as a
    a. zero balance account.
    b. wire transfer.
    c. depository transfer check.
    d. lock box.

11. A zero balance account is
    a. an empty bank account.
    b. a transfer of funds.
    c. an unauthorized checking account.
    d. an account with no balance until a check is drawn.

Discussion Problem

Background. Your 15-person interior design firm has been with the same bank since you founded the firm 18 years ago. You have never forgotten their help at the beginning, when they loaned you $2,000 for working capital, with your automobile as security, to get the firm started. Occasionally you have had to borrow for short periods of time to meet a payroll, and the bank has always been accommodating. Other than maintenance of your checking account, you have expected little from the bank, and you have seen the bank president rarely or only at social functions. You recently obtained an assignment as a consultant to a London architectural firm on a hotel project. The project is in Central America. You need help with such matters as letters of credit, foreign currency transactions, and foreign business procedures.

You approach your banker because the architectural firm has indicated that you must obtain a separate letter of credit for your portion of the project. The architect also asks you to open a bank account in London because you will be paid partially in pounds and will have expenses for the office you open there.

At a meeting with your local banker he tells you that he has little experience in foreign operations and directs you to another bank in a nearby large city.

Assignment. How should you establish a relationship with the new bank that will allow them to accommodate your needs now and in the future? List the kinds of information that the new bank will want to have. How would you organize the package of information to give to the bank?

2 BUDGETING FOR PROJECTS

Chapter Summary

- The advantages of a flexible budgeting policy
- Cost-based budgeting
- Other budgeting methods
- Projects that do not require a formal budget
- Assembling the team
- Increases in overhead rates
- Client price budgeting
- Four other ways to budget a project

Why Budget?

To properly control project costs it is essential that budgets be established and control mechanisms be in place to prevent surprises and unexpected cost overruns. The key to successful project control is to have an adequate reporting system that raises warning signals when projects are not proceeding according to plan. The warning signals should alert project managers to take corrective action in enough time to prevent costly overruns. Preparation of good project budgets is the start of this system.

2.1 WHAT TO LOOK FOR IN ESTABLISHING A BUDGET

When establishing budgets for design projects, the project manager must first examine the scope of the project to make certain that it is well thought out and clear to all parties. He or she needs to examine the time frame available to accomplish the task and to plan the work accordingly. Sufficient time must be allowed for project management tasks, concept reviews, and quality control checks. The project manager must also look at the total project budget and make some allowances for contingencies wherever possible. If the project is priced such that the total budget does not have an allowance set aside for contingencies, then the principals in the firm must be aware of it, since these are the projects that often have overrun costs.

Use the following checklist to establish project budgets. Many design firms incorporate this type of a checklist as part of the procedural steps to be followed when a project is assigned to a project manager.

YES	NO	
☐	☐	Is scope of work clearly defined?
☐	☐	Are client responsibilities spelled out as well as the responsibilities of the design professional?
☐	☐	Is the time frame for the project realistic?
☐	☐	Are labor rates based on the latest information available and adjusted to include the time period when the work will be accomplished?
☐	☐	Have reimbursable expense rates been verified with the financial manager to ensure responsibleness?
☐	☐	Is there a letter of agreement from each consultant indicating his or her price?
☐	☐	Has profit on the project been determined in accordance with firm policy?
☐	☐	Is there a contingency allowance?
☐	☐	Has enough time been included for project management?
☐	☐	Has allowance been made for learning time needed by any new people assigned to the project?
☐	☐	Has the budget been compared with the budgets of any similar projects completed recently?
☐	☐	Has the budget been reviewed by a principal in the firm?
☐	☐	Has the financial manager reviewed the budget?

When Not to Budget

Budget controls and procedures are important, but there are times when a full-blown project budget is not necessary. Small projects that are completed quickly generally do not have to be budgeted in detail since the total contract amount controls the level of expenditure. Often the client needs the work on an emergency basis, which requires a maximum effort in a short period of time. In this case, the focus is on getting the work done with overtime where necessary and cost is not the primary concern. Another case is where there is an open-ended contract to be performed on a time and materials basis. These "blank-check" contracts are usually small.

The point is that budgeting procedures should be flexible enough to accommodate all kinds of projects. There are certain types of projects where detailed budgets are not necessary. A flexible budget policy will encourage the preparation of accurate and complete budgets for those projects that require them. On other projects they will be prepared to the extent necessary.

EXERCISE 2.1 ■

Looking at Your Firm's Budget

1. First and foremost, does your firm have a standardized budget procedure?

   _____

2. How do you handle contingencies?

   _____

   _____

3. Which projects have cost overruns?

   _____

   _____

4. Are your budgeting procedures flexible?

   _____

5. What would be the advantage of making your budgeting more flexible?

_____

_____

6. Before you continue this lesson, list four weaknesses of your firm's budgeting process that you'd like to change.

1. _____

2. _____

3. _____

4. _____

2.2 COST-BASED BUDGETING (ADDITIVE)

Cost-based budgeting is the method of preparing budgets by building up the elements of cost and then adding profit to arrive at a total project amount. It is the usual method used in preparing budgets for proposals to governmental agencies. The pricing data prepared at the time of the contract negotiations have now been refined, updated, and broken down into finer detail for the final project budget. Exhibit 2.1 is an example of a relatively simple budgeting form, and Exhibit 2.2 shows one that is more complex; both are illustrative examples. The degree of complexity in budgeting will be determined largely by the types of projects and the amount of control that the firm needs to exercise.

The project manager needs to look over the mix of people available to work on the project and determine the type and classification of people required. He or she needs to determine how flexible people are working in different areas and what levels of experience personnel need to make the best fit. In some cases the project manager needs to allow time for new people to gain experience on projects. If average salary classification rates were used in the pricing proposal, the project manager may have to examine the rates of individuals who are likely to be assigned to the project in order to detect any possibility of labor costs being higher or lower than anticipated.

In most instances the overhead rates used in the pricing proposal will be used to prepare the budget, and a single overhead rate should be applied to direct labor, a rate that covers fringe benefits plus general and administrative expense. It is important for the project manager to understand

WORKSHEET FOR DOWNWARD BUDGETING: FIXED FEE OR LUMP SUM PROJECTS

1. Total project value — $ 92,000

2. Desired profit — $ 9,200

3. Total project budget — $ 82,800

4. Direct costs excluding labor — $ 4,700

5. Amount available for direct labor and overhead — $ 78,100   6. Current nominal overhead rate 150 %

7. Amount available for direct labor

$$\text{Line 5} \div \left(1 + \frac{\text{line 6}}{100}\right)$$ $ 31,240

Personnel	Category	Hours	Hourly Rate	Direct Salaries
F. Jones	Principal	25	$ 40.00	$1,000
R. Smith	Senior Engineer	100	28.00	2,800
N. Turner	Senior Architect	112	25.00	2,700
L. Johnson	Junior Engineer	508	15.00	7,620
S. Strom	Designer	380	14.00	5,320
D. Sargent	Draftsman	1,010	10.00	10,100
N. Franklin	Typist	200	8.50	1,700

8. Total direct salaries (should be same as line 7) $ 31,240

Reproduced courtesy of Engineering-Science, Inc., Pasadena, California.

Exhibit 2.1   The downward budgeting approach begins with a total anticipated fee and serves to determine the number of man-hours that may be used by each member of the project team.

that the direct labor and overhead rates have been estimated in the price proposal and that the financial manager will be accumulating actual costs to compare with the budgets. Refer to Chapter 7 for an example of monitoring actual performance versus budget. Most of these reports can be prepared on a personal computer.

Sometimes costs over which the project manager has little control, such as overhead, get out of line with actual performance. For this reason, many firms compare budget with actual labor costs and reimbursable expenses only, and do not hold the project manager accountable for overhead variances. There is no one right way to report project control information. The important thing is that all employees understand the system and how it affects their performance.

Consultants' contracts should be written so that they abide by the same terms that apply to the prime professional. The

SAMPLE FORM FOR DETAILED BUDGETING BY TASK ELEMENT

Project Name: _Project C_   No. _0216_

| Labor | Time Period | | Personnel | | | |
| | Month | Month | Classification | | Daily | |
Task Element	Start	End	Assigned[1]	Mandays	Rates[1]	Amount
Preliminary Analysis	Sept.	Dec.	Prof. Staff A	10	$600	$6,000
			D	5	200	1,000
Schematics	Jan.	Feb.	Prof. Staff B	20	500	10,000
			E	10	150	1,500
Design Development	Mar.	June	Prof. Staff B	10	500	20,000
			E	20	150	3,000
Construction Documents	June	Aug.	Prof. Staff B	10	500	5,000
			C	20	400	8,000
			D	40	200	8,000
			E	40	150	6,000
Subtotal labor						$68,500

Exhibit 2.2 This report is used to budget a project by task or phase. In this case daily labour rates include overhead and profit. Note the detail requested in budgeting expenses. After the total is budgeted, provision is then made to break the budget down by months in order to compare with actual performance.

Direct expenses (Show calculations below)

Travel	Location	No. of R/T	Cost per R/T	Extension	
	Large City	_4_	_$500_	_$2,000_	
Subtotal travel					_2,000_

Subsistence	Location	No. of Days	Daily Rates	Extension	
	Large City	_4_	_$150_	_$600_	
Subtotal subsistence					_600_

Printing and drafting: In-house materials (Estimate labor separately and include under appropriate task element) _4,000_
Outside services (Include total price for both labor and materials) _6,000_

Data processing service (Complete subcontractors schedule below and enter total here) _1,000_

Communications (Telephone, telegraph, telex, cables, etc.) _1,000_

Subcontractors (Complete subcontractors' schedule below and enter total here) _10,000_

Temporary field/office help[2]

Total direct expenses _24,600_

Total direct expenses at 110% _27,000_

Contingency _*_

Total direct labor and expenses (Show monthly breakdown below) _$95,500_

Subcontractor Name	Brief Description of Work to Be Performed	Contract Terms[3]	Mandays or Hours	Rate	Amount
A Laboratory	_Soils Investigation_	_Lump Sum_			_$10,000_

Total labor and expenses (monthly breakdown)

Month	_Sept._	_Oct._	_Nov._	_Dec._	_Jan._	_Feb._	_Mar._	_Apr._	_May_	_June_	_July_	_Aug._
Total labor and expenses	_2,000_	_2,000_	_2,000_	_3,000_	_3,000_	_4,000_	_10,000_	_10,000_	_10,000_	_16,000_	_16,000_	_17,000_

*5% included in each task element.

Notes: [1] Personnel classification and rates

Officers	_$800_	Supervisors and technicians	_$150_
Project manager	_700_	Stenographic and clerical	_150_
Professional staff A	_600_	All other personnel at actual or estimated rates	
B	_500_		
C	_400_		
D	_200_		
E	_150_		

[2] Survey and coding personnel should be included under the appropriate task element. Use this line for additional personnel who cannot be readily identified, such as temporary help.

[3] Identify basis of payment, that is, fixed price, time and charges, and so on.

Submitted by	_JPG_	Date	_8/3_
	(Project Manager)		
Reviewed by	_TVJ_	Date	_8/12_
	(Project Officer)		
Approved by	_KMR_	Date	_8/18_
	(President)		

Exhibit 2.2   Continued.

CHECKLIST FOR PREPARING SUBCONSULTANTS' CONTRACTS

YES	NO	
☐	☐	Are the responsibilities of the consultant clearly defined?
☐	☐	Is the time frame for the work understood and agreeable?
☐	☐	Have you worked with the consultant before and are you acquainted with his or her work?
☐	☐	In your experience, has the consultant quoted a fair price? (If the price is too low, the quality of the work will suffer.)
☐	☐	Are payment terms defined and are they in accordance with your payment terms with the client?
☐	☐	Is the consultant familiar with the terms and conditions of your contract and is the consultant willing to abide by them?
☐	☐	Does your contract with the client provide for client approval of all consultants and has this been done?
☐	☐	Does your contract contain a provision for obtaining certificates of insurance from consultants and has this been done?

Exhibit 2.3 Subconsultants' contracts should be prepared with the same care and attention as client contracts.

project manager should review the consultant's contract with as much care as if it were a client contract. The project manager should make certain there is agreement with the price and work statement. Exhibit 2.3 is a checklist to be used when preparing consultants' contracts.

The amounts set aside for contingency planning and for profit in the pricing proposal are generally carried forward in the budget unless new information is obtained. Based on surveys of profitable design firms, at least 10% of all costs should be set aside for contingencies, and a target of 25–45% profit should be established on every project. Additionally a line item of 15% of the total cost should be set up for all project management activity. Any deviations in these areas should require approval from someone at a level higher than the project manager's.

EXERCISE 2.2 ▉▉▉▉▉▉▉▉▉▉▉▉▉▉▉▉▉▉▉▉▉▉▉▉▉▉

Understanding Cost-Based Budgeting

1. Cost-based budgeting is

_____

_____

_____

_____

2. The degree of complexity of a budget depends on the

_____

and the

_____

3. Consultants' contracts should be written so that they

_____

_____

4. The amounts set aside for contingency planning and for profit are generally

_____

_____

5. What amount should be budgeted for project management activities?

_____

_____

2.3 CLIENT PRICE BUDGETING (SUBTRACTIVE)

This method of budgeting is the opposite of cost-based budgeting. With subtractive budgeting you start with the total amount for the project and then subtract profit, reimbursable expenses, and overhead to arrive at an amount that is budgeted for direct labor. Dividing this amount by the weighted average salary rates of the people who will be working on the project produces the total budgeted hours available to do the work. The hours are then distributed to the departments and individuals who have been assigned to the project. An example of client price budgeting is shown in Exhibit 2.4.

CLIENT PRICE BUDGETING

Total project price	$ 20,000
Less: Profit (15%)	3,000
Overhead	9,000
Reimbursables	500
Contingency (5%)	1,000
Amount budgeted for direct labor	$6,500
÷ weighted average salary rates ($10.00)	650 Hours Available

(Hours)	
Architecture	500
Graphics	50
Interiors	100
Total	650

Exhibit 2.4 Using this work-sheet enables the project manager to quickly arrive at the breakdown of hours needed to complete the work within the established budget.

Generally, it is a good practice to budget a project using more than one method, since each method reinforces the other. The project manager may also have greater confidence in a budget that has been arrived at by more than one method.

EXERCISE 2.3 ■■■■■■■■■■■■■■■■■■■■

Discussion Problem

Background. Your firm has had difficulty controlling project costs. The managing principal is convinced that the project managers do not budget properly and that once the budgets are established they are not changed to accommodate changing circumstances. The excuse given is that there is usually lack of time and that budgets are busywork that do not directly contribute to the success of the project.

Although the firm has a computerized accounting and project control system, budgets are prepared by hand and then added to the project information in the computer. When changes occur on a project or adjustments are needed between phases, it is a time-consuming task to rework the budget. As a result many project managers ignore them, thinking that since the total project price has not changed, the changes in different phases will eventually work themselves out. Comparisons between the actual amount spent on phases and what was originally budgeted are often useless.

The managing principal asks the financial manager to develop a computerized program that can be incorporated into the project accounting system. Using the client price budgeting concept shown in Exhibit 2.4 and an electronic spreadsheet program, the financial manager arrives at a method of budgeting that is simple and easy to change. Client price budgeting emphasizes the labor hours and dollars needed to accomplish the work. The electronic spreadsheet program enables changes to be made in any elements of the budget and carried through to the total automatically. Manual calculations are thereby eliminated. Exhibit 2.5 is an example of a budget prepared by computer.

Assignment.   List the reasons for preparing a budget and the need for keeping it current as circumstances change on a project.

_____

_____

_____

_____

_____

_____

_____

Is time spent on project budgeting a legitimate project cost, or should it be included in overhead and spread to all projects?

_____

_____

_____

_____

_____

_____

_____

SAMPLE BUDGET REPORT

	Hours	Dollars
Direct Labor		
Schematic design		
Bill Smith	10	$ 400
Mary Jones	9	350
Etc.		
Total	80	$ 2,000
Design development		
Jay Taylor	5	$ 180
Sam Bailey	9	320
Etc.		
Total	175	$ 5,000
Construction documents		
Al Allen	20	$ 800
Joe Howard	9	350
Etc.		
Total	200	$ 6,000
Bidding negotiations		
Tom Green	9	$ 300
Walter Williams	13	400
Etc.		
Total	40	$ 1,000
Additional service		
Allen Smith	5	$ 180
Gene Bowles	10	350
Etc.		
Total	40	$ 1,000
Total Direct Labor		$15,000
Overhead		$24,000
Reimbursable expenses		6,000
Consultants costs		7,800
Total Costs		$52,800
Profit @ 33%		17,200
Project Price		$70,000

Exhibit 2.5 An electronic spreadsheet program, such as Excel or Lotus 1-2-3, allows you to make changes in any of the budget assumptions, with the computer making all calculations and extensions automatically, thereby eliminating considerable manual effort.

What are the pros and cons of each method?

Cost-Based Budgeting

Pros	Cons
_____	_____
_____	_____
_____	_____
_____	_____
_____	_____
_____	_____
_____	_____
_____	_____
_____	_____

Client Price Budgeting

Pros	Cons
_____	_____
_____	_____
_____	_____
_____	_____
_____	_____
_____	_____
_____	_____
_____	_____

2.4   FOUR OTHER WAYS TO BUDGET A PROJECT

There are usually four additional ways that budgets can be computed for any project. The first method is "zero-based" budgeting. You start with a list of tasks and estimate the man-hours and corresponding costs to perform the work. The second is "downward" budgeting, which involves starting with the amount of compensation that can be obtained and breaking out the various costs components to establish the number of man-hours that can be allocated. The third method of budgeting is the "unit cost" budget, or the use of "historical" cost data (other than man-hours) from previous similar projects, such as cost per sheet of drawings. The fourth method is the "staffing level" budget, which considers the number of people assigned to a job for a certain time period.

Each method provides a different perspective, and comparison of results from the four can be most revealing. This section describes how each of these methods is best used, its advantages and pitfalls, and finally, how the results of each can be used to establish the project budget.

Zero-Based Budgeting

Zero-based budgeting means that each task must be analyzed so that any cost associated with that task is developed by determining what the particular project requires. Zero-based budgeting typically uses the following approach:

1. Prepare a task outline of contract requirements.
2. Estimate man-hours by labor category for each task.
3. Estimate direct labor rates for each labor category.
4. Calculate direct labor costs for each task by multiplying results of steps 2 and 3.
5. Add overhead costs as a percentage of the direct labor cost determined in step 4.
6. Estimate other direct costs (such as air fare, printing, and subconsultants) for each task.
7. Add the appropriate contingency.
8. Add the desired profit.

The major advantages of zero-based budgeting are:

1. It forces the project manager to plan out the job.
2. It provides the project manager with baseline information essential for monitoring and controlling the project budget and schedule.
3. It obtains commitments from the individuals involved in estimating the level of effort required for each task.
4. It provides the information needed to calculate manpower requirements.
5. It provides information that can be valuable during fee negotiations or negotiations for contract modifications.

Despite the above inherent advantages, the zero-based budgeting method also contains two potential pitfalls. The first is that the project manager may tend to pile contingency upon contingency, ultimately overpricing the job and losing the bid. The second pitfall is failing to identify all the subtle costs that must be figured into the typical project.

To illustrate this second potential pitfall, let us define a sample project, which consists of sending a two-person crew to a power plant to collect smokestack samples for a one-month period. The obvious costs of this project are:

Two man-months for the field crew

Travel costs for the field crew to get to the plant

Two months of living expenses while on site

Stack sampling equipment rental for one month

However, a more careful analysis of the project requirements would reveal that the costs must also be included for such activities as:

Office coordination of activities

Meetings with the client

Mobilization and demobilization of sampling stations

Reduction of stack sampling data

Report preparation and printing

Maintenance of project records

Another example of hidden costs is an interior design firm that is asked to evaluate a client's existing furnishings and to integrate new furniture purchases with older furnishings before a move into a new office building. The obvious costs for such a project are:

Man-hours for a field inventory of furniture

Travel time to and from various client offices

Design time to select appropriate new furnishings

Drawing time to lay out old versus new furnishings

A closer scrutiny of such an interiors project would reveal that these additional costs must be included before budgeting the project:

Tagging of all old furniture for moving and locating in the new facility

Meeting time with client to review specific pieces of furniture you have selected

Cost of supplies for tagging and inventorying old furnishings

Expediting costs involved in the purchase of new furniture

Cash flow costs incurred if the firm purchases furnishings on behalf of the client

Replacement costs of furniture damaged or lost before or during a move, including the time to evaluate the problem and select another piece of furniture

When requesting proposals, most clients tend to consider only the obvious costs, ignoring the less visible items. It is the project manager's job not only to include all these hidden costs, but also to be able to explain to the client why they are necessary.

Downward Budgeting

The downward budgeting approach arrives at a total fee based on a percentage of construction cost, cost per square foot of building, or some other method not directly related to the level of effort required to perform the work. The desired profit, contingencies, overhead, and other direct costs are subtracted to obtain the dollar amount available for manpower. This amount is then divided by average hourly rates to obtain the total number of hours available for each labor category to perform required tasks.

The success of downward budgeting is based on determining the maximum possible compensation for the project, which requires two critical pieces of information. The first is the market price, or how much your competitors will charge for the same project. The second is the client's budget for the job. Estimating the market price means knowing who your competitors are, the nature of their pricing structure, the level of effort they will probably use for budgeting the job, and how hungry they are for work. Finding out the client's budget involves probing to determine the kinds of guidelines that the client usually uses (for instance, percentage of construction cost or dollars per square foot). In some cases, the client's budget may even be public information that can be obtained for the asking.

The major advantages of downward budgeting are (1) it is based on obtaining the maximum possible compensation and (2) it targets budgets that will (at least theoretically) meet the firm's profit goals. The primary disadvantages are:

1. It does not obtain a high level of commitment from the project team.
2. It does not provide the project manager with essential planning information.
3. It fails to identify jobs that cannot be done within the available financial limitations.
4. The hours left to do the work may not relate to the amount of time required for the various tasks.

Unit Costs Budgeting

Probably the most common use of unit cost budgeting is to determine the cost per sheet of design drawings. Other examples of unit cost budgeting tools used in design firms include cost per square foot of design drawings, cost per page for certain types of reports, cost per analysis for laboratory work, and cost per boring for soil investigations.

The main advantage of unit cost budgeting is that it provides an objective estimate based on actual historical costs for similar work. The major disadvantage is that no two projects are exactly alike. Even if they were, the second project would probably cost less because of the experience gained from the first. Also this method does not account for cost impacts resulting from changes in conditions that have occurred over the years. Examples of such changes include productivity increases resulting from computerization, additional work required by new government regulations, and improvements or reductions in efficiency resulting from staff changes.

Furthermore, the unit cost budgeting approach does not provide the project manager with the quality of planning information that can be obtained from the zero-based budgeting method.

Staffing Level Budgets

The fourth method of budgeting is to estimate the total size of the project team for each phase of the project. The budget is determined by multiplying the number of people by the length of time each will work on the project to obtain the total estimated man-hours.

The man-hours are then multiplied by average hourly rates to obtain direct labor costs. Overhead, other direct costs, contingency, and profit are added in the same manner as previously described for zero-based budgeting.

Staffing level budgeting works well for small projects involving few people for a short period of time. It is also useful as an independent check of the other budgeting methods described above. The major problem with staffing level budgeting is that it doesn't relate the costs to the tasks that must be performed.

2.5 AVOIDING COMMON PITFALLS

Following is a brief review of some common pitfalls that project managers often overlook when establishing project budgets, along with the suggestions on avoiding these traps.

Budgeting for Corrections

Most people budget for reviews, but overlook the fact that reviews almost always result in the need to make corrections. Identify review and correction tasks as separate activities in the task outline and budget them individually.

Activities Beyond the Contract Due Date

Projects hardly ever end on the contractual due date, even if all contract requirements have been met. There are questions from contractors, requests to attend City Council meetings, or requests for extra sets of drawings. The costs for these wrapping-up activities can be budgeted by including an appropriate amount in the project management task budget and planning to spend it after all the other tasks have been completed.

The Dangers of "Lowballing"

"Lowballing" is a practice in which a project is taken at a fee lower than the cost of doing the work, in the hope of obtaining a future fee increase. Consider the following example of lowballing on a typical time-and-expense project:

Total estimated cost	$80,000
Proposed compensation	$50,000

Estimated loss	$30,000
Anticipated additional fees	$50,000
Anticipated "profit"	$20,000

Because the practice of lowballing is a gamble, consider the above example in gambling terms. You have taken a bet that you will be able to double the originally negotiated fee without increasing your costs! If you really want to gamble, play the stock market! If you want to be profitable, avoid lowballing when budgeting projects.

2.6 DEVELOPING A PROJECTED EXPENDITURE CURVE

Once the project budget has been completed, the next step is to develop a projected expenditure curve. This curve will serve as the basis for projecting manpower requirements and monitoring schedule and budget status throughout the project. The expenditure projection is derived by apportioning each task budget into the scheduled time frame for the corresponding activity, as shown in Exhibit 2.6. Values can then be totaled for each project period (monthly in the example) and summed up to estimate the cumulative expenditures throughout the project duration (as illustrated in Exhibit 2.7. These expenditures can then be plotted on a curve such as that shown in Exhibit 2.8.

Remember that this curve represents not only the projected expenditures, but also the estimated rate of progress for the project—a concept that can be displayed graphically be defining the total project budget to equal 100% completion and then establishing a progress scale (percent complete), as shown in Exhibit 2.8. The resulting graph will thus serve as the baseline against which the status of the project may be measured.

FINAL EXAMINATION—CHAPTER 2

Multiple Choice

1. When establishing a project budget, the project manager must first examine
   a. the scope.
   b. the site utilities.
   c. the building.

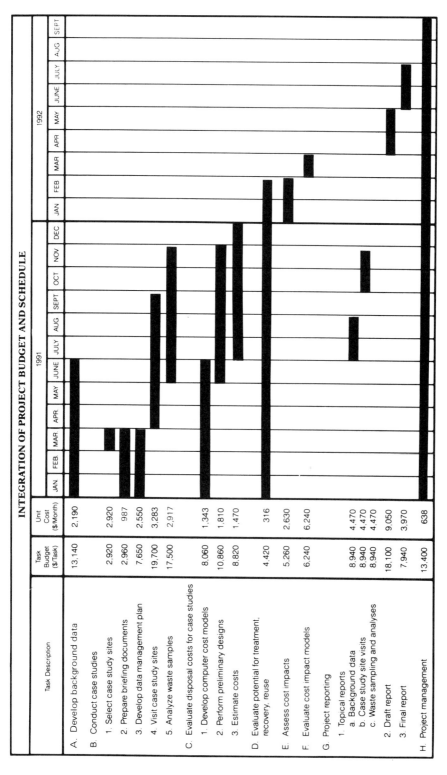

Exhibit 2.6 Using a common task outline for the scope, schedule, and budget (as shown in this example) is a prerequisite to development of a projected expenditure curve. Determining unit cost often helps in the calculations.

    d. none of the above.

2. A full-blown project budget is not necessary for
   a. large projects that are completed quickly.
   b. small projects that take long time periods to complete.
   c. small projects that can be generated quickly.
   d. none of the above.

3. Cost-based budgeting is
   a. a simple budgeting method.
   b. a complex system of cash accounting.
   c. taking the elements of cost and then adding profit to arrive at a total project amount.
   d. none of the above.

4. Additive budgeting is
   a. cost-based budgeting.
   b. client price budgeting.
   c. a reporting method.
   d. all of the above.

5. Many firms do not hold the project manager responsible for
   a. labor costs.
   b. reimbursables.
   c. overhead.
   d. none of the above.

6. Consultants' contracts should
   a. be completely different from the prime professional's.
   b. abide by the same terms that apply to the prime professional.
   c. be reviewed daily.
   d. none of the above.

7. Any deviation from the original contingency planning and profit amounts must be approved by
   a. the project manager.
   b. the project assistant.
   c. the project manager's superior.

8. Client price budgeting is
   a. subtractive.
   b. additive.
   c. the opposite of cost-based budgeting.
   d. a and b only.
   e. a and c only.

CALCULATION OF PROJECTED EXPENDITURES

Task Description	Task Budget ($/TASK)	Unit Cost ($/MONTH)	1991						
			JAN.	FEB.	MAR.	APR.	MAY	JUNE	JULY
A. Develop background data	13,140	2,190	2,190	2,190	2,190	2,190	2,190	2,190	
B. Conduct case studies									
1. Select case study sites	2,920	2,920			2,920				
2. Prepare briefing documents	2,960	987	987	987	987				
3. Develop data management plan	7,650	2,550	2,550	2,550	2,550				
4. Visit case study sites	19,700	3,283				3,283	3,283	3,283	3,283
5. Analyze waste samples	17,500	2,917						2,917	2,917
C. Evaluate disposal costs for case studies									
1. Develop computer cost models	8,060	1,343	1,343	1,343	1,343	1,343	1,343	1,343	
2. Perform preliminary designs	10,860	1,810						1,810	1,810
3. Estimate costs	8,820	1,470							1,470
D. Evaluate potential for treatment, recovery, reuse	4,420	316	316	316	316	316	316	316	316
E. Assess cost impacts	5,260	2,630							
F. Evaluate cost impact models	6,240	6,240							
G. Project reporting									
1. Topical reports									
a. Background data	8,940	4,470							4,470
b. Case study site visits	8,940	4,470							
c. Waste sampling and analyses	8,940	4,470							
2. Draft report	18,100	9,050							
3. Final report	7,940	3,970							
H. Project management	13,400	638	638	638	638	638	638	638	638
Total Monthly Costs			8,024	8,024	10,944	7,770	7,770	12,497	14,904
Cumulative costs	173,790		8,024	16,048	26,992	34,762	42,532	55,029	69,933

Exhibit 2.7 Spreading the task budgets throughout their respective durations will enable you to estimate the total projected cost for each month. These monthly costs will provide you with projection of cumulative costs throughout the scheduled duration of the project.

												1992	
AUG.	SEPT.	OCT.	NOV.	DEC.	JAN.	FEB.	MAR.	APR.	MAY	JUNE	JULY	AUG.	SEPT.
3,283	3,283												
2,917	2,917	2,917	2,917										
1,810	1,810	1,810	1,810										
1,470	1,470	1,470	1,470	1,470									
316	316	316	316	316	316	316							
					2,630	2,630							
							6,240						
4,470													
		4,470	4,470										
				4,470	4,470								
								9,050	9,050				
										3,970	3,970		
638	638	638	638	638	638	638	638	638	638	638	638	638	638
14,904	10,434	11,621	11,621	6,894	8,054	3,584	6,878	9,688	9,688	4,608	4,608	638	638
84,837	95,271	106,891	118,512	125,406	133,460	137,044	143,922	153,610	163,298	167,906	172,514	173,152	173,790

Exhibit 2.7 Continued.

PROJECTED EXPENDITURE CURVE

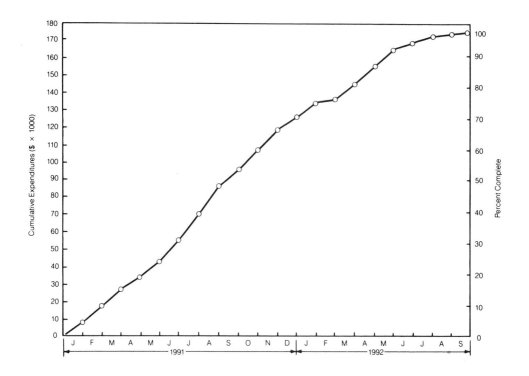

Exhibit 2.8 The cumulative costs calculated in Figure 2.7 can be plotted to obtain a projected expenditure curve. Setting the total budget to correspond to 100 percent will enable you to establish the ''percent complete'' scale on the right side of the graph.tive durations will enable you to estimate the total projected cost for each month. These monthly costs will provide you with projection of cumulative costs throughout the scheduled duration of the project.

9. In subtractive budgeting, you
   a. subtract labor.
   b. subtract reimbursables.
   c. subtract overhead.
   d. all of the above.
   e. none of the above.

10. It is advisable to
    a. use additive budgeting only.
    b. use subtractive budgeting only.
    c. use both methods.
    d. none of the above.

3

PRICING TO MAXIMIZE PROFITS

Chapter Summary

- What a project manager needs to prepare an estimate
- How to use "escalated" rates
- Estimating for unforeseen contingencies
- Establishing a profit policy
- Roles the financial manager plays in pricing projects
- Value pricing in a competitive environment
- Procedures to control project expenses
- Three other methods besides cost of service to develop price

Two Key Roles

For a firm to adequately price its services to achieve profits, two individuals—the project manager and the financial director—must play key roles.

3.1 PROJECT MANAGER'S ROLE IN PRICING

The project manager must develop a realistic estimate for the project that allows for an adequate profit margin. In today's competitive environment this is often difficult to accomplish, particularly when a project is being negotiated with a governmental agency or a large commercial organization that deals with many design firms. Worse yet, if the project manager has not been part of the negotiating process and is given a job to do for X dollars, he or she is at an even greater disadvantage. Nevertheless, after the contract has been awarded it is up to the project manager to establish a detailed budget and to produce a quality product, delivered on time and within budget.

NARRATIVE REPORT ON COMPLETED PROJECT
(INCLUDE IN PROJECT FILES)

September 17

TO: Operations Manager
FROM: Project Manager
SUBJECT: Design of Replacement for Boston City Hospital

The following report is provided for the completed project file on the referenced project.

Type of Project

On February 20, Contract No. ABC-123 between our firm and Professional Associates, a group of doctors, was signed to do the preliminary study, concept design, and master space plans to replace the 150-bed Boston City Hospital with a new facility. Our firm was designated as prime professionals for the project, and we used Jones Engineering, Bill Smith and Associates (facilities consultant), and Ray Edwards, a specialist in hospital interiors, as consultants.

The preliminary study was to begin April 1, but because of delays caused by the owners' inability to agree among themselves, the work did not start until May. Through the use of overtime, we were able to bring the project back on schedule, and it went out for bids within two weeks of the date originally decided.

Type of Contract

We agreed to provide the above service in two parts. The preliminary study was to be done on an hourly basis and the concept and master space plans on a lump sum.

Project Schedule

The preliminary study was completed on June 1 at a cost of $10,000. After review, the owners decided on August 1 to proceed with the concept design and master space plans and we agreed on a lump sum of $100,000. Final plans were completed and reviewed on January 1.

Project Team

Bob Turner served as project manager on the project and was assisted by Sam Bailey. David Eagle worked closely with the subconsultants and was responsible for coordination of their work.

Project Costs

Our firm did the preliminary study and was budgeted $50,000 for the design phase of the project. Using our standard multiplier, which provides for a 20% profit, we earned $2,000 profit on the study. Direct labor for design amounted to $15,000 and reimbursable expenses were $6,000. Total project costs were $48,000 when a 1.8 multiplier for overhead was taken into account. Billings to the client for our portion of the work summed $50,000. Thus, a 4% profit on cost was realized.

Exhibit 3.1 This report is often the only record of certain information that is not included elsewhere in the project files.

The final budget versus actual hours were:

Category	Budget	Actual	% Used
Principal architect	20	20	100
Project manager	200	240	120
Associates	100	150	150
Staff architects	400	430	108
Drafters	200	210	105
Secretaries	80	50	63
	1,000	1,100	110%

Summary

Additional hours were spent in the design phase to accommodate several changes in the clinical and kitchen facilities that were requested by the client. We felt we were entitled to an additional fee for these changes, but the client tended to be difficult throughout the project and insisted it was our misunderstanding of his original intentions. We think that a lot of the problems were caused by the client's lack of experience in working with architects on building projects.

The project gave us an opportunity to work on a highly visible project in a small city. I felt that the client was finally pleased with our efforts and would contact us if we could be of any assistance to them in the future.

Exhibit 3.1 Continued.

To assist in preparing an estimate for pricing purposes, it is important that the project manager has a well-defined project scope, and that the client clearly understands that any scope changes will require an adjustment in the project price. It is also necessary to have help from past experience in estimating project costs. Hence it is useful, when the project is finished, to ask the project manager to prepare a narrative in the form of a brief memorandum describing the project, the team that worked on it, financial results, and a summary of the team's experience. These data are very useful to project managers when pricing similar projects or additional work for the same client. A sample report is shown in Exhibit 3.1.

When pricing a project, the project manager must be certain to use escalated rates for labor and overhead—that is, the rates should be those that will be in effect during the time the work will be accomplished. Exhibit 3.2 shows how labor rates should be escalated. The important point to remember is that forward pricing should be based on documented evi-

EXAMPLE OF CALCULATION OF LABOR RATE ESCALATION

Situation

1. Current base salary rate for senior engineer is $29/hr and $18/hr for drafter.
2. Estimated project start date is six (6) months from today.
3. Estimated project period is eighteen (18) months.
4. Based on firm's wage increases and the current economy, the estimated increase for both employee classifications is 9%/year.

Problem

What is the estimated hourly rate for these classifications for the project period?

Solution

Escalated rate at project start date, six months from today
$\qquad$ 9%/year for 1/2 year = 1.045

Escalated rate at project completion, two years from today
$\qquad$ 9%/year for 2 years = 1.188 (compounded)

Use average rate for escalation during the project period
$$\frac{1.045 + 1.188}{2} = 1.1165$$

Escalation on base salary:
$\qquad$ Senior Engineer $29 x 1.1165 = $32.30/hr
$\qquad$ Drafter $18 x 1.1165 = $20.10/hr

Additional Considerations

1. Given project team members, is the average rate for employee classification a representative figure, or should we use a specific employee rate?
2. Are man-hours spread evenly over the project period or do more hours need to be expended toward the beginning or end of the project?

> **Exhibit 3.2** When using the formulas make certain that the items included under "additional considerations" are answered and included with the work-paper calculations.

---

dence showing how prices have increased in the past and are likely to increase in the future. Of course, known increases in certain overhead items, such as payroll taxes and insurance premiums, should be factored in using actual amounts rather than estimates.

In larger firms, the question sometimes arises whether to use a single firmwide overhead rate or separate rates for each office or profit center. In most instances, the single firmwide rate is preferable if it can be negotiated because it is less sus-

TELEPHONE REIMBURSEMENT RATE CALCULATION

Item of Cost	Monthly Amount
1. New AT&T Equipment, $29,126 10 year depreciation	$242.72/month
2. Directory advertising	15.24/month
3. Taxes/Insurance/Maintenance	142.80/month
4. Receptionist time to place long distance calls, 20% × 675/month =	135.00/month

1. AT&T/month	$242.72
2. Directory/month	15.24
3. Taxes/Insurance/Maintenance/month	142.80
4. Receptionist/month	135.00
Total/month	$535.76

As a percent of average monthly toll calls = 51.02%
Hence use a multiplier of 1.5 to recover telephone costs

Exhibit 3.3 This is an example of how to price reimbursable telephone expenses in order to recover a portion of the fixed charges in the reimbursement. Otherwise fixed charges are included in overhead. When you use this method of reimbursement, it is important that the firm use it consistently on all projects.

ceptible to wide fluctuations, and a uniform rate is more realistic when work is transferred to different offices.

Reimbursable expenses, which are rapidly rising items, also need to be escalated based on past experience. Exhibit 3.3 shows a calculation of telephone reimbursement that can be used to justify factoring long distance telephone charges by a rate of 1.5 to recover fixed charges. Exhibit 3.4 is a calculation of a reimbursement rate for computer charges. Both of these calculations emphasize the recovery of costs through direct charges to projects. They are useful techniques, but remember that any costs recovered directly through job charges must be excluded when calculating the firm's overhead rate. This is extremely important since firms can unwittingly duplicate the same charges in direct and indirect costs and then be faced with a significant roll-back in their overhead rate if it is ever audited. Exhibit 3.5 lists various types of reimbursable expenses.

In developing the estimate it is important to include an amount for contingency planning. It is the tightly estimated projects with no contingency allowance that are most likely to overrun. No one can say exactly how much of the estimate should be set aside for contingencies, but a bench mark that some people use in 5%. The fact that some amount is pro-

COMPUTER REIMBURSEMENT RATE CALCULATION

			Monthly Amount
1. Lease of equipment/month			$ 596.15
2. Service agreement/month			200.00
3. Software cost:			
Structural software	$1,500	(allotment for future)	
Job cost	350		
Accounting	1,500	Depreciate in 60 months	
Total	$3,350	Cost/month =	55.83

4. Rental Space 9′ × 8′ = 72 sq. ft.
@ $8+ per sq. ft. + 20% for anticipated yearly cost increase
Total/month = 9.60 × 72 sq. ft. =   691.20

5. Utilities (included in rent)

6. Insurance/month   2.50

7. Cost of running parallel

a. Double time sheets	$ 960.00	
b. Double bookkeeping	2,000.00	
c. Initial setup		
1. New input each job	950.00	
2. Computer training	2,400.00	
3. Miscellaneous other costs	500.00	
Total parallel setup cost	$6,810.00	
Amortize in 2 years		283.75

	Total Monthly Cost	$ 1,829.43

Working hours/month =	174 hours
Actual cost/hour =	$10.52/hour
50% efficiency = 2 × actual cost =	$21.04/hour
If it is treated as an employee, the changeable rate to cover indirect expense and profit would be 2.5 times cost	
Hence 2.5 × 21.04 =	$52.60/hour
Actual charge rate used =	$60/hour

Exhibit 3.4   This method for arriving at an hourly rate for computer charges includes all related costs in the rate rather than in overhead. When these charges are excluded from overhead, projects that do not require computer services are not burdened with the costs.

vided, depending on what the project can afford, is the important point.

The project manager generally plays a part in the contract negotiations, unless he or she is assigned after the project is awarded. In the negotiating sessions it is important that the project manager have the preliminary estimate worked out in advance so as to be in a position to know when and where to negotiate for a reduction in scope if the price must be reduced.

LIST OF REIMBURSABLE EXPENSES

Common reimbursable Expenses

Auto
Air travel
Computer
Fax machines (in/out)
FedEx (and other overnight mail carriers)
Reproduction
Printing
Telephone
Travel and subsistence

Other reimbursable Expenses

Other fees that directly relate to a project may be charged as reimbursable expenses as long as the firm follows a consistent policy with all clients:

Books/maps/charts (purchased for a project)
Courier service
Liability insurance (when increased policy limits are requested the extra costs may be charged to the project)
On-site facilities (cost of trailer, office, administrative personnel)
Postage (large identified mailings)
Professional registration (where needed in order to proceed with the work)
Miscellaneous (any other charges directly related to the project)

Exhibit 3.5 It is advantageous to identify reimbursable expenses and charge them separately. However, the other costs involved in accounting for reimbursable expenses need to be weighed against the alternative of recovering these costs in overhead.

The project manager must also recognize the importance of earning an adequate profit on each project. Profit must be included the same as any other element of "cost," and it must be recognized that any percentage set aside for contingencies must not come out of profit. Members of the firm should understand the meaning of profit, simple as this may sound. Profit is not something that goes in the owner's pocket— it supports the firm during times of low business activity, it pays for unallowable costs, such as interest and promotional expense in government contracts, it buys new equipment, it pays for losses on projects, and it supports the firm's growth and expansion into new areas.

Generally, a profit policy is established on a firmwide basis for various types of projects, and project managers should be well versed in it. The policy may have different rates for different types of work, but usually profit should relate to the

EXAMPLE OF PROFIT POLICY FOR DIFFERENT CONTRACT TYPES

Profit Range

Cost Plus Fixed Fee   **15–20%**

Where there is no risk of not recovering full costs, use the mid-range. Where an up-set limit is imposed, use 12–15%.

Lump Sum   **25–40%**

Depends on competition, degree of difficulty. Needs clear scope of work and agree-ment on additional charges for extras.

Multiplier/Billing Rates   **20%**

This profit is built into quoted rates. Overhead rate used in this calculation must be examined to make sure it conforms with current actual overhead rate.

Cost Plus Fixed Fee   **20%**

Where there is no risk of not recovering full costs, use the mid-range. Where an up-set limit is imposed, use 12–15%.

Special Projects, Such as Expert Witness Testimony   **35%**

The firm does not actively solicit this work because it is time consuming for the principals. Therefore, a higher-than-normal profit is added to the rates charged and certain minimums established regardless of the time spent in court.

Exhibit 3.6   Profit policies should be tested periodically against the firm's actual profit experiences to determine whether the policies can be reasonably attained.

degree of risk on a project. For example, a cost plus fixed fee contract generally carries a lower profit margin than, say, a lump sum project. An example of a profit policy is shown in Exhibit 3.6.

The profit percentage should be taken on all items of costs. Some firms mark up reimbursable costs, including consult-ants' costs, by a factor of, say, 15% when incorporating them into the overall price for the project. The 15% factor is not a profit in the usual sense, and clients should be made to un-derstand this. The 1993 *Professional Services Management Journal* survey established the median markup in the indus-try to be 17%. The markup covers the firm's costs for ac-counting and for managing these items. In some cases the profit policy of the firm needs to be reexamined, particularly on projects requiring a high concentration of effort in a short period of time. When a large portion of the firm's resources must be mobilized quickly to finish a rush project, this project should be estimated at a higher margin of profit than others.

Once the profit policy is established there will still be deviations based on competitive factors and there may even be times when a firm will take a project knowing it will incur a loss. In this case the firm may be trying to enter a new market, or it may be willing to forego profit in order to keep the staff busy and to cover overhead. The important point is that a decision has been made by the principals of the firm to knowingly deviate from the policy, and therefore the losses will not come as a surprise. Poorly priced projects that, for a host of reasons, result in overruns and losses are to be avoided when determining pricing.

EXERCISE 3.1

Measuring the Project Manager's Role in Pricing

Multiple Choice

1. A realistic estimate for a project allows for
   a. adequate additional services.
   b. adequate profit margin.
   c. adequate negotiating room.
   d. none of the above.

2. Forward pricing should be based on
   a. historical costs.
   b. documented evidence showing the rate of increase in the past.
   c. Known overhead, payroll, and tax increases.
   d. none of the above.
   e. a, b, and c.

3. Reimbursable expenses should
   a. not be projected.
   b. be projected based on past experience.
   c. be estimated in advance.
   d. a and b only.
   e. b and c only.

4. Profit is
   a. something that goes into the owners' pocket.

   b. what supports the firm during periods of low activity.

   c. a means for paying for unallowable expenses in government contracts, for equipment and losses.

   d. a and b only.

   e. b and c only.

Consider This:

1. The typical profit percentage for your firm's project is _____ %.

2. By what percentage do you believe you could increase that profit? _____ %

3. What would you establish as a firmwide profit policy?

_____

_____

_____

4. List four reasons why your projects don't make their profits now.

   1. _____

   2. _____

   3. _____

   4. _____

5. Next, list four ways you could tackle the problems listed in (4) above.

   1. _____

   2. _____

   3. _____

   4. _____

3.2 FINANCIAL MANAGER'S ROLE IN PRICING

The financial manager plays a significant role in pricing. He or she should review all cost proposals, not only to assure accuracy, but also to determine that the correct rates and profit margins are applied. The financial manager should also verify the payment terms and make certain that all salary and overhead escalations have been forecasted and applied properly.

If the firm uses standard billing rates that factor up direct hourly salary rates by overhead and profit, the financial manager, in conjunction with the project manager, must make certain that the client understands what is included in the billing rates. The financial manager must also verify that the standard billing rates realistically reflect the salary averages for the various classifications of personnel.

The financial manager also checks the accuracy of reimbursable expenses when reviewing cost proposals. He or she should make certain that the rates for automobile mileage, fax transmission, printing, and so on keep current with inflation. After the project is underway, the financial manager must see to it that people working on the project charge expenses to it, rather than to an overhead account. Procedures should be established so that no expenses are paid without proper approval. The project manager should be responsible for approving all charges to projects and the manager in charge of each overhead function, such as marketing, should be responsible for approving charges affecting these budgets. In smaller firms, the principal in charge of operations should approve all overhead expenses.

Pricing Methods and Techniques

While there are a number of methods for pricing design services, the one most usually used is based on cost. That is, all elements of cost are built up, including direct labor, overhead, and reimbursable expenses, and a profit is added to arrive at an overall contract price. Interestingly, most other professionals, including doctors and lawyers, do not price their services this way. Rather, their services are priced using a combination of factors ranging from "what the traffic will bear" to "loss leaders" that attract new clients with a special introductory offer.

The development of price from cost factors plus profit is acceptable, but it is only one method of arriving at price. Other methods include market price: that is, the price at which similar projects are being performed. Obtaining this information is not as difficult as it appears, particularly if you stay attuned to activities in your market and learn the price of projects you were not awarded. Market price may not necessarily be the price you can hope to obtain for a number of reasons, principally competition from others, but it is still important to know what it is in order to help make pricing decisions. Closely related to market price is value pricing, or what the project is worth to the client. An important element in determining value is the amount of construction and operating cost savings that can accrue to the owner from the efforts of the design professional. For example, a design that maximizes energy conservation in a building can save the owner a considerable sum over the life of the building. This amount can be computed by comparing building operating costs against standards developed for similar buildings. Obviously, these factors need to be taken into account and made known to the client, even when the design professional is not fully reimbursed for these efforts.

A fourth element in the pricing decision is what the client can afford to spend. In some instances this information may be obtained through various sources of market intelligence, and in some instances, the client might be tempted to come right out and tell you. Regardless of how the information is obtained, it can be a significant factor when deciding to pursue a project and can save a great deal of costly marketing effort on projects that are not worthwhile.

The point to remember is that developing a price from cost is just one element, and it is helpful to know other elements, as well as the client's perception of price, before arriving at a final figure. An example of developing a price based on different methods is shown in Exhibit 3.7.

EXERCISE 3.2 ■

Discussion Problem

Background. Your interior design firm has just incurred a $10,000 loss on a project for a small motel chain. When questioned, your project manager says that the start-up costs on this project were higher than expected because of troubles the project manager had in getting the right people assigned to the project. This sounds like an excuse, so you ask to review the data that were used to arrive at the price quoted the client.

The first thing you discover is that there was no allowance for contingency, and the estimate was underpriced by about $10,000 for the amount of work to be done. You were not shown this estimate before (the financial manager is not routinely given an opportunity to review and check the figures), and when questioned, the project manager admitted that he

EXAMPLES OF DEVELOPING PRICE FOR SERVICES

Based on Cost

The scope of work is analyzed, and from a detailed estimate of the number of hours required during each phase of the project, the following costs are summarized:

Direct labor	$ 10,000
Overhead	17,000
Reimbursables	5,000
Consultants	+ 10,000
Total cost	$ 42,000
Profit	+ 8,000
Total price	$ 50,000

Based on Market Price

The client is a large developer of small, inexpensively constructed, single-story shopping centers. Over the years, the client has compiled cost data on various architects' costs and profit in order to price these projects. The client expects an architectural firm of the size interested in these projects to have a multiplier of 2.5 times direct labor, which allows for a 7% profit factor in the price expected to be quoted. The client makes this information known to any architect who asks.

If your firm is able to meet these criteria and if it wishes to develop this work, it can submit proposals for these projects on the basis of market price.

Based on Value Price

Your engineering firm has special expertise in the design of research and development laboratories for the pulp and paper industry. An overseas manufacturer is interested in establishing a large facility on the East Coast of the United States. A laboratory will be built first, and the manufacturer wishes to engage the engineer to conduct a preliminary feasibility and site location study. The manufacturer's U.S. representative wants you because of your reputation among pulp and paper manufacturers.

Depending on competition from other engineering firms with this capability, you may be able to price this project on the basis of value to the client. Consider the level of expertise you can offer, and then set a price based on what this knowledge can save the client in terms of being able to quickly establish a presence in the U.S. market.

Exhibit 3.7 Developing a price for services using other methods besides costs serves to reinforce the accuracy of the final figure.

had not reviewed it with a principal of the firm. The firm has been very busy lately and the project manager has been working directly with this client for six months on several projects. He had been quoting estimates for several small motel projects, and since the work was accomplished within budget and on time the client was satisfied and none of the principals questioned the arrangement. This time the project manager received a call to prepare an estimate for a rush project, and in his haste to respond, he overlooked a $7,000 item for computer charges.

Assignment. List what is wrong with the firm's procedures and what you would do to correct them. How would you correct this situation without having the project manager lose initiative in serving the client?

What kinds of reports would you ask the project manager to make for you in order to analyze the reasons for the loss?

_____

_____

_____

_____

_____

_____

_____

_____

_____

_____

3.3 VALUE PRICING IN A COMPETITIVE ENVIRONMENT

The Price Life Cycle

This section explains the concept of value pricing, beginning with the definition of the price life cycle. Basically the problem today is that simply by entering a bidding situation, you are admitting that the "product" you offer has reached the end of its product life cycle, because competitive bidding only occurs at this point in the life of a "product." In the current economy, and presumably for many years to come, traditional design services are viewed as a commodity. Good de-

PRICE Lifecycle

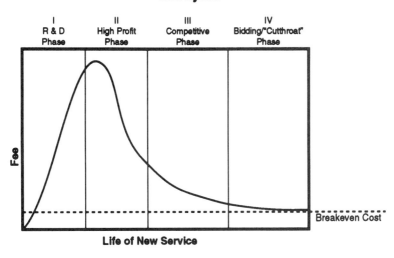

Exhibit 3.8

sign is expected. Quality is understood. So what are your selling points? How do you get out of the bidding arena?

First and foremost, the service you provide must be viewed by your clients as new, and then you can charge whatever you wish, people will seek you out, and you won't have to bid.

The graph in Exhibit 3.8 represents the life cycle of a product or service as it is developed, enters the market, and then becomes competitive. The difference between the break-even line on the price scale and the revenue flow curve represents a firm's level of profitability.

Stage I: Research and Development

The first stage in the price life cycle is the research and development stage, section I on the graph in Exhibit 3.8. As can be seen this stage costs a firm money, and represents a loss because it does not produce any income. The price life cycle on the graph, and the firm's revenue, are still below the break-even point.

Stage II: Profit Maximization

After developing a newly defined, highly sought after service, you are in high demand (Section II in Exhibit 3.8). When your service is unique, new, and no one else provides it, you can charge whatever you want for it. This is the innovative stage. This is where you would like to stay without any competition. However, the only way to stay here is to continually offer new products and services, about every 18 months.

Stage III: Price Competition

The third section (III) on the price life cycle chart is the competitive phase. This means your service has "peaked" because competitors have discovered how to produce or provide your product/service and offer it at a low price. Now, you have to lower your price to keep getting projects. This is generally where traditional architectural and engineering services end up.

Stage IV: Cutthroat

The final phase (IV) is the bidding, or "cutthroat" phase. In this phase, you try to stay competitive by bidding the lowest price. As can be seen from the chart, the bidding phase is the least profitable place to be. How do you avoid even getting near the point of bidding?

Where Do You Stand?

If the services you offer are traditional architectural or engineering services, it's time to reevaluate your image. You are positioned at point C on the chart and bidding will be inevitable. Invest in new services, new ideas, change your name, develop a niche market or specialization. You will lose money while learning how to sell the new service, but once you cross the break-even line you can sell this new service at an increasing fee until competition enters the market at point A. As more and more competition enters the market, note how both the potential fee and profitability on a new service decline until the new service becomes mature (traditional).

To stay out of the bidding arena, you must not be perceived as performing the *same service as everyone else.* Whenever bidding is used as a selection criterion, the client perceives all firms asked to bid as being equal. Thus, just by being asked to bid, you know that you have not positioned your image in the marketplace for maximum compensation. To that client you are just another A/E firm offering "bodies" to do traditional work. Price becomes the only differential.

How to Get to the Top

There are three ways to get to the top of the price life cycle (Exhibit 3.8):

1. *Be Truly Innovative.* Be the first one with a new idea. This is a risky approach to take. Sometimes your professional colleagues start to mention ethics. True innovation is also difficult to achieve. You may be called a maverick, unprofessional, or unethical by your peers. People may not like you or may not perceive you to be part of your profession.

2. *Copy Someone at the Top.* Look at a profitable firm, and copy it. Look, for example, at how fast facilities management has grown.

3. *Repackage your Services.* Organize your services into "bundles" to produce unique "products," which you can price profitably. You'll still be perceived by your clients as unique and service-oriented. Consider, for example, construction managers: these individuals are making money off of a new service that architects and engineers had been giving away for hundreds of years! And they are making more money than design professionals!

Continue Creating New Products

Redefine the firm's services in terms of client needs instead of professional practice. No one cares if you are an "architect" if no one "needs" architecture. Clients still need a whole array of design-related services, even if they are not building new structures. Examples include:

1. Financial analysis.
2. Market analysis.
3. Site investigation.
4. Regulatory approvals.
5. Lending negotations.
6. Presentation materials.
7. System management.
8. Americans with Disabilities Act (ADA) compliance audits.

9. Other regulatory reform compliance audits.

10. Hazardous waste disposal studies, and more.

To determine what new services would be appropriate for you to develop, survey your clients. Keep in touch with past clients. Identify new needs and serve them before someone else does. Try removing the traditional words "architect" or "engineer" from your firm's name. Instead call your firm "facilities management consultants," "program managers," "children's needs specialists," "hospital care design specialists," or some such. Remember that clients today want you to be a specialist. They feel they are being taken care of if you are a specialist, they trust you if your track record shows you've worked with other clients in their industry.

Once you've developed a new service, you can price your service according to whatever the market will bear, or based on its market value. When you stop selling your services based on the hours it takes to finish the project, and present truly innovative services, then you'll be able to charge higher prices. That is value pricing in a nutshell.

3.4 EIGHTEEN WAYS TO GENERATE CASH

In too many instances, architectural and engineering firm profits are all on paper. Where do they go? They get funneled to problem projects, new marketing ideas, and more. But with design firms feeling the cash crunch today, you really need to build up a cash pool so you're not levered to the point of near bankruptcy. Here are 18 ways to generate cash resources.

1. Attack Accounts Receivables

This is an obvious area to attack, but be sure you do it the right way. Don't instruct accounts receivables people to make calls or send duplicate invoices: Go straight to the source. Sit down with your clients, and explain exactly where you stand and why you need to get paid. Face to face contact is worth 1000 brownie points! Telephone calls and letters are not effective.

Get your project managers involved. Have them contact troubled accounts, or set up meetings with the troubled accounts. Bring the project manager to these meetings with you. Suggest payment schedules that accommodate both you and the client. If they cannot manage a $50,000 payment, then break it up into $10,000 or even $5000 per month. If you don't ask for it, you won't get it.

2. Work-in-Process

Do not allow any account to sit unbilled, regardless of its troubles. Often project managers will hold off on billing troubled work-in-process . . . for fear of upsetting the client. This is no longer acceptable—you cannot afford to let any account go unbilled these days. You've got to make payroll, cover overhead, and pay the rent, too.

Try this process:

1. Sit down with your project managers and ask for all billing data on troubled accounts.
2. Next, set up a meeting with each of the clients, bringing the project manager with you.
3. Resolve the trouble, and keep the bills going out and getting paid monthly.
4. If they're balking at payment, stop work. Payment must go on, and they must believe that you will work it out, no matter what the trouble.
5. Take this as an opportunity to build a better relationship with the clients in question.

Payment should be tied to a prearranged monthly schedule, and not to project cost accounting. Take a look at your accounting system. Many accounting software packages contribute to unsteady cash flow because they tie accounts receivables to job cost accounting. How often has your firm held up $500,000 in monthly billings waiting for one time card?

A good accounting system should divorce accounts receivables from job cost accounting. The job accounting system should track all project time and expenses, and the invoicing system should run independently on the first of each month. Your invoicing system should be based not on percent of the work that is complete, but on a prearranged payment schedule agreed upon during the contract negotiations. This type

of payment system provides optimum cash flow, particularly
if you establish greater lump sum payments up front.

3. Get Paid for Changes!

The biggest mistake design professionals make in relation to
changes is in trying to collect on changes when it's too late.
Any client will argue a change you're trying to collect on after
the fact, especially when it's three to six months down the
line. In addition, collecting for changes after the fact makes
your firm appear poorly managed.

The smartest system for dealing with changes is to preprint
a company changes form, and to require authorization for
each change. A change form should contain a place for your
signature, and a space for the client's approval signature. Do
not proceed with any change until you receive a signed
change form from the client.

If you're on a tight schedule and you feel that you cannot
afford to wait the two or three days it might take to obtain the
client's signature, then print a statement directly on the form
that says, "If we do not receive other instructions within 24
hours of receipt of this notice, then the change is hereby approved and we will proceed with the work described above."
Of course, check with your attorney to be sure you are stating
the stipulation correctly.

Another alternative to getting approval is to carry a portable fax with you wherever you go, and maybe even to give
the client a portable fax for the job duration (build this into
the job cost). In this way, you can be sure that the client has
access to you and can fax approval directly at any time.

4. Separate Reimbursable and Fee Invoices

Another item that unnecessarily holds up cash flow is reimbursables. How many times has a $50,000 client payment
been held up because an erroneous $.97 telephone call is in
dispute. This is an exaggeration, but the point is that reimbursables should not be part of the monthly payment agreement. Consider using three invoices: (1) your monthly payment, (2) an invoice for subconsultants, and (3) an invoice
for reimbursables. This may appear to be a more confusing
format, but the cost is low in comparison with the cost associated with the holdup of a $50,000 payment.

5. Don't Reveal Your Reimbursable Markups!

Design professionals are like terrible poker players—they sit down at the table and eagerly show all their cards. They reveal to the client all of their costs, all of their markups, and generally give away too much of the game.

Consider what happens when you go to a gas station and get a quart of oil for $3.00. You'll pay a markup on the oil without even thinking that you could run to the nearest hardware store and pick up a quart of oil for $1.29, open your hood, and put it in yourself. But when you need a quart of oil at the gas station and you're in a hurry, you don't think about it. You just order the quart of oil and pay the $3.00! Suppose, however, that the attendant said, "Look buddy, I'm going to charge you $3.00 for this. That's a markup of $1.71, okay? Just wanted you to know." Of course, you'd run right across the street to the hardware store, buy the quart for $1.29, and put it in yourself.

Whenever you reveal your actual costs you are opening yourself up for negotiation. Take a lesson from the gas station attendant and create flat prices for each reimbursable item. For example, rather than listing the cost of each telephone call you made for the client and then showing your markup multiplier, charge a flat fee for calls within a specific radius. For each call within a 50-mile radius, charge a flat $10 or $15, regardless of how long you are on the telephone. Charge another flat fee for calls within a 100-mile radius. Don't forget that each telephone call you make and receive has hidden costs—the cost of your telephone system, your receptionist, and the hourly rate of the person making the call.

And don't provide backup unless you're asked for it. Consider putting a clause in the contract stating that for every sheet of backup requested, you will charge the client an additional $100. This fee covers the cost of digging up the backup, the hourly rate of the project manager who must spend time looking for it, and the hourly rate of the accounting person who assists in sending it out. Again, these are the hidden costs that kill design professionals in business.

6. Give Frequent Raises

Giving frequent raises in these turbulent times is not only a morale booster, but another way to generate cash. Consider the increase in fees you could collect if you gave monthly raises (in smaller increments), rather than annual ones.

Turn to your company's spreadsheet program and perform the following two-year salary analysis. For the first year, bill one individual out at 200 hours per month at your existing multiplier for twelve months. That's 2400 hours of the person's salary rate, multiplied by your annual multiplier. At the end of the year, give that employee a raise of 12%. Then bill him or her out for the same number of hours for the next year period. At the end of the two year period, add up all the cash you've raised in that time.

On a separate spreadsheet, perform the same exercise, assuming that you give out a 1% raise each month for the two-year period. Total the revenue and you will find that you have generated 18% more revenue. This is just for one individual!

Obviously, you may not be able to give out monthly raises for accounting reasons. However, you might consider giving more frequent raises, because every time you give your employees a raise, you're giving the firm a raise as well.

Consider the other implications of monthly raises: you'll be known as the only design firm around that offers monthly raises—an added benefit to potential employees and present top performers.

7. Renegotiate Your Rental Lease

Capitalize on the recession's effect on real estate values. Don't pay more than you have to. Try renegotiating your lease or moving to another building to cut cash. Move from a triple net lease where you pay the rent, the taxes, and the utilities, to a single net lease where you pay only one lump sum for rent and the owner covers taxes and/or utilities. If you have let go a portion of your staff, then rent a smaller space. Renegotiate now while landlords are desperate to lock in tenants for the next five to six years.

8. Consolidate Your Borrowings

Many financial management firms and banks, as well as the Small Business Owners Association, are offering opportunities to consolidate your borrowings. Obtain a loan to consolidate all of your borrowings. If you are now borrowing at two points above the prime lending rate, have an extended credit line, have loans for CADD equipment and automobiles, and your balance sheet shows differing rates for each one, consider the merits of borrowing one lump-sum long-term note to consolidate.

Another way to consolidate your loans is to borrow from your pension plan. Federal regulations have relaxed recently to make this practice possible. The advantages are: (1) you negotiate your own rate of interest, and (2) you can obtain a fixed, rather than an adjustable rate. In this way, the interest you pay is going back into the plan, and, in essence, you are paying yourselves. Of course, you should first consult your attorney and your accountant.

9. Stretch Your Payables Ethically Starting Today

If you're really in a cash crunch, be sure to communicate with your creditors and suppliers. Write them all a letter today stating that rather than penalize one of them by not paying one, you would like to negotiate a new payment plan over a longer period to pay off all your debts. Obviously utility companies cannot be flexible, but oftentimes computer and equipment terms can be rewritten. When times are tight, explore your alternatives, communicate with your creditors, and set new payment plans. Suppliers and creditors know all too well these days that getting paid something is better than getting paid nothing at all.

10. Fire a Nonperformer Today

Unfortunately in any economic circumstance there are always a number of people in your firm who are just not productive workers, who kill time incessantly, and who are not motivated beyond 8 to 5 and the paycheck. They do not reach out into the client community to help you get more business, and they do nothing to boost their image within the firm. Take action on one of these persons today, and you'll save yourself time and aggravation.

This is no time to hold on to a nonperformer. There are millions out there in the job market and if your employees are not willing to go the extra mile for you, there are plenty out there who will. In fact, the "hiring" market is "good" for you, and you might even be able to find workers who will not only go the extra mile, but who'll take you another ten miles themselves. These are the top performers of the 90s, and they are out there. Get rid of someone today that you know you should have let go six months ago.

11. Stop Work on Losing Projects

All firms have losing projects, projects that should be quickly evaluated and put to rest, one way or another. Here's a way of ranking your work load to identify the losing projects:

1. Rank all existing projects starting from the top third (most profitable) to the middle third, and down to the bottom third (least profitable).

2. Remove the present project managers from the losing one third projects and place a principal in charge of each one. Motivate the principal to finish them up as fast as possible. The longer you let problem projects remain unfinished, the more money you lose.

Use your principals and your top performers to whip the problem projects into shape. Sometimes it just takes a new perspective to solve a lingering problem.

And above all else, do not initiate changes on losing projects unless you know in advance that you'll get paid for them.

12. Stop Writing $12,000 Proposals for Projects You May Not Get

In today's economy, the bid wars are losing battles, and too many design professionals out there today are submitting bids and proposals for projects that they wholeheartedly know they won't get. Or there are 40 other bidders. Or you don't have any contacts with the client.

Instead, start today to improve the quality of your proposals. Look at every lead and consider carefully whether or not you are truly capable of receiving the work. And embark on a networking plan that will guarantee you a higher percentage of work.

A network can be built relatively easily, and contacts are out there just waiting for you to meet them. Sit down today and draw up a plan for directing market research toward getting to know potential clients better. Join civic groups and client associations (your professional affiliations are not getting you any work!). Run for local offices, to spread name recognition. Zero in on client contacts.

13. Get Your Principals to Sell

Don't forget the value of selling your principals. Clients like to talk to people with the authority to make decisions. They want specialists, so get your specialists to sell. Clients do not want to talk to a greenhorn who was a drafter last week and is a project manager this week. Put your principals on the line, get them out of the nonbillable status. Gone are the days of nonchargeable principals. The most successful firms have principals with 60–65% chargeability ratios.

14. Use More Temporary Staff

If your revenues start growing again, don't staff up, staff down. Take advantage of retirees looking for part-time positions, mothers returning to the workplace, students who have almost, but not quite, completed their degrees, or contract architects, engineers, or drafters.

This can improve cash flow because: (1) it eliminates costly health care benefits, (2) it eliminates vacation, sick, health, or holiday pay, and (3) you can let temps come or go on an as-needed basis.

15. Increase Liability Insurance Deductibles

Many firms are still carrying unnecessarily low deductibles such as $25,000 on a $1 million policy. If a lawsuit should occur, you'll invariably use up the deductible very quickly. But how many lawsuits occur? Take some time to evaluate how much you can afford to lose. Deductibles today run as high as three years' worth of a firm's profitability. If your firm's profit is $50,000 a year, you can probably afford a $150,000 deductible, because a firm can finance that deductible over a five- or eight-year period.

16. Renegotiate Your Health Insurance Premiums

Recessionary times also impact the health industry. Take advantage of your leverage and find a private health company that can beat all of the other premiums being offered. Investigate plans through your professional affiliations, because the plans are larger and can cover more for less.

One architectural firm I know of has self-insured itself for every employee expense below $50,000. Their claims rate has gone down significantly as has their total cost for insurance. In the event of a catastrophe, the firm also has catastrophic policies for long-term or costly services only.

17. Eliminate Overhead Personnel

Eliminate personnel in your firm that cannot be charged directly to projects, or seek to assimilate them into chargeability. Directly charge secretaries and bookkeepers to projects, especially for state, local, and federal agencies where this practice is allowed. Eliminate the positions that cannot be charged directly to projects. Investigate the cost of a phone mail system that will answer the telephone rather than hiring a receptionist.

18. Postpone all Postponable Expenses

Put off for three months any expense that you can. For example, if you were just about to spend $30,000 producing a new company brochure, put it off. According to the *Professional Services Management Journal's Financial Statistics Survey,* accounts receivables turnover can be as high as 74 days, and work-in-process turnover as high as 40 days. This means that three and four months pass between the time a firm begins a task and the time it generates cash. If it takes three months to get paid, then postpone payment of capital expenses three months.

Some Final Notes

> *Get Paid in Advance.* From this day forward, ask every client to pay money in advance on all new contracts or all new phases of existing contracts. Place that money into an escrow account or savings account to be applied to the last payment. Ask for advances for all expenses such as pass-through engineers, travel, and so on. These are legitimate reimbursables. Some international contracts are paid entirely in advance.
>
> *Brainstorm.* Call your ten key people into the conference

room today and ask them to think about ten ways, each, that the firm can generate cash now. Set a date for one week from today to sit with these people and brainstorm.

Safeguard Cash Reserves. Once cash is raised, safeguard a portion of it by putting it into a Certificate of Deposit for a one year period. Build your cash assets.

Don't Procrastinate. Those who manage cash most effectively are those who don't procrastinate. Procrastinators in a tight economy will inevitably fail. Don't procrastinate at calling a client for fear of upsetting the relationship. Don't put off firing the nonproductive employee, calling the bank for a loan, calling the Small Business Owners Association for a loan. Seek necessary channels to improve your cash flow. Waiting another day will only cost you money.

FINAL EXAMINATION—CHAPTER 3

Multiple Choice

1. A project manager needs the following items to prepare the estimate:
   a. the firm's costs for past projects.
   b. the firm's profit policy.
   c. figures on escalation rates of future costs.
   d. all of the above.
   e. none of the above.

2. Reimbursable expenses are
   a. not foreseeable.
   b. projected in advanced based on past projects.
   c. not important.
   d. a and b only.
   e. b and c only.

3. Profit is not
   a. the supporting cash for the firm in hard times.
   b. a means for paying for unallowable expenses.
   c. something that goes into the owner's pocket.
   d. funding for computers and equipment.

4. Typical markup for contingencies is
   a. 1%.

    b. 2%.

    c. 5%.

    d. 10%.

    e. 20%.

5. In using billing rates, the client must understand
   a. what is included in billing rates.
   b. how much each person in the firm makes.
   c. reimbursable expenses.
   d. all of the above.
   e. a and b only.

6. Market price for projects is influenced by
   a. what the client can spend.
   b. nothing in particular.
   c. the price the competition is charging.
   d. a and c only.
   e. b and c only.

7. Developing a price from a cost
   a. depends on many factors.
   b. depends on client's perception of price.
   c. doesn't work.
   d. a and b only.
   e. a and c only.

8. The amount to allocate in a budget for project management is
   a. 5%.
   b. 10%.
   c. 15%.
   d. 20%.
   e. 25%.

Discussion Problem

Background. Your 15-person environmental consulting firm has primary expertise in waste water treatment facilities and general cleanup work. Its projects are split about evenly between private and government work.

Your firm uses a number of fee schedules to price the work according to the wishes of your clients and the type of work as follows:

    Schedule A: Percentage of construction costs.

    Schedule B: Actual salaries times a 3.0 multiplier that

includes overhead and profit. Other direct costs are marked up by 15%.

Schedule C: Billing schedule based on standard rates for each classification of personel, that is, junior engineer, intermediate engineer, and so forth. Other direct costs are marked up by 15%.

Schedule D: Special rate schedule for assignments requiring a high degree of senior staff time, such as expert witness testimony. Rates for all technical personnel are the same as the highest hourly rate shown in Schedule C. Support personnel are billed at the highest hourly rate for support personnel. Other direct costs are marked up by 15%.

Assignment: When would you use a multiplier (Schedule B) rather than a standard billing rate (Schedule C)? List the advantages and disadvantages of each. Under what circumstances would it be appropriate to quote a lump sum fee arrangement?

List the considerations involved in undertaking an assignment requiring expert witness testimony. How would you justify the higher fee schedule to a client?

_____

_____

_____

_____

_____

_____

_____

_____

_____

_____

_____

_____

_____

_____

4

CONTROLLING LABOR AND OTHER PROJECT COSTS

Chapter Summary

- Elements of a good salary administration plan
- How to determine bonuses
- Points to consider before reducing staff
- Principal causes of project overruns
- How to control overruns

Controlling Labor Costs

Since labor makes up such a high percentage of the costs on a project, controlling labor costs will go a long way toward controlling all other project costs.

4.1 CONTROLLING PROJECT LABOR COSTS

Project labor costs need to be controlled through careful budgeting and careful supervision, particularly of the less experienced staff members. Each person should be given an individual budget allotment by the supervisor so that everyone is aware of what is expected in a given number of hours. If there is a problem with the budgeted hours it should be discussed and resolved, if possible in advance. In many cases the budgets will have to be adjusted, but it is better to make these adjustments in advance before the work is started. Afterwards there is less flexibility for trade-offs.

Controlling Firmwide Labor Costs

Labor costs also need to be controlled on a firmwide basis, and this is accomplished through good personnel practices. Most successful firms now recognize the need for a human resources function managed by a professional, if the firm is of a size to support it. Hiring and retaining good people is the responsibility of the human resources manager in a larger firm. In smaller firms this responsibility is given to the principal in charge of operations or administration. He or she is responsible for recruiting and recommending proper salary levels for the various categories of personnel in the firm based on surveys and other data. These salary scales must be competitive with those in the marketplace as well as those within the firm. Salary increases should be budgeted and based on a number of factors, including (1) prior years' increases, (2) cost of living, (3) competition, and (4) the financial resources of the firm. Exhibit 4.1 is an example of how data on previous years' salary increases are compiled. Most importantly, the decision on salary increases should include the immediate supervisor's evaluation of the individual.

To set up a good salary administration plan you should determine ranges for different categories of personnel. Note that the ranges overlap at the top of each classification in order to permit a certain amount of salary increases without necessarily having to promote an individual to the next higher category. A written salary administration policy should accompany the ranges and outline the firm's philosophy and procedures for administering the program. The policy and ranges should then be distributed throughout the firm, and all individuals should know their classification and the requirements needed to advance.

One important method for controlling labor costs is to convert nonbillable to billable time whenever possible. Support staff, such as secretaries and word processing operators, should charge their time to projects whenever they work long enough on a single project to make this worthwhile. Likewise, principals should charge their time directly whenever they are contributing to a project. In this case communication is most important so that project managers know and accept the help they are receiving from the principals.

Bonuses are a widely accepted method of motivating employees, and if used properly they can contribute greatly to the success of the firm and to the proper control of labor costs. Bonuses should be paid on the basis of merit and should generally be large enough to signal an important re-

CALCULATION OF PERCENTAGE INCREASE IN SALARIES

Fiscal Year Ending _____

Classification	Number of Employees	Amount (Beginning of Year)	Amount (End of Year)	% Increase
Division manager	1	$40,000	$45,000	
Department manager	2	70,000	74,000	
Senior engineer	4	125,000	130,000	
Engineer/Designer	6	150,000	152,000	
Junior engineer	7	140,000	150,000	
Specialist	—	—	—	
Senior drafter	1	25,000	28,000	
Drafter	3	54,000	60,000	
Senior technician	1	20,000	22,000	
Technician	—	—	—	
Secretary	2	30,000	35,000	
Administrative support	2	35,000	40,000	
Total firm	29	$689,000	$736,000	7%

Exhibit 4.1 This analysis should include employees who worked for the entire period. Employees who were promoted during the year would tend to depress the percentage increase in those categories affected and may require a separate analysis if significant.

ward. They should be limited to those people who have made a significant contribution to the firm. To the extent possible they should be directly related to the profitability of the firm and to the individuals responsible for that profit.

When labor costs must be reduced through terminations and layoffs, most firms have found that good communications between management and staff become even more important than usual. The people affected must be told quickly and in a straightforward manner, and those not affected must be told as well. Otherwise rumors will circulate and the people you are trying to keep will often leave on their own.

Eleven suggestions for determining how to terminate employees, which have been used in several firms, are shown below:

1. *Terminate Nonperformers.* This should be the policy in good times as well as bad, but it is especially important for the morale of an organization to let these people go first in a downturn.

2. *Correct Existing Salary Inequities.* If anyone's pay is out of line with responsibilities for whatever reason, cutbacks and terminations are a good time to correct the situation.

3. *Eliminate Overtime.* Obviously, in slack periods overtime should be cut back or eliminated consistent with the requirements of on-going projects. Those people who have counted on a certain amount of overtime to supplement their income will be particularly affected, but an overall policy change is fairest to all.

4. *Loan Personnel to Other Firms, if Possible.* This is a good solution when practicable, but during slack periods in the economy few employers need extra help.

5. *Reduce Working Hours.* This is also a fair across-the-board solution, but it is often disruptive in a professional services firm where people depend on each other in the course of their work. While the office is open during regular hours, people working shorter hours will not be around for portions of the day.

6. *Reduce the Number of Secretaries per Officer/Manager.* Obviously, each position needs to be evaluated and plans made for doubling up on duties whenever possible. The reduction in number of support staff is one place to start.

7. *Encourage Voluntary Leaves of Absence.* Through good communication with staff it may be possible to identify people who, because of their personal situations, would be willing to take a leave of absence without pay.

8. *Promote Vacations With/Without Pay.* This is another area where some short-term savings in labor costs are possible.

9. *Institute Salary Cuts/Deferrals.* When decisions are

made to cut salaries, it is important for the staff to know that management is included and is taking the largest percentage deductions.

10. *Identify Labor-Consuming Tasks/Bottlenecks and Correct Them.* If there are any procedural or operating situations where personnel are not being used effectively or where some people have to wait around for others to complete certain tasks, these problems should be corrected.

11. *Cut Diagonally Across All Levels in the Organization.* Most specialists in human resources suggest that it is better to reduce staff at all levels in the organization when reductions are necessary, rather than cutting only the junior levels.

EXERCISE 4.1

Controlling Labor Costs

Multiple Choice

1. Each person in the firm should be given
   a. an individual budget allotment by the supervisor so each is aware of what is expected.
   b. no guidelines, so each is tested based on his or her abilities.
   c. a labor chart.
   d. none of the above.

2. In a small firm, the person responsible for controlling labor cost is
   a. the project manager.
   b. the CEO.
   c. the principal in charge of operations or administration.
   d. all of the above.

3. To set up a good salary administration plan, you should
   a. determine levels of need.
   b. set up ranges for different personnel categories.
   c. look at past records.
   d. all of the above.

4. One way to control labor costs is to
   a. charge more time to overhead.

    b. charge less time to projects.

    c. convert nonbillable to billable time when possible.

    d. none of the above.

5. Bonuses should be

    a. directly related to the profitability of the firm.

    b. limited to those who have contributed significantly to the firm.

    c. large enough to signal reward.

    d. paid on the basis of merit.

    e. all of the above.

6. When layoffs are necessary in a firm

    a. communications must be open.

    b. people affected must be told quickly.

    c. people not affected must be told.

    d. a and c only.

    e. a, b, and c only.

4.2 CONTROLLING OTHER PROJECT COSTS

Costs other than labor on a project, such as computer and report preparation costs, are controlled by the budget. Often these expenditures are not made equally throughout the project, which is why budgets must be broken down by month or reporting period to compare with actual expenditures. The level of detail needed to control reimbursable expenses, for instance, varies by firm, and each firm has to decide which expenses are likely to overrun and which should therefore be monitored separately. For example, computer costs can become a significant item of expense on a project and can easily get out of hand if not watched. The amount budgeted for costs generally associated with the final stages of a project, such as report or document preparation, can also be used up before the project is completed unless budgeted separately and set aside. Experienced project managers recognize the importance of controlling reimbursable expenses and will carefully watch the charges that they approve for payment against their projects.

If the overhead rate must be increased because it was not correctly forecast when the budgets were prepared, that is not the project manager's fault. He or she cannot be held accountable for it. This will become obvious in the project reporting system when the various elements of costs are isolated. The difference caused by a variance in overhead should be eliminated when judging the project manager's performance on the project.

EXERCISE 4.2

Other Project Costs

True or False

T F   Costs other than labor are controlled by the budget.

T F   Nonlabor costs are expended equally throughout a project.

T F   Computer expenditures are easily controlled, preventing cost overruns.

T F   The amount budgeted for final costs can be consumed before the project is completed and should be set aside.

T F   It is not very important to control reimbursable expenses.

T F   The project manager is accountable if the firm's overhead rate is increased.

4.3   PROJECT OVERRUNS

Overruns occur when costs get out of line with the budget for any number of reasons and when they cannot be recovered from the client. In that case the project may incur no profit or even suffer a loss. Regardless of the reasons for the overrun the cause is the same—poor estimating or inadequate project management.

In some cases, the overrun may not be the fault of the project manager if he or she has been overruled in decisions by higher management. That is then an organizational problem. However, most firms now recognize the importance of the strong project manager type of organization, which gives complete operating authority and responsibility to the project manager. In that case, the project manager accepts responsibility for project losses. Exhibit 4.2 is a checklist for controlling project overruns.

CHECKLIST FOR CONTROLLING PROJECT OVERRUNS

YES	NO	
☐	☐	Are procedures in place for review of contracts for technical, legal, and financial aspects?
☐	☐	Are project managers involved at the beginning in contract negotiation and pricing?
☐	☐	Are budgets prepared for each project where appropriate and breakdowns required by month so that comparisons can be made with actual performance?
☐	☐	Do project managers have control over all charges to their projects (including labor and expenses)?
☐	☐	Are meetings held regularly with project managers and principals to discuss the status of projects?
☐	☐	Are project managers encouraged to report problems early so that corrective action can be taken?
☐	☐	Is a financial summary prepared on completion of each project and reviewed with the principals and project manager?
☐	☐	Are project managers graded on their ability to control costs as part of their performance evaluations?
☐	☐	Does the firm encourage project managers to seek further training in project management?
☐	☐	Do project managers read and understand the financial reports prepared for them?

Exhibit 4.2 Note the preventive measures that can be taken to avoid project overruns.

A good project control system, in which progress on the job is compared against the budget and there are reports often enough and in sufficient detail for the project manager and others to recognize potential trouble spots, will go a long way toward preventing project overruns. Simple manual systems can be useful for smaller firms. However as a firm grows and projects are added, it becomes necessary to keep track of such data by computer. Timesharing and service bureaus are available for this task, or the firm may decide to purchase an in-house computer and software to run the system. There are several reference sources available to help in selecting software specifically developed for the design professional.

Projects overruns are a painful and expensive lesson when they occur, and it is important that they be a learning exercise for everyone. Principals in the firm need to know who the capable project managers are, the ones who can be trusted to perform well. Experienced project managers need to learn to read early warning signals. Less experienced project managers need to learn from their mistakes. Fault finding is not nearly so important as learning why the loss occurred and what can be done about it in the future so that it will not happen again.

EXERCISE 4.3

Discussion Problem

Background. Your ten-person interior design firm has been losing projects to a larger architectural and interior design firm located across town. Many of these clients have been of long standing. When asked, several clients have explained that your costs have risen so rapidly over the last few years that your services have lost their competitive advantage. Clients cannot justify paying a higher price for work that is not that much superior in quality.

You examine your recent project estimates and budgeting forms and everything looks to be in order. Your overhead rate has increased from 1.5 to 1.8 over the last two years, but it still appears to be comparable with other firms according to some recent survey information you obtained. Salary rates also appear to be about what others are paying for comparable skills. Upon examination of time accounting reports, you notice that it takes people longer to accomplish certain tasks than you think necessary. Some of the problem can be traced to the turnover of personnel and the extra training required of new employees. In other cases, it appears that overall staff productivity is not keeping pace with that of other firms.

To track the costs for training new employees, you establish an overhead account for orientation. Project managers are instructed to have new employees charge this account when they are receiving instruction.

Assignment. What are the advantages of isolating and accounting for training costs? What kinds of training should every new employee receive? What actions should be taken to improve productivity and make the firm more competitive?

List the ways in which a design firm can measure productivity.

_____

_____

_____

_____

_____

_____

_____

_____

_____

_____

_____

_____

_____

_____

_____

_____

FINAL EXAMINATION—CHAPTER 4

Multiple Choice

1. A project overrun can be an organizational problem when
   a. overhead rates decline.
   b. project managers are not careful.
   c. the project manager's decisions are overridden by management.
   d. none of the above.

2. The strong project manager organization gives
   a. corporate control to project managers.
   b. complete operating authority to the project manager.
   c. reward to strong project managers.
   d. all of the above.

3. Experienced project managers know when overruns will occur because they know how to
   a. detect changes.
   b. read early warning signs.
   c. read reports.
   d. none of the above.

4. To set up a good salary administration plan, you must
   a. look at past records.
   b. determine levels of need.
   c. set up ranges for different personnel categories.
   d. all of the above.

5. In a smaller firm, the person responsible for controlling labor costs is
   a. the CEO.
   b. the project manager.
   c. the principal in charge of operations/administration.
   d. all of the above.
   e. none of the above.

6. One way to control labor costs is to
   a. charge less time to projects.
   b. charge time to overhead.
   c. convert nonbillable to billable time when possible.
   d. none of the above.

True or False

T F Labor costs of less experienced staff should be closely controlled.

T F Each person should receive an individual budget allotment for each project.

T F Hiring and firing is the responsibility of the principal in charge of operations.

T F Salary increases are based only on performance.

T F A written salary administration policy is not necessary.

T F Support staff should never charge their time to projects.

T F Bonuses are a widely accepted method of motivating employees.

T   F   Layoffs require little communication to staff.

T   F   People affected by a layoff should be notified last.

T   F   People not affected should not be told about a layoff.

T   F   Vacations without pay are one way to save labor costs short-term.

5 CONTROLLING OVERHEAD COSTS

Chapter Summary

- Danger signals that indicate rising overhead costs
- Typical overhead rates
- Fixed and variable costs
- Controlling unauthorized purchases
- Insurance for professional liability
- Controlling marketing expenses
- Encouraging budgeting initiative
- Fifty Ways to Control Costs

Danger Signals

When overhead costs begin to climb significantly there is generally a reason. However, if a firm can recognize certain danger signals in advance, it can save itself the diminished profits or losses that are likely to occur.

5.1 HOW TO RECOGNIZE DANGER SIGNALS

One tip-off that overhead costs are not in line with your estimates is that there are wide variances from established budgets. Another is unexpected losses in certain profit centers. There may be unexplainable cost increases in certain overhead accounts. These are danger signals that circumstances are not under control.

Rising indirect labor costs and a corresponding decline in utilization rates (the percentage of direct or chargeable labor to total salaries) are another indication that overhead costs are on the increase. Sometimes there may be significant charges to overhead labor accounts, such as administration or marketing, by people who normally should be charging most of their time to projects. If the firm has an account called "unutilized time" for time that cannot be legitimately charged to anything else and if there are significant charges to this account, then that is obviously a danger signal. If there is not enough work to keep the staff busy and people are required to use vacation and sick time, that is another indication that overhead costs are likely to rise. If there are significant project overruns, then that is a sign of lack of proper control that is bound to be reflected in overhead.

Overhead is usually calculated monthly and compared with the budgeted overhead rate established at the beginning of the year. It should be compared on a cumulative year-to-date basis to avoid month-to-month distortions. Generally, an overhead rate is established at the beginning of the year and is not changed unless there are significant changes in the firm's operations. The overhead rate should be compared with the firm's historical experience as well as with that of other firms of similar size and characteristics. *The PSMJ Financial Statistics Survey for Professional Services Firms,* sponsored by *Professional Services Management Journal* (PSMJ), is a good source for comparing overhead rates and other statistical information. Write to PSMJ, Ten Midland Avenue, Newton, MA 02158, for more information. Exhibit 5.1 is a checklist of items to consider in controling overhead costs.

Low profitability or losses may be the ultimate signal that overhead costs are climbing out of control. On the other hand, it may not be an overhead cost problem at all, but rather a revenue problem caused by not enough work or lack of project control. Therefore, while it is important to monitor overhead closely, the financial manager should be familiar with the other danger signals in order to discover and report the real reasons for any problems that may arise.

Nature of Overhead Costs

Before examining ways to control and reduce overhead costs, you need to understand the concept of fixed and variable costs. While all costs are variable given a sufficient period of time, fixed costs are those that do not vary with the volume of operations. Some examples are rent and depreciation expenses that essentially remain unchanged as the firm's

CHECKLIST OF ITEMS TO CONSIDER IN CONTROLLING OVERHEAD COSTS

YES	NO	
☐	☐	Do I receive information in time enough to take corrective action to prevent losses?
☐	☐	Are project managers aware of their financial performance, and are they constantly monitoring project performance?
☐	☐	Are overhead budgets carefuly controlled and not exceeded without advance explanation?
☐	☐	Is management "cost conscious," and is that attitude conveyed to the rest of the staff?
☐	☐	Is there a report on administrative time that identifies the various categories such as marketing and administration?
☐	☐	Do the principals of the firm charge sufficient time to projects?
☐	☐	Are controls in place so that time shown on timesheets reflects what people are actually doing?
☐	☐	Is the support staff of the proper size when compared with other similar firms?
☐	☐	Is there enough work scheduled ahead to keep people busy and not worrying about staff reductions?

Exhibit 5.1 Note the emphasis on preparing budgets and then comparing actual costs against budget.

revenue increases or decreases. On the other hand, variable costs do change with volume; some examples are supplies and telephone charges, which are somewhat related to the amount of work performed. While variable costs may be easier to control in the short run, fixed costs should not be overlooked when examining ways to make permanent reductions.

It is important to know who has responsibility for controlling costs. In most firms the responsibility for controlling project costs rests with the project manager. Fixed costs should be under the control of the financial manager and variable costs under the control of department or profit center managers. Depending upon how the firm is organized, there may be some variations in this arrangement, but the important point is to assign responsibility so that someone in the organization is looking at individual costs and watching for signs of unusual increases.

EXERCISE 5.1 ▩

Items to Consider in Controlling Overhead Costs

Multiple Choice

1. Which of the following are overhead cost danger signals?
   a. unexpected losses in certain profit centers.
   b. unexplained cost increases in certain overhead accounts.
   c. wide variances from established budgets.
   d. all of the above.
   e. none of the above.

2. Declining utilization rates and _____ indirect labor costs indicate increasing overhead labor costs.
   a. rising.
   b. declining.
   c. stable.
   d. erratic.

3. If people are required to use vacation time and sick time, it is an indication that
   a. there is not enough work to keep people busy.
   b. overhead costs are likely to decline.
   c. overhead costs are likely to rise.
   d. all of the above.
   e. a and c only.

4. Overhead is usually calculated
   a. weekly.
   b. biweekly.
   c. monthly.
   d. semiannually.
   e. at the beginning of the year.

5. The budgeted overhead rate is established
   a. weekly.
   b. biweekly.
   c. monthly.
   d. semiannually.
   e. at the beginning of the year.

6. Low profitability or losses may be a sign of
   a. a revenue problem caused by not enough work.
   b. a revenue problem caused by lack of project control.
   c. overhead costs climbing out of control.
   d. all of the above.
   e. none of the above.

7. Fixed costs are those that
   a. are fixed according to the rate of inflation monthly.
   b. are fixed according with the volume of operations.
   c. do not vary with the volume of operations.
   d. all of the above.

8. When examining ways to make permanent reductions, one should consider
   a. fixed costs.
   b. variable costs.
   c. all of the above.
   d. none of the above.

9. Responsibility for controlling costs belongs to
   a. the project manager.
   b. the financial manager.
   c. department or profit center managers.
   d. all of the above.
   e. a and b only.

10. It is important to assign responsibility for controlling costs so that someone in the organization is
    a. monitoring petty cash.
    b. looking at individual costs.
    c. watching for signs of unusual increases.
    d. all of the above.
    e. b and c only.

5.2 COSTS NOT AFFECTING PERFORMANCE

When taking action to control overhead costs, concentrate on meaningful areas. That is, first examine costs of significant size so that any reductions achieved will make an impact on total overhead costs. Otherwise, efforts at cost reduction will be dissipated over an assortment of minor savings that do not amount to much in total. People then become quickly discouraged with the effort. It is also a good practice to begin in areas that do not affect the firm's operating performance. Cuts in these areas are the least painful to make.

Idle Time

YES   NO

☐   ☐   Is idle time of staff members controlled?

☐ ☐ Are projects monitored to see that excessive time is not spent by some individuals and departments?

☐ ☐ Are charges to overhead accounts, such as marketing and administration, carefully controlled by the people in charge of these activities?

An obvious area to examine first is idle staff time, which is probably the largest waste of money. Either the people should be made productive or else the staff should be reduced. In order to make judgments about this, manpower staffing forecasts, as described in Chapter 7, are vital and should be updated at least monthly over a three month period.

Purchasing

YES   NO

☐ ☐ Is purchasing controlled so that only one or two people in the organization can purchase supplies and authorize payment?

☐ ☐ Are purchase orders used for all expenditures except routine purchases?

☐ ☐ Are quantity discounts taken on purchases?

Purchasing is another area that should be brought under control Purchasing should be centralized within the organization with only one or two people authorized to buy supplies and equipment. This will enable the firm to take advantage of quantity discounts and to shop for the best price, as well as to control unauthorized purchases. Arrangements should be made for emergency purchases by people who run short of supplies when working outside regular office hours, but the large routine purchases should be tightly controlled. The firm should consider the use of a purchase order system if the volume of purchases warrants it.

Another arrangement that some firms have used successfully is that of hiring a single vendor for all purchases of high-volume items, such as reproduction or drafting supplies. The firm should calculate what it spends in a year for these supplies and then ask several vendors what discounts they will give if all the firm's business is placed with one supplier. Of course, the firm should only make this offer to vendors that it has used in the past and who have proven their reliability.

General Liability Insurance

YES	NO	
☐	☐	Does the firm have one broker for all insurance?
☐	☐	Does the broker survey the market to be certain that the firm is purchasing coverage most economically?
☐	☐	Is the broker routinely notified when new equipment is acquired or office space is to be increased or decreased?

Insurance is another overhead cost area that should be examined for possible savings, or at least periodic increases should be controlled. The firm's insurance broker should be pressed to get the best insurance coverage for the money, since that is the broker's primary purpose. Competitive bids should be obtained for both the employee benefit insurance and the firm's general liability coverage at least once every two years and every year in cases where rates are rising significantly. The firm should try to place all its insurance with a single broker, if possible, so that the total amount is significant enough for the broker to be encouraged to work on the firm's behalf. One good technique for employee benefit insurance is to see if the firm can become a part of a "group within a group"—that is, to place its group insurance within a larger group to take advantage of lower member rates. Members of the American Consulting Engineers Association, the American Institute of Architects, and most other professional societies, either locally or nationally, have similar arrangements, or they should be encouraged to obtain them from a group insurance carrier.

Professional Liability Insurance

YES	NO	
☐	☐	Does the firm have a loss prevention program in which all senior staff members participate?
☐	☐	Are nonstandard contracts reviewed by legal counsel?

☐   ☐   Do principals understand what the professional liability insurance covers and how it is different from general liability?

Professional liability insurance is generally the largest element of insurance cost. While there is little a single firm can do to affect these rates, some things are possible. The firm can participate in loss prevention programs sponsored by the insurance carrier, it can train its own personnel in loss prevention to maintain a good experience record, and it can shop around when various carriers are competing for this business. The problem with switching insurance carriers is that the firm has exposure on past projects that must be covered for a long period. Another drawback to changing carriers is the volatile insurance market, where carriers enter and leave the market periodically, so that coverage with a new carrier may not be automatically renewed.

One way of achieving some reduction in professional liability premiums is to find out how they are calculated. If they are based on gross revenue encourage clients to accept invoices for service directly from consultants rather than having them pass through the firm's books when the firm is acting as prime professional. The firm can still monitor the consultant's work and act in every way as prime professional on the project, but by elimination of pass-through accounting, the firm's revenues are thereby reduced. This can represent a significant savings.

Another way to reduce professional liability insurance premiums is to investigate the use of project professional liability insurance. In this case the carrier agrees to insure only a particular project and the firm can then claim that premium as a reimbursable expense on the project. If clients will agree to this, then they do not have to bear that portion of the overhead rate that includes professional liability insurance on all other projects. This procedure is sometimes useful for larger projects, if your insurance carrier writes this type of coverage.

Another recent development is the use of a single insurance carrier by both the design professionals and the contractor on a project. This prevents disputes between insurance companies if there is a claim, and it can result in lower premiums for all.

Another interesting development is the attempt by several firms to get together to form this own captive insurance company, which is owned by the firm or firms it insures. The captive insurance company invests its own premium income and pays its own claims and can save its owners significant sums of money by handling claims up to a certain limit. The captive insurance company lays off or reinsures the larger losses with other insurance carriers in case of catastrophe. The drawbacks to forming a captive company are that it requires a substantial premium income to support its operations, so it is available only to the largest firms. There are significant administrative expenses as well; in effect, you are going into the insurance business, because you're dependent on the group's experience to determine your premium expense.

It is good to know about the newer developments in the insurance market and then to check with your broker to determine if they are appropriate for your firm.

Exhibit 5.2 is a checklist of insurance coverages that can assist you in structuring a comprehensive program with the assistance of your broker.

Office Space

YES   NO

☐   ☐   Has the present office space been examined recently to see whether it is crowded or excessive?

☐   ☐   Does the firm have a plan for its future space requirements?

☐   ☐   Are leases reviewed and decisions made well in advance of expiration dates?

☐   ☐   Could the firm swap excess space with someone to cut costs for other services?

Space requirements are another area that should be examined to keep overhead costs under control. The firm should try to anticipate its space needs as it grows to avoid having to take space at another location. Operating out of two locations can be expensive because of the need to duplicate office services. This is one area in particularly where a long-range business plan comes in handy.

Lease arrangements should be made with some provision for growth through subleasing adjoining space or contraction depending on space needs. The firm, for example, must decide whether to stay at its present location or move well in

CHECKLIST OF INSURANCE COVERAGE AVAILABLE
TO PROFESSIONAL SERVICE FIRMS

Package Policy

1. *Multiperil Policy*: Provides comprehensive property and general liability insurance tailored to the needs of the insured and subject to a package discount from premiums for similar insurance written under separate policies. Building coverage and personal property coverage are available on a named peril basis or an all-risk basis. An automatic increase in insurance endorsement may be attached to keep coverage in line with inflation. Earthquake coverage where appropriate is available by endorsement. Loss of earnings, rents, and extra expense may also be covered by endorsement, as well as employee dishonesty and money loss.

2. *Business Owners' Policy Program*: Available for an office building, but subject to certain restrictions. Property coverage is on a replacement cost basis, and there is no coinsurance clause for all risks or named perils protection. Loss of income insurance and comprehensive liability insurance are included.

Building Property Damage

1. *Fire Insurance*: For design professionals who occupy their own buildings.

2. *General Property Form*: Applies to described structures and all permanent fixtures constituting a part of the structures.

3. *Builders' Risk Form*: Available to indemnify professionals who erect their own building for loss or damage from specific perils while under construction. Insurance applies only in course of construction; a permanent policy must be written upon completion, at which time the builders' risk policy is cancelled pro rata.

4. *Replacement Cost Endorsement*: Provides for full reimbursement for the actual cost of repair or replacement of an insured building without deduction for depreciation. The standard policy indemnifies on an actual cash value basis.

5. *Extended Coverage Endorsement*: Covers property for same amount as fire policy against all direct loss or damage caused by windstorm and hail, explosion, riot and civil commotion, aircraft, vehicles, and smoke.

6. *Vandalism and Malicious Mischief*: Written by endorsement with the extended coverage endorsement and extends the policy owner to cover loss or damage caused by vandalism or malicious mischief.

7. *Demolition Insurance*: For an additional premium, extend the fire policy to cover a loss resulting from the enforcement of any state or muncipal law that necessitates, in rebuilding, the demolition of any part of the insured building not damaged by fire. Study your local regulations on this point.

8. *Glass Insurance*: Insures replacement of plate glass windows and structural glass broken or accidentally or maliciously damaged. Glass is used extensively on the front of modern office buildings, and it should be insured if it appears on your offices.

9. *Flood Insurance Policy*: Protects owners against financial loss from floods. Flood insurance is written in areas declared eligible by the Federal Insurance Administrator.

10. *Sprinkler Leakage*: For buildings equipped with sprinklers, insures against all direct loss to buildings or contents as result of leakage or freezing or breaking of sprinkler installations.

11. *Earthquake Insurance*: Covers loss caused by earthquake, an important coverage in areas where earthquakes occasionally occur.

> **Exhibit 5.2** Package policies that ensure more than one hazard are less expensive than individual policies covering the same risks, and should be obtained whenever possible.

12. *Boiler and Machinery Insurance*: Insures against direct damage and loss of income from boiler mishaps.

Contents and Personal Property Damage

1. *Fire Insurance*: For a tenant who wishes to insure contents, improvements, and betterments under a single policy.
2. *Office Personal Property Form*: Provides all-risk coverage on contents of offices at named locations; applies to improvements and betterments as well as personal property.
3. *Extended Coverage Endorsement*: Applicable to contents and personal property just as it is to real property.
4. *Vandalism and Malicious Mischief*: Determine whether the additional expense of this extension is warranted by the location of the occupied building.
5. *Replacement Cost Endorsement*: Provides coverage on the basis of replacement cost for owned property.

Professional Activities

1. *Scientific Instruments Floater*: Intended for scientific instruments of a portable nature; insures each instrument listed on an all-risk basis.
2. *Accounts Receivable Policy*: Protects the insured against loss resulting from the inability to collect accounts receivable when the books of record have been destroyed, lost, or damaged.
3. *Valuable Papers*: Covers loss or destruction of valuable papers such as financial data, specifications, client lists, construction plans and blueprints, and manuscripts.
4. *Rental Value Insurance*: For owners of buildings. Protects building owner against loss of income where rentals have been interrupted or rental values impaired by the occurrence of any of the hazards insured against.
5. *Leasehold Interest*: For tenants. Protects against loss caused by having to rent property at a higher rate in the event the lease is cancelled as a result of the occurrence of any hazard insured against.
6. *Extra Expense Insurance*: Insures against payment of additional expense of operating in temporarily rented quarters due to damage to building or contents by fire or other insured hazard.
7. *Broad Form Comprehensive General Liability*: When added by endorsement, extends basic comprehensive general liability insurance to cover a number of additional hazards. Ask your broker for details about this coverage.
8. *Worker's Compensation*: Mandated by the state for varying amounts.
9. *Business Auto Policy*: The business counterpart of the personal auto policy; be sure to include coverage for employee cars and rental cars used on business.
10. *Umbrella Liability Insurance*: Provides protection against third-party claims not covered by underlying general liability and automobile liability policies and provides excess limits of insurance for claims.
11. *Fiduciary Liability Insurance*: Pays legal liability arising from claims for alleged failure to prudently act within the meaning of the Pension Reform Act of 1974.
12. *Partnerships*: Provides cash to carry out a buy-or-sell agreement in the event of the death of a partner. The advice of an attorney is customary in tying the insurance in with a carefully worked-out agreement.
13. *Key Man Insurance*: Reimburses business for financial loss resulting from death of a key person in the business.
14. *Professional Liability Insurance*: Covers errors and omissions.

Exhibit 5.2   Continued.

advance of the lease's expiration. It is important to review the lease and note any milestone dates when notices must be given to the landlord. An analysis of various alternate locations needs to be made and the real estate market tested so that the firm is in a position to make the proper decision when the time comes.

Accounting/Legal Services

YES	NO	
☐	☐	Are you satisfied with the accounting/legal services you are receiving?
☐	☐	Is the cost comparable with what others are paying for similar services?
☐	☐	Does your accountant/attorney keep you informed of the latest tax matters that are important to you?

If the firm is audited by an outside certified public accounting firm, the cost of this service can be significant and it should be examined. As with insurance, the firm should make certain that the money spent on this is giving the most value. Periodically it may be wise to test the market to determine what other firms charge for this service. In some cases, particularly with smaller firms, a regular audit may not be necessary. The accountant may then be asked to "review" the firm's books and records at a significantly lower charge. In that case the accountant will do less work and will not certify as to the fairness of the financial statement presentation, but this narrower examination may be sufficient for the firm's purposes. It will largely depend on whether the firm has a bank loan outstanding and whether the bank will accept a review in place of a complete audit.

After significant items of expense have ben reviewed, small items should not be overlooked for possible savings, particularly if these items can be looked at in a systematic way by means of a checklist. For example, Exhibit 5.3 is a checklist for reviewing business forms, which can be helpful when investigating all the forms used throughout the firm.

CHECKLIST FOR BUSINESS FORMS

YES	NO	
☐	☐	Do you have a business forms' control program to avoid excess duplication and clerical effort?
☐	☐	Do you have a forms committee to control forms and improve the paper communication between departments?
☐	☐	Do you know how many different forms you use?
☐	☐	Do you know the actual usage for each form?
☐	☐	Have you identified "key forms," that is, forms without which your operations are severely curtailed?
☐	☐	Do your external forms present the image you wish to project?
☐	☐	Do you schedule your requirements to avoid the expense of "rush" orders?
☐	☐	Do you have specifications written for economy in printing?
☐	☐	Do your suppliers maintain your forms inventory?
☐	☐	Do you know the cost per square foot of your forms storage area?
☐	☐	Do you keep a perpetual inventory of all forms to insure that you never run out of a given form?
☐	☐	Do you receive sufficient notice prior to depletion of your forms' inventory?
☐	☐	Do you have a business forms' identification guide, that is, a list of management-approved business forms?
☐	☐	Have you used a business forms' audit guaranteeing a 10% decrease in actual business form costs?
☐	☐	Do you have an accurate computation of usage to ensure that the proper quantity is printed and thereby avoid obsolescence and excess inventory carrying costs?
☐	☐	Does each of your forms have a number and revision date?

Exhibit 5.3 Business forms are a useful tool, but care should be taken to see that only the minimum number and variety are used in a manner consistent with the size of the firm.

EXERCISE 5.2 ████████████████████████████

Cutting Costs

Multiple Choice

1. Staff idle time can be reduced by
   a. firing employees.
   b. preparing a cash flow chart.
   c. sharing financial information with staff.
   d. preparing man-hour staffing forecasts.

2. Purchasing can be brought under control by
   a. getting quantity discounts.
   b. centralizing purchasing operations.
   c. financing a loan.
   d. none of the above.

3. A firm's insurance broker should be pressed to
   a. reduce insurance coverage.
   b. increase insurance coverage.
   c. get the best insurance for the money.
   d. none of the above.

4. You can reduce professional liability premiums by
   a. finding out how they are calculated.
   b. investigating the use of project professional liability insurance.
   c. obtaining one insurance carrier for both contractor and design firm.
   d. all of the above.
   e. a and b only.

5. A captive insurance company is
   a. underinsured.
   b. owned by the insurance company.
   c. owned by the firm.
   d. none of the above.

6. You can reduce office space to
   a. consolidate operations.
   b. reduce overhead.
   c. avoid moving.
   d. none of the above.

7. The cost of auditing your firm
   a. is well worth any price.
   b. could not be reduced.

    c. could be analyzed and perhaps reduced.

    d. none of the above.

5.3 COSTS AFFECTING PERFORMANCE

After you review the various costs that do not affect performance, it is then necessary to examine others that will impact the firm's operations.

Marketing

YES	NO	
☐	☐	Are marketing costs reviewed and approved by a single individual in the firm?
☐	☐	Is there a budget for marketing (time and expenses)?
☐	☐	Are marketing costs compared as a percentage of total revenue with those of other similar firms?

Marketing costs are a significant item of overhead expense, and this is a very sensitive area to cut. Perhaps the best way is to examine these costs from the standpoint of whether or not the firm is directing its marketing effort in the right channels. Costs should be verified to make certain that they are really going for marketing activities. The marketing director should be responsible for his or her costs and should approve all time and expenses charged to that budget. One area to scrutinize in particular for possible savings is that of "entertainment," particularly if the firm cannot realize any real payoff for some of these expenditures.

Support Staff

YES	NO	
☐	☐	Are all personnel on the support staff fully used on meaningful work that benefits the firm?
☐	☐	Are secretaries assigned on the basis of need by the person requiring them?
☐	☐	Is turnover of support staff comparable with that of similar firms?
☐	☐	Could more use of part-time help cut costs?

Support staff expenses are another area to look at in controlling costs. The firm needs to decide on the level of operations it wishes to maintain and then see what, if any, costs can be cut back. It may be possible to combine some functions, but the reductions should not decrease overall efficiency.

Fringe Benefits

YES	NO	
☐	☐	Does the firm conduct an anual review of its fringe benefits policies?
☐	☐	Are comparisons made with the fringe benefits provided by other similar firms?
☐	☐	Are employees aware of what the firm is paying them in fringe benefits above salary?
☐	☐	Could employees pay a portion of health care insurance?

Fringe benefits is an area that cannot be cut without hurting morale, but it should not escape an overall review. The employee benefit plan, for example, should be at least as good as that of other firms in the area in order to retain personnel, but as the costs increase, it is expected that employees will share in that increase. Benefit reductions can be made if they are communicated properly and thoroughly to the staff and as long as the staff recognizes them as fair to all and contributing to the financial health and stability of the firm.

EXERCISE 5.3

Reducing Costs with Impact on Operations

Multiple Choice

1. The best way of examining marketing costs is to
   a. hire an assistant.
   b. consider a new marketing director.
   c. determine if they are directed to the proper channels.
   d. all of the above.

2. One area of marketing that can be analyzed for potential savings is

    a. mailing costs.
    b. entertainment.
    c. printing.
    d. telephone calls.

3. Support staff expenses, when reduced, should
    a. be across-the-board cuts.
    b. not decrease overall efficiency.
    c. not be expected to reduce overhead.
    d. all of the above.
    e. a and b only.

4. Fringe benefits are difficult to cut because
    a. you might decrease morale.
    b. you might lose coverage.
    c. you're losing people each time you do it.
    d. none of the above.

5. Benefit reductions can be made
    a. if they are communicated properly.
    b. if they are thoroughly explained.
    c. as long as they are fair to all.
    d. all of the above.
    e. none of the above.

5.4 IMPLEMENTING A COST REDUCTION PROGRAM

When you review overhead costs and decide on what cuts should be made, it is important to recognize that large sweeping cuts, which may relieve a temporary loss, will not be effective in the long run. Such cuts will eventually have to be restored if the firm is to operate efficiently. Therefore, it is important to look at the long-term effect of any cost reduction program. The firm should remember not to try to over-control operations so that people lose initiative. In addition, long-term staff development needs may have to be reduced, but they should not be eliminated altogether or the firm will ultimately suffer for it. In addition to cutting costs, the firm should look for ways to raise revenue, such as entering new markets.

Exhibit 5.4 is a checklist to use when reviewing various overhead accounts for possible cost reductions.

CHECKLIST FOR REDUCING OVERHEAD COSTS

1. **Accounting fees**
   a. Year-end audit
   - Renegotiate the fee each year
   - Obtain quotations from other firms.
   - Ask to have your in-house accounting staff prepare as many work-paper schedules as the auditors will allow

   b. Annual income tax return
   - Do most of the return in-house and ask tax accountant to review.

   c. Quarterly payroll tax returns
   - Perform in-house.

2. **Debt service**
   - Investigate other banks for better terms.
   - Get faster client payment.
   - Collect on change orders.

3. **Insurance**
   a. Property/liability
   - Keep coverage at an adequate rate and ask insurance company to provide temporary endorsements for clients who require higher coverage during the time their projects are being worked on.
   - Obtain quotations from other firms.
   - Promote good loss experience through in-depth communication with staff.
   - Arrange for higher deductibles.
   - Obtain discounts with packaged policies.

   b. Group Insurance
   - Obtain quotations from several firms.
   - Investigate professional society insurance programs.
   - Share more of the cost with employees.
   - Set up higher deductibles.

   c. Officer's life insurance (funds buy/sell)
   - Make sure the coverage is term insurance, not whole life.
   - Obtain quotations from other firms periodically.
   - Investigate self-insurance for a portion or all of the risk.

4. **Outside services**
   a. Retirement program consultation
   - Use in-house accounting for completing administrative forms and reports.

   b. Branch office services
   - Negotiate short-term agreements.
   - Review quotations from many real estate firms.
   - Investigate whether branch office is the most effective alternative.

Exhibit 5.4 Do not overlook suggestions from your staff as an important source of ideas for reducing overhead costs.

5. Rent/lease

    a. Building

- Review market rates periodically.
- Try to negotiate a limit to the escalation clause at renewal date.
- If real estate market is soft, negotiate with a new landlord for free rent, minimum escalation rate, short-term lease, and moving costs.
- Eliminate old files to reduce need for storage space.
- Make floor plan efficient to reduce need for space.

    b. Equipment

- Share equipment with other firms rather than rent equipment that may be idle most of the day.

6. Employment agency fees

- Investigate alumni organizations, newspaper advertising, and competition.

7. Dues for professional organizations

- Limit to management or else eliminate.
- Ask that employee who is an officer in a professional organization be reimbursed by the organization for related travel.
- Share cost with employees.
- Eliminate or reduce number of meetings attended.
- Set up policy of no spouses/family attending at company expense.
- Institute policy of no entertainment costs charged to firm.

8. Supplies

- Investigate quantity discounts for large purchases.
- Get quotations from many suppliers.
- Control inventory of drafting and field supplies.
- Do not store copy paper in copy room to avoid unnecessary waste.

9. Postage/delivery

- Does every item have to be mailed first class?
- Ensure that postage scale is properly calibrated.
- Control overnight deliveries.

10. Fax

- Control hotel fax costs.
- Charge for both inbound and outbound.
- Install coded access numbers to control personal use.

11. Telephone

- Use more faxes to cut long distance charges.
- Cut lines and/or equipment.
- Change billing status with telephone company.

Exhibit 5.4 Continued.

EXERCISE 5.4 ■■■■■■■■■■■■■■■■■■■■■■■■■■■

Reducing Your Overhead Costs

1. What is the fee you paid for your year-end audit last year? Can it be reduced?

   _____

2. What about fees for annual income tax return and quarterly returns?

   _____

3. Assess your insurance coverage. List the kinds of coverage your firm has, the corresponding amounts, and the premiums you pay:

Coverage	Amount	Premiums
_____	_____	_____
_____	_____	_____
_____	_____	_____
_____	_____	_____
_____	_____	_____
_____	_____	_____

   Can you reduce any of the premiums?

   _____
   _____

4. Assess your outside services. What outside services did your firm use last year, and how much did they charge?

Service	Charges
_____	_____
_____	_____
_____	_____
_____	_____
_____	_____
_____	_____

5. Consider the amounts you pay for building rental and office equipment. List your expenses here and then determine which are too high, which are truly necessary, and which could be reduced or renegotiated.

Item	Charges
_____	_____
_____	_____
_____	_____
_____	_____
_____	_____

6. What costs were incurred for employment agency fees over the past year? Could you better use these fees on alumni organization, newspaper advertising, or competition?

_____

_____

7. Professional dues: List all of the organizations you belong to and the dues you pay. How many are absolutely necessary? How many get work?

Organization	Dues
_____	_____
_____	_____
_____	_____
_____	_____
_____	_____

8. Supplies: Take a look at the total amount spent for supplies for the past year. Could you benefit from quantity discounts?

_____

_____

9. Postage/delivery: Consider how your pieces are mailed. Have you had your postage scale properly calibrated? What was the number of overnight delivery packages you sent last year? How could this figure be reduced?

_____

_____

_____

5.5 OVERHEAD COST COMMITTEES

One technique for controlling overhead, which is used in some larger firms, is an overhead cost committee. Such a committee is generally established to accomplish the specific task of cutting overhead costs. Usually, the financial manager and several operating personnel are assigned to the committee.

Overhead cost committees can be very beneficial if they are used properly. If they can be formed before a crisis situation develops, they do not have to work on a "crash" basis. If senior management personnel are appointed to the committee and its recommendations are carried out, they can be very effective. The committee can serve as an educational forum for the financial manager to explain cost control to others. Very often this is the first exposure that technical people have to the financial operations of the firm. The committee can have a significant impact on performance if it is recognized that cost control is a never-ending task and the committee should work with each segment of the firm on a rotating basis so that all areas are eventually covered.

In smaller firms, the overhead cost committee can be made up of the principals, but the committee must operate separately from the general management of the firm and must meet separately for this purpose. Otherwise management problems and operating crises will crowd out the agenda, leaving no time for the important task of controlling overhead costs.

EXERCISE 5.5 ▬▬▬▬▬▬▬▬▬▬▬▬▬▬▬▬▬▬▬▬▬▬▬▬▬

Discussion Problem

Background. For several years the volume of revenues for Smith Engineers has been steadily increasing, but profit before taxes and discretionary bonus payments have stayed below 5%, as shown on the table below:

	Revenues ($000)	Expenses ($000)	Profit before Taxes ($000)	% Profit of Revenues
1990	$403	$394	$ 8	2%
1991	478	460	18	4
1992	492	472	20	4
1993 (est.)	526	514	12	2

SUMMARY OF KEY RATIOS

| | Participating Firms | | |
	Mean	Median	Smith Engineers
Net profit [before tax and distributions on net revenues] (%)	8.63	8.31	2.3*
Contribution rate (%)	60.1	61.1	59.4*
Overhead rate [before distributions] (%)	144	140	126*
Net multiplier (X)	277	2.70	2.09*
Net revenues per total staff ($)	41,415	40,115	24,338*
Net revenues per technical staff ($)	56,672	51,805	35,690*
Chargeable ratio (%)	64	63	59*
Total staff to marketing staff	381	53.1	48.1

*Indicates figure deviating from averages shown.

Exhibit 5.5 This extract compares key reporting ratios for firms participating in the survey with Smith Engineers. Definitions of the ratios are provided on the following pages. Asterisked items are outside the ranges and require further analysis.

Note that the estimate for 1993 is even lower. The managing principal is very concerned that the overhead rate has been steadily increasing and that it is out of line with that of other comparable firms. Although he has no hard numbers to support this conclusion, he bases his assumption on informal talks he has had with other principals at professional society meetings.

The managing principal has decided to look for ways to cut overhead and keep it down. Because this is a small firm and there is no one on staff to assist him, he discusses the matter with the firm's independent accountant. The managing principal is aware of the Financial Statistics Survey sponsored by the *Professional Services Management Journal*. He obtains the latest copy and gives it to the accountant to assist in the analysis. An extract of key ratios from this report is shown in Exhibits 5.5–5.7. The accountant prepares the analysis that compares the key overhead items for Smith Engineers with other firms in the study. The managing principal then decides to find out why the asterisked items were outside the averages shown in the report.

Assignment. List other reasons besides higher overhead that could account for the low profits. What are the advantages/disadvantages of comparing operating perfor-

EXPLANATION OF KEY RATIOS

Net Profit before Tax and Distributions on Net Revenues

This index measures net profit (income) before taxes and distributions based on net revenues. As a result, it bases profit percentage only on your own efforts and not on consultants and reimbursables. It is calculated before distributions for bonuses, profit-sharing, and the like.

Contribution Rate

The contribution rate is the portion of each dollar of net revenues remaining after all direct project costs (both labor and expenses) are covered. Thus, it is the contribution of each fee dollar to overhead and profit. The findings indicate that 60.2¢ (mean figure) or 61.1(median) of each $1 of gross income is available for overhead and profit. It is calculated by dividing gross profit by net revenues.

Overhead Rate before Distributions

The overhead rate is the percentage of total office overhead to total office direct labor. For each dollar of project direct labor spent, an equivalent of $1.44 (mean) to $1.40 (median) is spent for overhead. Overhead also includes that portion of the principals' time that is not chargeable to projects.

Net Multiplier

This is the effective multiplier firms achieve on direct labor in their most recent fiscal year (it is not the target multiplier). It is calculated by dividing net revenues by direct labor and is more meaningful than a gross multiplier (which includes consultants and reimbursables) in that it represents the actual multiplier you achieve on your own efforts. When determining a project fee, you first calculate the labor required, multiply the result by your net multiplier, then add consultants and reimbursables, and factor in any markups to achieve the total fee quoted to the client. The net multiplier thus covers your direct project labor, any other nonlabor project expenses, overhead, contingencies, and profit. The 2.77 (mean figure) indicates that the participating firms received $2.77 per $1 spent in direct labor (the median was 2.70).

Net Revenues per Total Staff

This index measures the dollar amount of net revenues each employee or part-time equivalent represents. It is calculated by dividing net revenues by your average total staff including principals and part-time equivalents. The average found in the survey was $41,515 per employee (including principals) and the median was $40,155.

Net Revenues per Technical Staff

This index is calculated by dividing net revenues by the average total technical staff (defined as including all planning or design professionals, technicians and

Exhibit 5.6 This list defines the terms used in the summary of key ratios in Exhibit 5.5.

job shoppers, who work on projects, including principals). The survey results indicate $56,672 in revenues per technical staff member (the median is $51,805). Many feel that this is a more accurate representation than revenues per total staff in that it assigns revenues to those who are directly responsible for generating them.

Chargeable Ratio

The chargeable ratio is determined by dividing total direct labor by direct labor plus sick leave, vacation, and holiday labor expense plus total indirect labor. A calculation could also be made based upon time (hours), but for survey purposes the dollar figure is more accurate. The average chargeable ratio was found to be 62 percent and the median was 63 percent. A net ratio could be calculated by omitting the vacation, sick leave, and holiday labor expense.

Total Staff to Marketing Staff

This is the number of staff per full marketing person (meaning those who spend at least 75% of their time on marketing). The median figure of 53.1 appears quite high when compared with other surveys that found this ratio to be about 22.1.

Exhibit 5.6 Continued.

---

mance with statistical surveys? What other methods could be used to analyze operating performance?

Analyze the data in Exhibits 5.5–5.7 to determine whether the managing principal was right in his assumption that overhead expense is the reason for the firm's low profitability. What are some other contributing causes?

_____

_____

_____

_____

_____

_____

5.6 FIFTY WAYS TO CUT COSTS

If you are facing a downturn in business, cutting costs becomes an essential part of your business strategy for staying alive. If business is steady, cutting costs is a quick way to increase profits. Regardless of the reason, you can cut costs in more areas and in more ways than you think. Following are 50

KEY OVERHEAD ITEMS
(Expressed as Percentage of Direct Labor)*

Line Item	Participating Firms		Smith Engineers
	Mean	**Median**	
Pay-roll Burden			
Mandatory payroll taxes	11.0%	11.1%	10.2%
Vacation, sick leave, holiday	14.1	14.2	10.4
Group insurance	6.1	5.8	6.6†
Annual pension expense	4.8	4.0	0
Bonus, incentive payments, profit sharing	14.9	10.8	4.3
All other fringe benefits	2.4	1.4	0
Total pay-roll burden	**48.7%**	**44.9%**	**31.5%**
General & Administrative			
Indirect (non-project) labor	46.4%	44.9%	51.2†
Cost of space	12.5	11.4	166.3†
Telephone	3.7	3.5	5.0†
Professional liability insurance	4.6	3.8	0.8
Interest on borrowed capital	4.3	2.5	1.0
Bad debt eepense	2.9	1.0	3.4
Total other general and administrative	35.7	31.5	31.6
Total general and administrative	**108.8%**	**105.9%**	**109.3%**
Total pay-roll burden	**159.4%**	**154.7%**	**140.8%**

*Individual items not additive.
†Areas needing attention.

Exhibit 5.7 This extract from the survey report shows individual items of overhead expense as a percentage of direct labor. The use of a percentage comparison is helpful in highlighting those areas where Smith Engineers is outside the survey's range.

ways you can cut costs now, contributed by accountant Joan Lautenschleger. Some you won't notice; others are more severe. Only you can decide which ones are right for your firm.

Finances

Use Least-Cost Accounting for All Long-Distance Telephone Calls. If your phone switch can't automatically send long-distance calls via the least-cost route, make sure employees know which option to use for which types of calls. If you have office-wide speed-dial numbers, include the access code for the desired carrier as part of the number dialed by each speed-dial code. In addition, review the call-billing plan applied by your long-distance carrier to your calls. It may not be the best one for your usage pattern. Choosing the right call-billing plan is as important as choosing a long-distance carrier.

Don't Pay Finance Charges. To avoid finance charges, the person paying the bills must first understand which finance charges can and should be ignored and which ones really do have to be paid (i.e., credit cards and utility bills). Then they must make sure that any bills in the latter category are paid on time. It's a good idea to charge all finance or late payment charges to a separate account so you can track how much you're paying.

Take Early Payments Discounts. These discounts should be taken whenever they're offered. If a supplier offers net 2/10 terms, the 2% you save is equal to a 24% annual interest rate (assuming you would have paid the bill anyway within 30–40 days). Unless you're financing your business through unusual sources or putting any spare cash in your bottom desk drawer, taking the discount will save you money even if you have to borrow to do it. Also, be sure to track these discounts so you know how much you've saved. Rather than simply recording the invoice at its net amount, record the full amount of the invoice to whatever expense category it represents, and record the discounted amount in a separate account.

Use Overtime as a Cushion. When business is slow, it's less expensive to assign another staff member to meet a deadline rather than to pay overtime to existing members of a project team. It also lets you keep productive staff members as long as possible. On the other hand, when your office is busy, it may be less expensive to pay overtime for a defined period of time than to hire another person with benefits and other overhead costs.

Cancel All Unnecessary Credit Cards. In addition to the obvious cost of the annual fee, credit cards give the individual cardholders the equivalent of check-signing authority. Once the expenditure has been charged, the company will most likely pay it, even if the expense would not have been approved had there been an advance discussion. In addition, the more credit card bills received by the company, the more checks that need to be written, and the more likely you are to incur finance charges.

Human Resources

Reduce Employee Education Costs. This can be done by having a speaker do in-house seminars for employees rather than sending individuals to outside seminars.

Offer a Reduced Work Week During Slow Periods. Depending on their personal circumstances, some employees may be willing to work a reduced work week for a period of time. Obviously, the savings associated with reducing the work week depend on an equivalent reduction in salary per week.

Selectively Reduce Staff. As unpleasant as it sounds, circumstances sometimes require staff cuts. Start first by not replacing anyone who leaves. If his or her function is essential, it may be possible to split the responsibilities among existing staff. Look for administrative positions that can be combined or eliminated. Offer selected staff the choice of moving into another position at a lower salary as an alternative to being laid off. Finally, don't offer special severance deals to one departing employee unless you're willing to offer the same deal to all employees in the same circumstances.

Take Workers' Compensation Audits Seriously. Your workers' compensation insurance premium is based on a separate rate for each category of employees and the gross payroll expense in each category. The rates vary enormously depending on the risk associated with each. Your total premium is estimated at the beginning of the policy year and adjusted based on the year-end payroll audit. While there's little question regarding the total payroll expense for each employee, there can be considerable questions regarding the category in which an employee belongs. When in doubt, auditors will choose the higher risk category. Your only defense is to understand the criteria, and be there to answer questions and review their assignments.

Insurance

Limit Payment to Lowest Cost Health Insurance Alternative. If your company is large enough to offer several health insurance alternatives, limit your payment to the least expensive choice and require employees choosing a more expensive alternative to pay the cost difference.

Add Service Charges for Extended Health Insurance. Employers are now required to allow employees to continue health insurance coverage at their own expense after terminating employment. You're also allowed to charge an administrative or service charge of up to 2% of the monthly premium. The service charge is intended to cover the administrative costs associated with extending coverage, but you may choose to regard it as a small reduction in your health insurance cost.

Manage Unemployment Insurance Costs. Your rate is based on the actual experiences of your firm. You ultimately pay for any benefits paid to former employees. There are several things you can do. First, respond to all wage requests. Wage requests are sent to former employers whenever someone applies for unemployment compensation. If there's a reason why this person isn't eligible or why your firm isn't responsible, this is your only chance to say so. Second, respond to wage requests on time. The response time is short, and most states impose a fine for not responding by the deadline. Be sure that someone actually looks at the benefit statements received. The statements list each person currently receiving unemployment benefits "charged" against your firm. This gives you a chance to catch mistakes.

Change Effective Dates on Employee Insurance. Review your policy regarding the effective dates of health, life, and disability insurance both at the beginning and end of employment. You may be able to reduce your costs by being less generous on the start date for certain insurance (i.e., life or disability) and the ending date for all insurance. Policies regarding continuation of insurance at company expense may have been established before federal law required you to make it available for an extended period at the employee's expense. Given the change in circumstances, your existing policy may be too generous.

Most insurers allow starting and ending dates throughout the month, so there's no administrative reason to extend coverage after an employee's termination date. If it's your decision not to provide certain insurance until after a certain period of employment, it can still be made available to new employees provided they pay for the entire cost during the waiting period.

Audit All Employee Insurance Bills. Most insurance bills list the employees covered and any changes in the current period. A few insurers only list changes, and the employer must maintain a list of who's covered. Regardless of the information provided on the bill, it should be reviewed each month to be sure you aren't paying for someone who should have been cancelled or that any new employees have been added. This should be done by the person responsible for administering employee benefits since it requires knowledge of personnel policies.

Mailing

Have One Person Meter the Mail. Someone who weighs and meters mail regularly is less likely to make mistakes in postage rates or actual operation of the machine. Having mail metered by one person at the end of the day also makes it easier to record the amount of postage to be charged to projects. Open access to a postage meter only encourages its use for personal mail.

Combine Courier Deliveries Whenever Possible. If there's a local engineer or architect with whom you do considerable business, you probably have frequent deliveries between your offices. If there's often more than one or two deliveries a day, establish a regular schedule. This will reduce the total number of deliveries, and you may also be able to negotiate a lower rate with the courier service by giving them a predictable schedule.

Eliminate Package Pickup Charges. Find out which companies charge extra to pick up packages at your office. (At least one major shipping company charges a weekly service fee for daily stops that can be eliminated by calling them for pickup when you have packages.) Other shipping companies charge a higher rate for any packages they pick up at your office and a lower rate for packages dropped in their collection boxes. Ask one staff member to collect all packages at the end of the day and walk/drive past a collection box on the way home.

Use a Postage Meter Instead of Stamps. Regardless of how small the office, a postage meter will probably save you money. Postage meters eliminate excess postage on pieces requiring an odd amount, the amount in the meter can't be lost or destroyed as easily as stamps, and it's easier to prevent personal use of a postage meter than to keep track of pieces of sticky-back paper.

Combine Overnight Shipments to the Same Destination. If overnight shipments are going to two different individuals at the same address, the individually addressed items can often be combined inside one large package and shipped as one item. In small offices where people tend to know what others are doing, this consolidation can be done informally. In larger offices, it can usually only be accomplished in the mailroom and requires packages provided by the overnight company be available only in the mailroom. (Note: the overnight shipper will not be your ally in this effort.)

Select Overnight Delivery Level Carefully. Each time employees complete an overnight delivery ticket, they choose a level of service (second day, next day, next day by noon, etc.). The normal reaction is always to check the same box, and you often end up paying more than necessary. The most effective way to eliminate this problem is to have all overnight delivery tickets completed in a central location. If this isn't possible, at least be sure that everyone completing them knows what they are doing.

Miscellaneous

Establish a Standard Allowance for Company Cars. If you must provide automobiles to principals, put a limit on operating expenses. Paying all operating expenses gives individuals no incentive to restrain those expenses. An alternative is to establish a lump-sum annual maintenance and operating allowance for each principal or an allowance per mile. In either case, the company's expense is limited to a predefined amount, and individuals benefit directly by controlling the costs associated with "their" automobiles.

Sell Unused or Excess Furniture. You may have unused or excess equipment or furniture because you have reduced size, upgraded items, or recently moved. Your trash may be another company's treasure. Obvious candidates to buy your "yard-sale" items are small start-up firms (put a notice in your local professional society's newsletter), students (post a notice at the local design school), or employees (post a notice on your bulletin board).

Eliminate Unnecessary Photocopy Expense. The number of photocopies made will increase directly with the number of copy machines you have, their speed, and the convenience of their location. If you have more copy machine capacity than you need, reduce it. Your rental contracts are probably one-sided (and not in your favor), but you may be able to terminate by paying a penalty or be able to replace one large machine with two smaller machines. For future reference, except with very large, high-capacity machines, it's better to pay a higher monthly rent for a shorter contract period to allow for flexibility in the future.

Sublet Part of Your Office. If you have more space than you need, you may be able to rent some of it. This will depend on the nature of the space, terms of your lease if you're a tenant, and services you're willing and able to provide. When looking for a tenant, don't limit yourself to other design professionals. Tenants from other professions may be able to pay higher rent and may be more self sufficient. If you're renting only a small piece of your office, remember that the rent per square foot can usually be considerably higher than your cost per square foot.

Reduce the Number of Subscriptions and Memberships. Review all your current subscriptions and memberships—the total cost may surprise you. Eliminate any duplicates, and make sure all subscriptions paid by the firm are actually received. Then assign one individual the responsibility of duplicating and/or routing the publications around the firm and filing them in the library. Second, eliminate any memberships or subscriptions that aren't essential. You can always add them back later.

Reduce Office Amenities and Freebies. Look around your office for amenities that are nice, but not essential. If you have flowers delivered weekly, perhaps they can be scaled down or replaced with a plant. Review the list of "consumables" such as tissues, coffee, tea, instant soup, hot chocolate, snacks, spring water, and aspirin. Don't overlook disposable items like plastic cups, paper plates, napkins, plastic utensils, and paper towels.

Outside Services

Use Competitive Bidding for Printing Jobs. This is especially helpful for jobs other than routine, daily work. This should include both blueprinting and any sizable photocopy jobs. Keep a list of four or five places to call for quotes. Giving them a chance to bid allows you to take advantage of those in slow periods. Your large rush job may just happen to coincide with another customer's large job not arriving when expected.

Perform More Tasks In-House. Determine which outside services can be performed in-house. Some may offer long-term savings, and some may offer a way to use an existing staff person during slack time. Services to look at include courier/delivery services, payroll and payroll tax returns, and preparation of routine corporate documents and routine schedules required for your year-end audit and tax filings. Also don't overlook the amount you pay to have a telephone jack moved, a computer relocated, or an extension changed on your telephone console.

Purchase Less Expensive Outside Services. Many outside services can't be eliminated entirely, but costs can be reduced. For example, accounting fees are affected by the frequency of statements, the nature of the statements (i.e., whether reviewed or audited), the level of staff performing the work, and the overall size and structure of the accounting firm you use. Similar considerations apply to legal fees. Find outside professionals who will help you do things for yourself, and whose price structure you can live with.

Negotiate Better Terms with Subcontractors. Although you should maintain good relations with your subcontractors and only subcontract work to firms whose quality you're comfortable with, this shouldn't eliminate negotiations. Dependence on a single source for a particular kind of work can be costly because it eliminates your ability to take advantage of other subcontractors' slow times. Also be sure your subcontracts generally reflect the terms of your contract with the client.

Service contracts

Shop for Alternative Service Contractors. Don't assume that your service contracts have to be with the company that originally sold you the equipment. For most equipment, there are other options. Often an independent service company is as reliable as, and less expensive than, the original vender. Alternatives usually exist for phone systems, PCs, typewriters, calculators, HVAC equipment, and software. Shop around and check references to find the best combination of price and service for your firm.

Eliminate Unnecessary Service Contracts. Some service contracts are essential—they're the only way to obtain reliable service when you need it. Other service contracts can be eliminated. Look for contracts on equipment that's inexpensive to replace, isn't used heavily, or for which you have a backup replacement for temporary use. For example, given the heavy use of word processors, you may no longer need a service contract on your typewriters. As another example, even though you may want to have a service contract on your telephone system, it could explicitly eliminate coverage of the actual phones given their low replacement cost.

Eliminate Service Contracts for Equipment You No Longer Have. Service contracts cover specific pieces of equipment (or software) that are generally listed as contract addendum. These lists should be reviewed carefully to eliminate items you no longer have or no longer use.

Write Off Any Equipment or Furniture You No Longer Own. If there are items presently carried on your books that you no longer own, the remaining depreciable cost of those items can be written off for income tax purposes. This will reduce your federal tax liability for the current year, and will reduce any state taxes that are based on income or asset values.

Suppliers

Shop for Lower Supply Prices. It isn't necessary to purchase all supplies from a single source, and it isn't necessary to purchase from the same source each time. Shopping for the right combination of price and service can save a considerable amount. Possible sources range from your standard office or drafting supply company (with whom you can negotiate for a discount), discount office supply warehouses, specialty mail-order catalogs, and local manufacturers. The key to effective price-shopping is motivation—if the person ordering supplies really wants to save money, he or she will find creative ways to do so.

Consolidate Supplies Inventory. Every employee needs a small personal inventory of frequently used supplies, but if that personal supply consists of complete boxes, it's probably too large. In general, box lots could be kept in a central area, and individuals should take only what they'll use in a reasonable period of time.

Recycle Supplies. When files and desks are cleaned or when records are put into storage, recycle items such as hanging files, pens, partially used writing pads, and partial boxes of leads rather than throwing them away. Many of these items are expensive, and the amount of time needed to reclaim them is minimal. Generally, the only way to encourage use of the recycled supplies is to be sure that new supplies aren't available until recycled items have been used.

Match Quality to the Need. When selecting equipment or supplies, buy the quality of product that is needed for a particular task or function. Keep in mind that matching quality of product to the task isn't the same as matching quality to the level of person using the product. For example, a principal who needs a small printing calculator for occasional use will be served quite well by an inexpensive model that would be inadequate for your bookkeeper. The same principle applies to everything, from pencils to computers.

Designate One Person to Order Supplies. Regardless of firm size, you'll save money by having one person responsible for purchasing supplies. Centralizing this task eliminates duplicate orders, prevents ordering excess inventory (i.e., ordering cases of paper instead of reams), and makes the company less vulnerable to telemarketing fraud or gimmicks. It also gives someone the ability to control the cost of supplies.

Return or Sell Excess Supply Inventory. After consolidating your supply inventory, you may find that you have a huge oversupply of certain items (probably due to a past ordering error) or a significant supply of things you no longer use. Standard items in unopened boxes or cases can often be returned to your normal supplier for at least partial credit, or you may be able to sell surplus supplies to another firm at a discounted price. Finally, don't overlook your own employees as potential buyers of unwanted or excess supplies, provided both you and your employees agree on a fair price.

Travel and Entertainment

Develop a Written Travel Policy. Your travel policy should clearly state what you'll pay for and what vendors are to be used. Negotiating a preferred rate with a hotel or rental car company is a wasted effort if employees don't use the hotel or company. Likewise, telling employees after the fact that you don't pay for theater tickets or in-room movies is an ineffective way to reduce costs and is unfair to employees.

Negotiate Discounted Hotel Rates. At a bare minimum, you should qualify for a hotel's published corporate rate, regardless of how frequently you use them. If you use a particular hotel frequently, a better rate can almost always be negotiated. If you don't travel to a particular city often, you can obtain better rates by staying with one hotel chain, or by booking through a large hotel consortium.

Reduce Meals and Entertainment Expenses. The easiest way to accomplish this is to establish a budget for each principal. Be sure the total of each principal's budget is less than the total you've spent in the past, and expenditures will be reduced without spending time and energy auditing individual expenses.

Use Discount Airfares. A large share of business travel is scheduled far enough in advance that some type of discount airfare is available. Many large firms with travel departments find most of the available savings result from purchasing discount airfares for overhead travel. However, some project-related travel is predictable and discount fares can be obtained.

Be Creative About Employee Activities. Employee activities, such as holiday parties, company picnics, or informal office get-togethers, are important even when business is slow and money is tight. Be creative, or ask employees to be creative, about finding inexpensive or free ways to relax and have fun together.

Use Credit Cards for Hotel Telephone Calls. Given the exorbitant markup by most hotels, there should be no long-distance calls placed through a hotel switchboard. Long-distance calls using any long-distance company's credit card will be less expensive because the hotel will only bill you for the call to the 800 access number (usually at the same rate as a local call).

Negotiate a Preferred Rate with One Rental Car Company. The greater your volume, the better the rate you'll be able to negotiate. It's therefore to your advantage to consolidate all your national business with one rental car company. If you frequently rent cars in your locale, you can usually find a small local company that will provide excellent service at reasonable rates. The point is, shop around, then develop a solid, working relationship with one reasonable company.

Utilities

Reduce Utility Bills. Survey your office to identify obvious places where electricity, gas, or water can be reduced. When you're finished, call the utility company. Many will conduct an audit of your office free of charge. In some areas, they'll even provide energy savings at their expense.

Audit Rates Charged by Utility Companies. The rate structure of most utilities is complex, and rates charged to customers depend on how each customer is classified. The utility company is required to provide information on the rate structure that applies to each customer classification, as well as criteria for inclusion in each classification. You may qualify for a lower rate structure. If you, you'll save in the future and may get a rebate.

Eliminate Excess Phone Lines. Outgoing telephone lines are a fixed cost that's usually forgotten the day after installation. You may be able to reduce the number of lines you have. If your phone switch can't provide information regarding the amount of usage on each trunk line, your local phone company can probably monitor it for you for a short time. As a crude measure, if you never get a busy signal when trying to make an outside call, you probably have excess lines. Keep in mind that as projects change, your usage needs change too. What made sense last year may no longer apply today.

Keep in mind that to cut costs, you have to know what they are. Start looking at the invoices you're paying, not just the total and the name of the vendor, but exactly what services or products were purchased and by whom. You may be surprised at what you're paying for.

FINAL EXAMINATION—CHAPTER 5

True or False

T F Low profitability is a sure signal that overhead costs are under control.

T F Fixed costs are those that do not vary with volume of operations.

T F Variable costs are not easier to control.

T F Purchasing should be centralized within a firm.

T F It is not advisable to hire a single vendor for all purchases of high-volume items.

T F It is an easy task to switch insurance carriers.

T F Using a single insurance carrier for both the design professional and the contractor can help prevent insurance disputes.

T F A long-range business plan can help you determine your space requirements.

T F Market testing for a new service is rarely necessary.

T F Reductions in support staff should not decrease overall firm efficiency.

T F Fringe benefits are difficult to cut without cutting morale.

T F A firm should not over-control operations because this practice will decrease morale.

Discussion Problem

Background. Your eight-person architectural firm has experienced a rapid increase in overhead rate at the same time that growth has leveled off because of a downturn in construction activity in your location. Recently you have been losing $5,000 to $10,000 per month on an accrual basis and your bank loan has been higher than ever before. Your forecasts indicate further losses in the months ahead. You have not had to reduce staff yet, but you are concerned about how long you will be able to keep everyone employed. Because of your small size, a layoff of even one person would be disruptive. Everyone understands the situation and has been working extra hours to keep the firm going.

You would like to examine all items of overhead in detail to see if there are expenses that can be trimmed. However, because of the press of current work and the need to make extra business development calls, there is really no time to accomplish this task. Besides, you are not familiar with what is included in many of the overhead accounts, as your bookkeeper has been handling this since you founded the firm.

You ask your other principal and the bookkeeper to meet with you on Saturday to review all items of overhead and discuss ways to achieve reductions. Based on what you have learned in Chapter 5, how would you go about preparing for that meeting?

Assignment. List the overhead expenses you would concentrate on to achieve meaningful reductions. How would you involve other members of the staff in an expense-reduction program? What other options are available in addition to cost cutting?

6

GETTING PAID

Chapter Summary

- The necessity for having sufficient working capital
- Invoicing the client
- Suggestions for expediting billing
- Signing a client's purchase order
- Performing a credit check on a new client
- Expediting payment
- A seven-step procedure to improve collections
- When to use a collection agent
- Managing cash flow problems
- Getting paid for changes

The Importance of Cash Flow

The importance of cash flow to a design firm cannot be over-emphasized. The rate at which cash enters and leaves the organization can determine the difference between success and failure, regardless of what appears on the financial statements. It is important that technical personnel understand the concept of cash flow and its implications in the overall financial health of the organization.

6.1 WORKING CAPITAL

The cash cycle in a design firm is much simpler than that in other types of organizations since a service firm does not have to be concerned with inventories in various stages of completion. However, labor must be paid immediately after it is performed and vendors of supplies and services must generally be paid within 30 days. This lag between the time the work is performed and when it can be invoiced, and still later paid, must be financed in one form or another—generally through a bank line of credit or through internally generated funds. In any event it is a cost to the firm. However, as a firm grows and the requirements for working capital increase, it becomes even more difficult to rely exclusively on a bank line of credit.

Banks expect to be partners to share and assist in the firm's growth, but, in a sense, they expect to be favored partners since a bank line of credit must be repaid for some portion of the year—generally 30 days. This demonstrates to the bank that the firm has enough financial strength to meet its obligations and growth objectives and is not completely dependent on outside resources.

Obviously, the faster a firm can invoice and collect for its services, the lower the amount needed for working capital. However, no matter how efficiently the firm operates, it will be limited in its growth prospects if it does not have sufficient working capital to support its operations. If we consider the usual operating pattern of doing work one month, invoicing for it the next month, and collecting for it the third month, then working capital would generally be required to support three months' sales. This figure, of course, varies with the nature of the firm's operations. (See Exhibit 6.1 for a diagram of the cash cycle.)

EXERCISE 6.1

Improving Your Firm's Cash Flow

1. What is your firm's average daily receivables?

_____

2. How could you reduce your average days receivables by 20% within the next 60 days?

_____

_____

3. Measure your days unbilled receivables by dividing work-in-process by average days revenues.

_____

Is your average days unbilled receivables less than 30 days?

_____

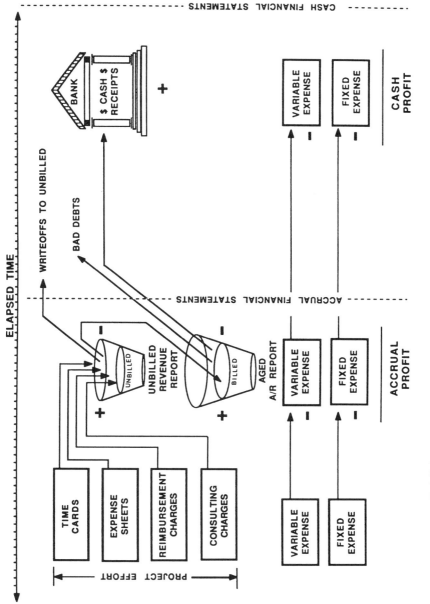

Exhibit 6.1 Relationship of accrual financial statements to cash financial statements.

What steps could you take to improve your average days unbilled receivables?

_____

_____

_____

_____

4. Do you continue to provide services to clients who are seriously delinquent?

_____

_____

5. Have you considered negotiating 2% 60-day discounts with your larger clients?

_____

6.2   EXPEDITING BILLING PROCEDURES

One area where a firm can take positive action to speed up its cash flow and lower its billing requirements for working capital is in invoicing clients. Invoices should be sent out as quickly as possible after the close of the accounting period.

A good rule of thumb is that invoices should usually be mailed by the 10th calendar day following the close of the month or end of the reporting period. At least most invoices should be out by that date. It is important to get into the client's monthly payment cycle early enough to avoid having to wait another month to be paid.

Expediting the Approval Process

One method to speed up the billing process is to make certain that invoice approval is handled expeditiously. It is important that project managers approve invoices before they are sent, but invoices should not be held up awaiting approval because a project manager is out of town or otherwise not available. Every project manager should designate an alternate person who can approve invoices when he or she is absent. In addition, deadlines should be established as a matter of policy when invoices must be mailed, and project managers should know that if invoices have not been approved by that date, they will be mailed regardless.

Standardizing Invoicing Procedures

Invoicing procedures should be standardized to the extent possible, and invoices should only be typed once. Exhibits 6.2, 6.3, and 6.4 are examples of typical invoice forms. It may be easier, in some cases, to have the project manager approve a marked-up draft of last month's invoice. The financial manager should see that all supporting documentation and

EXAMPLE OF TYPICAL INVOICE FORM
(Multiplier Type Project)

12/31

TO:	Alvin Development Company	
PROJECT:	Design of Entertainment Park (No. 83-025)	
INVOICE PERIOD:	December	
REFERENCE:	Letter of Agreement dated 6/30	

	Hours	Dollars*	Extension
Labor Charges			
Principals			
Sid Harrell	10	$2,400	
John Clay	13	2,625	
Project Managers			
John Smith	9	1,350	
Etc.			
Total Labor Charges			$10,500
Reimbursable Expenses			
Travel		$ 260	
Telephone/Fax		$ 350	
Etc.			
Total Reimbursable Expenses		$ 980	
Consultant Costs			
Structural Engineer			$ 2,500
Amount Due This Period			$13,980
Outstanding Invoices			4,000
Total Amount Due			$17,980

Exhibit 6.2 Note the inclusion of outstanding invoices on the current invoice as a reminder that these have not yet been paid.

progress reports that are required are included and submitted along with the invoice, because the financial manager is the one most concerned with mailing the invoices on time. Using a standard preprinted invoice form will also expedite typing, or if invoices are prepared on a word processor, it will be a simple matter to insert the proper figures each month. It is also important to avoid sending backup or supporting documentation unless the client specifically requests it. The amount of detail requested on each invoice should be decided upon at the time of contract negotiation, and clients should be encouraged to accept a standard one-page invoice without documentation. Most will, but there will be others,

EXAMPLE OF TYPICAL INVOICE FORM
(Published Billing Rate Project)

12/31

TO: Alvin Development Company

PROJECT: Design of Entertainment Park (No. 83-025)
INVOICE PERIOD: December
REFERENCE: Letter of Agreement dated 6/30

	Hours	Dollars*	Extension
Labor Charges			
Principals	10	$2,600	
Project Managers	18	$2,800	
Etc.			
Total Labor Charges			$12,600
Reimbursable Expenses			
Printing			$ 450
Consultants' fees			
Structural Engineer			$ 5,000
Amount Due This Period			$18,050
Outstanding Invoices			3,500
Total Amount Due			$21,550

Exhibit 6.3 A standardized invoice form permits invoices to be prepared quickly. To save time, if additional information is required by the client, it should be included in a progress report prepared by the project manager at the same time the invoices are being prepared.

particularly governmental agencies, which require special forms for invoicing, and these needs, of course, have to be accommodated. Preparing special-purpose invoices to meet the client's need is an extra overhead service and involves extra time and expense, which should be brought to the attention of the client even if the firm cannot be compensated for this expense.

Use of Discounts for Prompt Payment

Another consideration in efficient billing procedures is the use of discounts for prompt payment of invoices. Discounts are not widely used by professional service firms because they reduce the already slim profit margins. Offering a dis-

EXAMPLE OF TYPICAL INVOICE FORM
(Percent of Construction Project)

12/31

TO: Alvin Development Company

PROJECT: Design of Entertainment Park (No. 83-025)
INVOICE PERIOD: December
REFERENCE: Letter of Agreement dated 6/30

Estimated Construction Cost $2,000,000
fee @ 6%   120,000

Phase	% of Fee	Fee ($)	% Completed	Fee Earned
Schematic design	20	$24,000	30	$ 7,200
Design development	30	36,000	10	3,600
Etc.				
Amount Due This Period				$ 10,800
Previously Invoiced				3,000
Current Amount Due				$ 7,800

Exhibit 6.4   The figure shown under "% completion" should be based on a technical evaluation of the work effort and the amount yet to complete. It should not be based on the hours spent versus the total budgeted hours.

count is expensive as shown in Exhibit 6.5. While discounts would undoubtedly speed up the turnover of accounts receivable, there are some drawbacks, principally the many cases where clients will take the discount but not pay within the prescribed period. This requires re-invoicing for the discounted amount, at the risk of raising a dispute with the client, or else absorbing the loss, neither of which is a completely satisfactory solution.

Rather than offering discounts, it is preferable to ask for and obtain advance payments whenever possible. Depending on the practice of other similar firms, it is advantageous to obtain in advance either a portion of the payment or a retainer that is then credited against the final payment.

Important of Payment Terms

One payment method to avoid is the procedure that requires payment upon completion of particular milestones or stages of completion. This procedure often requires the firm to de-

CASH DISCOUNTS:
HOW TO USE THEM AND WHAT THEY REALLY COST

When interest rates are high, the question of cash discounts given or received by design professionals as an incentive for prompt payment becomes important. Cash discounts mean one of two things:

1. A discount given by the design professional to the client who pays during the discount period.
2. A penalty paid by the design professional who doesn't pay the supplier during the discount period.

If the terms of the discount are stated, it is possible to calculate the annual rate of interest lost by the design professional who fails to take the discount given.

$$I = \frac{D}{(G - D)\,(T/365)}$$

I = Annual rate of interest
D = Amount of discount
G = Gross amount of the invoice
T = Time difference between discount and net payment date in days

If, for example, in the case of a design professional's bill for $500 with the terms of 2% discount if paid within 10 days and the net amount due in 30 days, then:

D = 2% of the gross value of the invoice ($10)
G = Gross value of the invoice ($500)
T = Time difference between the discount and net payment date (20 days)

The formula then becomes:

$$I = \frac{\$10}{(\$500 - \$10)\,(20/365)}$$

I = 37.24% per anum

In this example, the client should take the discount as long as the interest rate is higher than what it costs to borrow funds from the bank.

Exhibit 6.5   As a matter of policy and good business practice most firms take discounts whenever they are offered.

lay invoicing beyond the end of an accounting period, further straining the requirements for working capital.

Payment terms must be clearly defined in the contract and should generally call for monthly invoices and payment within 30 days. Retainers should be withheld from the last payment whenever possible.

It is most important when working under a government or commercial purchase order to recognize that purchase orders were designed primarily to purchase material. They were not designed to purchase services. Therefore if the firm is not careful, it may find that the purchase order was written to provide for payment upon completion of the work. Additional clauses may have to be typed into a purchase order to allow for progress payments.

Obtaining Credit References

To avoid late payments and eventual bad debts, it is wise to ask for credit references from all potential clients for whom the firm has never worked before. In this case the client is coming to the firm requesting work and there should be no hesitation in asking for credit references. This is done all the time in other businesses. The bank references should include the name of the banker who handles the potential client's account. When you need a reference, remember that the banker is often more comfortable and will give out more information if he or she is dealing with another banker, so it is often a good practice to ask your banker to obtain the credit check for you. The potential client's banker will generally comment on the length of time the account has been open, average balances maintained, and a brief description of any borrowing and repayment history.

Since banks usually do not give a "bad" credit reference, the negatives to look for in examining the reference are as follows: whether any loans have had to be renegotiated, whether the client has been with the bank only a short time, and whether the banker does not know the client very well. In many instances it is necessary to "read between the lines" in judging a potential client's credit status. If a potential client is reluctant to give a bank reference, or if the bank has been instructed not to give out information, then the firm will have to make its own judgment before proceeding.

EXERCISE 6.2 ▉▉▉▉▉▉▉▉▉▉▉▉▉▉▉▉▉▉▉

Examining Your Billing

1. Calculate the annual interest rate lost if you fail to take a 4% discount on a supplier's bill of $1250.

2. On what day of the month should invoices be mailed?

_____

3. Project managers should designate an alternative person to approve

_____

_____

4. Backup should not be sent with invoices unless

_____

_____

5. Payment terms must be clearly defined in the

_____

_____

6. A retainer is useful because

_____

7. The most professional way to check a potential client's credit is

_____

8. Warning signs of bad bank credit include:

1. _____

2. _____

3. _____

6.3 COLLECTING RECEIVABLES

The ability to collect receivables quickly requires considerable effort, but it is vital in this economy where cash flow is so critical. This means that all invoices beyond the current period must be vigorously pursued. Clients must be reminded of any outstanding amounts on current invoices, and separate periodic reminders must be sent out to any clients who do not receive current invoices.

The financial manager should review the accounts receivable list monthly and make certain that something is done to expedite payment on each past due account. In some cases, he or she may know the problem and the reason why a client cannot or will not pay. But the financial manager still needs to investigate the progress that is being made toward reaching a resolution. Project managers must also be involved in the collection process and should work closely with the financial manager to follow up on late payments. The financial manager should not hesitate to get help from anyone in management, including the managing principal if necessary, whenever payment can be expedited in this manner. It is also important for the financial manager to report the status of unpaid invoices periodically to the principals of the firm so that they can help in the collection effort. Project managers will also be more eager to help if they know that a status report on unpaid invoices is sent to the principals each month.

Invoicing for Interest

Collecting interest on late payments is still not widely accepted among professional service firms, but it has been receiving increased attention in recent years. Contracts should be written to provide for interest on late payments, and the interest rate should be whatever it costs the firm to borrow. It is then important to invoice for the interest whenever payments are late.

For the firm to be able to invoice for interest on late payments, this procedure must be discussed during the negotiations, agreed to by the client, and then written into the contract. The interest charges should be clearly identified on the invoice and compounded each month. It is also a good practice to cite the clause in the contract and to show the interest calculation on the invoice, so it will not serve as another excuse for a late-paying client to contact you and request a further explanation. One other tactic to keep in mind is that it is sometimes wise to give up the accumulated interest in exchange for a quick and complete settlement of the outstanding amount. In this case, the interest becomes a useful bargaining chip.

Prime Professional/Consultant Relationships in Collection Efforts

In some cases where your firm is a consultant and the prime professional has not yet been paid, it is difficult to press for collection. However, there are still some actions that can be taken. If the prime professional has not been pursuing the collection as actively as you think he or she should, offer to help, particularly if you have done work for the client previously or have contacts in that office. In certain situations the prime professional will accept your offer, particularly if the amount you have outstanding is more than the prime professional's at that time. In any case anticipate these kinds of delays and try to build them into your costs whenever possible. Finally, you should remember the experience when going after future work and decide if the carrying charges offset the potential profit from the work.

The opposite situation occurs when you are the prime professional and have not been paid and consultants are calling you. In this case make certain to follow up with the client and report back your findings to the consultant. You should then pay the consultant promptly after you are paid in order to maintain cooperation.

Contacts in Clients' Office

The financial manager should have a contact to call in the client's office to check on the status of invoices, particularly where there are large on-going relationships. In some cases it may even be necessary for the financial manager to visit the client's office and "walk through" invoices, getting the necessary approvals along the way, particularly in some governmental agencies. This walk-through experience will be helpful in expediting the payment of future invoices.

At times it is difficult to collect the first invoice on certain projects because the invoicing routines have not yet been established. In that case, it is wise to invoice for the first pay-ment as soon as possible. This means that if the project started in the middle or toward the end of the month, it is well to send the first invoice at the end of the month even though it may be quite small, in order to get the payment rou-tine established.

Collection Techniques

A step-by-step technique that involves calling the client and asking the right questions at various stages of the collection process is described as follows:

First Call

1. Have you received our invoice? This question not only assures you that the invoice has arrived but also gets it to the top of the paying pile because the client has to search for it when the inquiry is made.

2. Is it correct? This question can resolve any discrepancy immediately so you do not have to wait for the invoice to be reviewed in the normal course of the client's pay-ing routine.

3. Do you require any supporting documentation? This question, in conjunction with 2, will tend to assure you that the invoice will receive approval without unneces-sary delay.

4. When can we expect payment? This is the first subtle reminder that you are looking for payment.

Second Call

5. We have not received payment. Is anything wrong? This question, asked after payment has not been received within the normal payment terms, is a request to re-solve any differences as quickly as possible.

Third Call

6. Shall we stop work? This is a stronger reminder deliv-ered after waiting, say, two to three weeks after the sec-ond call.

Fourth Call

7. We have stopped work. Shall we call our attorney? At this point there is a potential bad debt situation that must be resolved quickly before matters reach a point of no return.

In addition to calls, follow-up letters should be sent to all clients whose invoices are past due. It is very important to have a written record of attempts to collect past-due invoices in case the matter ever gets to court. Exhibit 6.6 shows some sample collection letters.

Use of Attorneys/Collection Agents

Before a client relationship becomes particularly difficult and payment is seriously past due, it is important to make certain that there is no dissatisfaction with the work. Often a delay in payment can be the first indication that there is a problem. If it is strictly a payment problem and reminders are not working, it may be necessary to stop work or at least threaten to do so until payments are brought up to date. As a last resort, the firm may have to use the services of a collection agency or attorney, but by this time there should be no expectation of future work. Collection agencies and attorneys should be engaged as soon as possible after the firm determines that it has a potential bad debt, because the more time that passes the less likelihood there is of collecting anything on the account. It is well to use a single collection agency for all past-due invoices because design firms rarely have enough poor accounts to justify a full-time collection person. You should obtain liens and judgments against clients who do not pay their bills, but throughout the collection process you must balance the amount at stake and the cost of proceeding versus the likelihood of collection.

SAMPLE COLLECTION LETTERS

First Reminder

Dear Client:

In reviewing our accounts receivable I note that our invoice number 118 in the amount of $2,000 is 30 days past due. Enclosed is a copy of the invoice and I would appreciate your taking action to expedite payment.

Signed,

Second Reminder

(Project manager should speak to client before it is sent.)

Dear Client:

On March 6th I wrote you regarding our invoice number 118 in the amount of $2,000 (copy enclosed). This invoice is now 60 days old and seriously past due. Please call immediately if there is some problem of which we are unaware. Otherwise, we will expect your check by return mail.

Signed,

Third Reminder

(Project manager should know reason for delay by now. If it is a case of the client simply refusing to pay, this letter should be sent.)

Dear Client:

Our invoice number 118 in the amount of $2,000 (copy enclosed) is 90 days past due and we must now take action to collect it. This is to notify you that if payment is not received by (date) we will turn this account over to our attorney for collection. We must take this action since we can no longer afford to carry past-due accounts.

Signed,

(Be sure to take action on the date specified in the letter.)

Exhibit 6.6 Use of standardized collection letters at specific intervals speeds up this procedure considerably.

EXERCISE 6.3 ████████████████████████████████

Analyzing Your Collections Process

1. Interest may be collected on late invoices only if you

_____

_____

2. When you are a subcontractor and the prime contractor has not yet gotten paid, you can offer to

_____

_____

3. When you are the prime professional, you can keep consultants happy by

_____

_____

4. You notify the client that you are going to stop work only after

_____

_____

5. Often a delay in payment indicates that

_____

6. Below, list your firm's process for collections. Be sure to include every step from initial concern through "collection."

1. _____

2. _____

3. _____

4. _____

5. _____

6.4   THE IDEAL COLLECTION LETTER

A sale is not a sale, goes the saying, until you collect the money. Which means that all too much of the selling "done" today will in fact remain undone a month from now.

In 1989, the most recent year for which figures are available, 6,000 U.S. collection agencies chased unpaid bills totalling $72.3 billion. (The sum of all past-due accounts receivable, most of which aren't handed to agencies, is much higher.) They recovered $13.3 billion—or 18%—and after skimming an average fee of 34% of the amount collected, they passed along $8.8 billion to their clients. The upshot? Send an agency after a dollar you're owed and you can expect to get $.12 of it back. The moral? Collecting is hard, but it pays to do it on your own. And it pays to be good at it.

Jim Ullery, customer financial services manager, at Albany Ladder, in Albany, NY, has a policy of extending credit to small time contractors who've never even borrowed money from a bank. The company extends credit early and often in order to maintain its market share. The upshot is that he must collect debts early and often as well. Ullery offers two secrets to successful collecting: First, recognize that it's a process, not a one-step demand. Albany Ladder pursues debtors with a program of phone calls, notes, letters, negotiations, and, if necessary, legal maneuvers. Second, Ullery says, it's important to empathize. "When we make the decision to give customers money . . . we really become a co-signer. So now my role in collecting is to help."

Exhibit 6.7 is an example of Ullery's ideal collection letter.

6.5 CONTROLLING ACCOUNTS PAYABLE

Proper control of the bill-paying function is the other side of the cash management picture. It is important that bills be paid on time but no sooner than necessary. This means that all discounts should be taken whenever offered because the effect of a discount of 2% for payment within 10 days is the equivalent of an interest savings of 37%, as was shown in Exhibit 6.5. Bills that offer no discount should be paid within 30 days. Not only does this protect the credit reputation of the firm, but in many cases, vendors are now adding charges for late payment of bills.

In the past, many vendors used to offer discounts, but they are rare today because of economic conditions. Whenever discounts are offered, you should be careful to abide by the payment terms so as not to cause ill will with vendors.

It is important that the firm maintain its credit reputation in order to receive proper service from vendors. It is also im-

Albany Ladder
1586 Central Avenue
Albany, NY 12205

Scott G. Debtor
966 Inman Way
Indianola, NY 12205

Dear Mr. Debtor:

Re: Past due balance: $4,656.32

In a very few days from now, our accounts are due for auditing and decisions must be made on those that are seriously past due.

As you might imagine, the choice whether or not to place an account with our collection agency is one which we weigh with a good deal of care—especially in your case.

Your goodwill, after all, has always been important to us: That is why we are reluctant now to take any action which might jeopardize your credit standing and cause you embarrassment or added expense. Your contract stipulates that you will be responsible for collection and legal fees.

Yet, I think you will agree that our position is a fair one: we have been happy to extend you credit based on your promise to pay according to our terms. Since then, we have contacted you numerous times without response, and now we must consider the possibility of placing your account with our collection agents or a law firm.

Still, I am hopeful that you will act promptly and forward us your check IN FULL IMMEDIATELY. That is why I am going to suspend further action until March 15, 1994.

It is important, however, that I hear from you by then. Otherwise, a decision must be made that I am sure neither of us wants.

Very Truly Yours,
ALBANY LADDER COMPANY, INC.

Jim Ullery
Customer Financial Services Manager
File No. 12340

518-859-5335
800-354-7368
FAX 518-869-0588

Exhibit 6.7

portant that the firm's credit reputation with banks and credit-reporting agencies, such as Dun & Bradstreet, be maintained so there are no problems with new vendors. Furthermore, it is not unusual for a prospective client who has never worked with the firm to investigate the firm's credit reputation in order to see if it is reputable and is the type of corporate citizen that the client wishes to engage.

If the firm is experiencing cash flow problems and is having difficulty paying its bills, credit experts advise that the problem should be discussed with suppliers before they start calling you. It is best to pay off all smaller accounts and then work out payment terms for the larger accounts. When a firm gets itself into this kind of situation it can expect to be placed on a cash-only basis with many of its suppliers. However, when the firm makes an honest effort and works itself out of this position, many of its suppliers will once again grant credit terms because of the competitive nature of the suppliers' business.

Accounts Payable Procedures

The bill-paying function in most firms is generally a clerical or an automated task, which means that management must set procedures for others to follow:

1. It is important to establish times for paying bills so that they do not accumulate interest for late charges.
2. The people handling this function should understand the terms established by the vendor and whether the vendor wants to be paid upon receipt of individual invoices or monthly on receipt of a statement that lists the invoices sent during the month.
3. All bills should first be verified against prior payments to the vendor to avoid duplicate payments.
4. Consider a two-step procedure for better internal control: One person should prepare the bills for payment by checking for duplicate payments, assembling the supporting documentation, noting approvals on documents, and coding for payment, while a second person reviews and approves the documentation and prepares the checks.

EXERCISE 6.5 ▰▰▰▰▰▰▰▰▰▰▰▰▰▰▰▰▰▰▰▰▰▰▰▰

Discussion Problem

Background. Average borrowing from the bank has been steadily increasing in your 30-person architectural firm. You are rapidly approaching the limits of your $100,000 line of credit. Several times you had to exceed the limit for short periods when you were waiting for checks from clients. Your bank has been very accommodating, but your interest expense has risen by $10,000 this year. Client invoices are generally mailed during the third week after the close of the accounting period. From conversations with principals in other firms, you recognize that this is an excessive delay and you want to improve it.

You discuss the problem with your business manager and discover that invoices are usually typed three times before they are finally mailed. This is because project managers frequently revise the invoices several times after reviewing the total figures. Often they do not want to charge for the time of individuals who have not contributed sufficiently to the project in spite of the hours having been listed on time sheets. They also take exception to certain reimbursable expenses, particularly computer charges that they feel are excessive. Therefore managers do not hesitate to change invoices several times until they are satisfied.

You arrange a meeting with the project managers and business manager to resolve the problem.

Assignment. List the problems to be discussed at this meeting. What changes in procedures would you institute to resolve the problem? How would you monitor the situation so that you know how much time and expenses are not being charged to clients by the project manager's adjustments to invoices?

_____

_____

_____

_____

_____

_____

_____

_____

_____

_____

_____

_____

_____

6.6 GETTING PAID FOR CHANGES

Generally when thinking about getting paid and structuring your invoice system, you don't think enough about getting paid for changes. Yet changes can be costly and obviously impact the bottom line if they are not funded. Following are some suggestions on getting paid for changes that you should devise up front, before anyone signs the contract.

Have a Form

First of all, devise a form for internal use that requires every change to be recorded, priced, and approved by the client. Inform the client in the contract that this form will be presented for each and every change. Include a line for a signature from the client representative, and require return within a specified time period. For time sensitive changes, you might include a clause on the form stating that "If we do not hear from you within 24 hours after receiving this form, we will assume that this change is authorized and will proceed with the change." If you do include such a clause, however, be sure to point it out to the client in advance, at contract signing time.

Be Up Front

As stated above, changes should be addressed during contract negotiations. Here's a strategy that works:

1. Ask clients if they expect there to be changes in the design
2. Give them statistics from your historical data that show the average number of changes per project, the average

percent that every project has no matter how well executed

3. Inform them that because you know some changes are inevitable, a certain number of changes are free (give a specific number). Tell them they will receive the change form mentioned above, but it will have no dollar amount listed. The same policy applies to the free changes as to the paid changes; however, clients rarely balk at authorizing free changes.

4. Tell them clearly that after the specific number of changes are used up, they will receive the same form mentioned above, with a dollar amount listed. Explain in very clear terms how they must authorize the change.

If you follow these steps, you will have no problems getting paid for changes. Make changes part of the normal process of contract negotiations, and you'll have no problems getting paid for them.

FINAL EXAMINATION—CHAPTER 6

Multiple Choice

1. The rate at which cash flow enters and leaves the organization determines
   a. the number of receivables.
   b. the rate of interest.
   c. the difference between success and failure.
   d. none of the above.

2. The cash cycle in design firms is simpler than in most businesses because
   a. there is no exchange factor.
   b. a service firm has no inventories to track.
   c. financing is easier to obtain.
   d. all of the above.

3. The faster a firm can collect for its services
   a. the faster subcontractors can get paid.
   b. the better the cash flow of the firm.
   c. the lower the amount needed for working capital.
   d. all of the above.

4. A typical invoice should include
   a. one lump sum for all services.
   b. labor charges only.
   c. reimbursables and labor broken down separately.
   d. all of the above.

5. A cash discount is given
   a. when a client pays within a certain time period.
   b. to encourage prompt payment.
   c. as a penalty when the supplier does not receive payment.
   d. all of the above.
   e. none of the above.

6. It is not necessary to send backup unless
   a. the client specifically requests it.
   b. you want to.
   c. the firm traditionally sends it.
   d. none of the above.

7. Preparing special invoices to meet the client's need is
   a. recommended.
   b. a god way to enhance relations.
   c. an extra overhead service and should be discouraged.
   d. none of the above.

8. A drawback of giving discounts in exchange for prompt payment is
   a. that it may not speed payment.
   b. the client may take the discount but still not pay within the prescribed period.
   c. part of the payment is not held in advance.
   d. none of the above.

9. The best way to obtain a client credit check is to
   a. call the client's banker yourself.
   b. have your attorney call the client's banker.
   c. have your banker call the client's banker.
   d. all of the above.

10. Charging interest on late payments can be a useful bargaining chip when
    a. you settle for getting the invoiced amount and give up the interest.
    b. you are intent on getting paid.
    c. you insist on involving a collection agency.
    d. none of the above.

11. The best way to assure that you get paid regularly is
    a. to be as courteous as possible.
    b. to be as stern as possible.
    c. to maintain a personal contact in the accounting department.
    d. none of the above.

12. You should not call in an attorney or collection agency until
    a. you don't care about the client.
    b. you've weighed the cost of proceeding against the probability of getting paid.
    c. you've given up.
    d. all of the above.

13. When you can't pay your suppliers, you should
    a. wait until they call you.
    b. be prompt with payment.
    c. call them before they call you.
    d. all of the above.
    e. none of the above.

7

PLANNING AND MONITORING PERFORMANCE

Chapter Summary

- Strategic planning elements
- The importance of the annual business plan
- The pitfalls of "top-down" budgeting
- Budgeting and the annual business plan
- "Realization budgeting" and its use in a professional service firm
- Capital budgeting
- Labor cost monitoring for efficient use of personnel
- Importance of monitoring consultant's costs
- The difference between cash and accrual accounting
- How to value work in progress

The Importance of Planning

Planning and monitoring performance are important to firms of all sizes as organized methods for controlling operations. However, the method by which a firm accomplishes its planning is also important. In this lesson, you'll receive guidance in the foremost task of financial management—the planning stage—and learn how to monitor the performance of that plan.

7.1 STRATEGIC PLANNING ELEMENTS

Almost any business of any size periodically engages in strategic planning. In many firms, however, planning focuses heavily on numbers and doesn't include assessment of the strategic market position of the business. And you can trace most management problems directly to poor planning. Without adequate planning, your organization moves slowly, awkwardly, and without direction.

The strategic market position is that market share that a company can obtain in selling its service or product. Within the total marketplace, how much business will your company obtain? The main focus of your strategic planning process should involve (1) defining the market share for each "product" or "service" you sell, (2) determining how to successfully "sell" that product or service to get that market share, and (3) planning how to deliver your service cost effectively.

Include All Elements

The strategic planning process is made up of six main elements. Coordinate these elements so there is no conflict among them. The six elements are:

1. *Mission and Culture Statements.* The mission statement should capture the essence of what you want your business to be. It should be unique, succinct, and tailored to the exact service your firm provides. It shouldn't be a middle of the road statement ("XYZ Associates is a unique firm"). Instead, state specifically what the firm is trying to accomplish. For example, "We work only for hospital clients that are going to build major hospitals in the next 20 years."

2. *Marketing Plan and Direction.* Clear, concise, and measurable are the key goals of the marketing plan. A standard plan should be well researched and give all the statistical data about clients in the market and dollar volume. As well as being measurable, large firm marketing plans target strategies and techniques for attacking the market, from call reporting to presentation strategies to proposal strategies. In addition, a marketing plan should contain detailed personnel plans, naming specific individuals, to implement the work. Market research in advance of producing the plan is a must!

3. *Financial Plan.* This plan targets expenses and revenues and is simply stated. Forget about making a "financial management system" with all kinds of paperwork and red tape. Instead, identify the key financial measures to monitor monthly each project's success, and

then design a simple, one-page report to communicate this information to yourself and to others.

4. *Organizational Plan.* The organizational makeup of a firm can be one area of constant debate. If you have a typical organization, you have principals at the top, and some type of project manager or department managerial structure, with support staff falling below them. The best type of organizational structure is the market-focused team approach—an organizational structure that places the project manager not on top of others, but as the main point of client contact, with a pool of technical resources and support staff falling below. This structure makes your firm into a market-focused firm, rather than an internally driven organization. With a more client-driven organizational focus, you've got your top people in constant touch with the marketplace, day in, day out.

5. *Human Resources Plan.* Success in this area depends on the ability to staff your organization with employees who believe in what you are doing, with the motivation and skill to take your ideas to a higher level than even you can conceive. Human resources planning should not be simply recordkeeping for vacation and sick time, but a plan that includes staffing, recruitment, position planning, performance appraisal, career planning, training, compensation/rewards/benefits, employee assistance, and records. Focus in this plan on the kinds of individuals you wish to attract, and your methods of attracting them.

6. *Leadership Transition Plan.* The general problem with transition in a service business is that you cannot just sell your firm and leave. Clients buy your service because they feel they are buying you. How do you introduce a new leader? Consider who can carry your vision into the future. What kind of qualities do you look for in a leader? At some points, you may feel that choosing a leader right now is not possible. Just be clear with yourself on the issue, and let the issue go. If you decide that you need to look for a leader, don't limit yourself to first tier managers or the employees you currently have. Look for someone with leadership qualities, much like your own. Managers are often good followers, but are they good leaders?

One other element of successful planning is flexibility. Successful firms plan regularly, then adjust, modify, update, criticize, mold, and work on variations of business plans. Planning should be participatory, ongoing, and recognized as critical to your success.

7.2 WEAKNESS OF "OLD-FASHIONED" BUDGETING

All too often planning is equated with budgeting, and the scenario for the budgeting process goes something like this: The managing principal or chief executive officer calls in the management staff for a discussion about operations for the following year. Generally a certain amount of controlled growth in the organization is expected, and depending upon the economic climate and the anticipated competitive situation, an overall picture develops, say, on the order of 10–15% growth in revenues and profits in an ordinary year. In a smaller firm the principal in charge of operations develops a budget to meet these goals. In many cases the press of current business does not permit enough time to consult with project managers or anyone else in the organization. The budget is prepared "to please the boss."

In a larger organization the management staff is set to work to develop their individual budgets, and the financial manager is responsible for consolidating these budgets into a firmwide total. Most operating managers will tend to budget their operations conservatively, because they do not want to miss their goals and appear to be less than high achievers. They expect others to pick up the slack and achieve the goals originally decided upon. Since no one does, the firmwide budget may not bear any resemblance to what was discussed in the budgeting meeting. Depending on the managing principal's method of operation, in many cases the financial manager is sent back to the department heads with instructions to revise the budgets to conform to what was originally agreed upon.

In discussing the managing principal's wishes with the department heads, the financial manager may be told the reasons for the conservative estimates, such as completion of certain projects with no likelihood of others taking their place or increased competition from other firms. The financial manager may then find him- or herself in the positions of a go-between, relaying instructions and excuses back and forth. Budgeting accomplished in this manner is "old-fashioned" in the sense that it is directed at the top with little participation by the staff. As a result the staff does not feel any responsibility for the results. Budgets are often unrealistic, and they quickly get out of line with actual results, so that comparisons between actual and projected budgets are meaningless. This kind of budgeting is not a useful management tool.

EXERCISE 7.2 ████████████████████████████

Pitfalls of Top-Down Budgeting

1. What is one chief reason why budgets are prepared from the top and not the bottom?

   _____

2. Why do most operating managers budget conservatively?

   _____

   _____

3. Whose job is it to ask operating managers to revise conservative budgets?

   _____

4. Why is top-down budgeting considered to be "old-fashioned"?

   _____

   _____

5. What is the result?

   _____

6. What causes budgets to quickly get out of line?

   _____

7. Can you compare top-down "projected" to actual budgets?

   _____

7.3   BUDGETING AS PART OF AN ANNUAL BUSINESS PLAN

In order for budgeting to become a meaningful exercise, it must be part of an annual business plan. The annual business plan coordinates all elements of the planning process, of which budgeting is only one part. The annual business plan puts less emphasis on expense control and more on profits. It ties expenses to revenue projections prepared by the most knowledgeable people in the organization so that budgets are realistic. They are then easier to accept and implement.

As shown in Exhibit 7.1, the annual business plan includes goals and objectives for the firm and individual plans for marketing, operations, finance, personnel, facilities, and administration. The individual plans are prepared by the heads of these functions and coordinated through periodic discussions so that a meaningful document emerges and fits in with the overall goals established at the beginning of the planning process by the managing principal. After input has been obtained from everyone on the management team, the planning document is more realistic, but most importantly, it allows everyone to work toward the same goals. Tracking actual performance against the plan then becomes meaningful. Exhibit 7.2 describes the elements in the planning process by defining the various terms most often used. Exhibit 7.3 is an example of an annual business plan that might be developed by a firm. Exhibit 7.4 is a useful checklist of questions to ask during the planning process.

EXERCISE 7.3

Preparing a Meaningful Budget and Annual Business Plan

Multiple Choice

1. The annual business plan puts less emphasis on
   a. expense control and less on profits.
   b. profits and more on expenses.
   c. expense and more on profits.

2. An annual business plan should tie
   a. profits to revenue.
   b. expenses to revenue projections.
   c. knowledgeable experts to budget control.

3. A business plan includes
   a. goals and objectives for marketing.
   b. finance and operation projections.
   c. personnel, facilities, and administrative planning.
   d. all of the above.

SAMPLE OUTLINE OF ANNUAL BUSINESS PLAN

1. Goals and Objectives of the Organization

List answers to such specific questions as where does the firm want to be in five years, how does it expect to get there, what steps in the growth process *are* to be achieved and by when?

2. Marketing Plan

Outline the firm's philosophy on marketing and the organization structure needed to accomplish the marketing plan. Outline tools of the marketing effort and what items need to be produced and expanded. List anticipated project awards by specific marketing areas and dollar amounts. List specific clients wherever possible, amounts expected to be acquired, and estimated dates.

3. Operations Plan

List steps to be taken to achieve goals of completing projects on time and within budget. For example, does the firm have a project manager's manual to train new project managers? Outline the procedures to be followed to maximize use of personnel, including sharing of personnel by departments or operating groups. Summarize quality control procedures to be followed. Then develop a monthly forecast of fee income by projecting the balance to be earned on existing contracts and the anticipated earnings on new business acquisitions as outlined in the marketing plan.

4. Financial Plan

Based on current backlog, expected new business acquisitions from the marketing plan, and estimated staff capacity, develop a projected income statement and balance sheet for the new year. Develop budgets by operating groups to tie into income statement.

5. Human Resources and Organization Plan

Develop estimates of the number of new employees to be hired based on operating and financial plans, taking into account expected employee attrition. List skills needed and expected levels of compensation. Determine where, how, and when these people will be hired. List any techniques or changes in employee benefit plans that may help the firm retain good people.

6. Ownership Transition Plan

Outline support staff requirements needed to accomplish transition plan.

> **Exhibit 7.1** Use this outline as a starting point from which to begin the planning process.

ELEMENTS OF PLANNING

1. **Goals.** Broad statements that describe the nature of the firm and what it hopes to accomplish:

   Example for a large firm: "We see oureselves as problem-solvers for clients in all aspects of engineering."

   Example for a small firm: "We want a reputation as the premier architects of low-rise office buildings in this state."

2. **Objectives.** In general terms what the firm hopes to accomplish over the next five years.

   Example for a large firm: "We want to become a multidisciplined engineering firm serving clients throughout the United States. We will serve these clients through regional offices located in key cities around the country."

   Example for a small firm: "We need to broaden our capabilities by offering an interiors architectual service to clients."

3. **Strategies.** In more specific terms, what has to be done to obtain the objectives.

   Example for a large firm: "We need to open an office in Atlanta to serve as a base for clients in the Southeast."

   Example for a small firm: "Search for a small (up to five person) interiors firm for acquisition or else hire someone to provide this capability and organize a staff."

4. **Tactics.** Very specific actions that need to be taken, including time and budget constraints.

   Example for a large firm: "During the next six months we will open an Atlanta office, staffed by four people currently working on the XYZ project and will budget $250,000 over the next 12 months for a marketing effort that will make the office 50% self-sufficient by the end of the year."

   Example for a small firm: "During the next six months investigate possible acquisition prospects through contacts at the state society and through friends. If nothing definite, begin search for candidate for employment (offer at least $45,000 for at least six years experience in managing a small interiors department)."

   Exhibit 7.2 Goals and objectives are difficult to establish because they are the foundation on which the firm is built.

EXAMPLE OF AN ANNUAL BUSINESS PLAN FOR A LARGER FIRM

I. INTRODUCTION

A. Methodology

This annual business plan was developed as follows:

1. Five employee task forces, each consisting of five members, with one from each division, were appointed by the president to study basic issues and topics and to make recommendations to a general Business Planning Committee. The task force efforts were coordinated by the personnel director.

2. A general planning committee meeting was held Saturday, October 28, to hear the reports and recommendations from the five task forces and to participate in general discussions. Extensive notes of the meeting were taken.

3. The personnel director took these notes plus the written reports from the task forces and prepared a draft of the corporate goals and objectives (Sections II and III) for review, modification, and approval of the executive committee.

4. The executive committee sent a copy of the proposed corporate goals to each division/office manager for review and suggested modifications.

5. Each division/office manager provided his or her own objectives and plans for review and approval of the executive committee.

6. The controller and division/office managers prepared budgets for the year (not included in this report).

7. These efforts were combined, reviewed, and approved by the executive committee.

B. Purposes of the Annual Business Plan

1. To provide guidance for the officers and managers of the firm to follow in its management of the organization.

2. To be used as a communications tool for the general Business Planning Committee and for all staff. It is intended to be both a road map and a document subject to review and revision throughout the year.

C. Current Status of the Firm

1. Given the apparent success of the firm, it seems essential to review the current strengths and weaknesses to use as building blocks for this year and subsequent years.

Strengths

1. The firm has been in business since 1965 and has established an excellent technical reputation.

2. It is larger than most (perhaps 85%) of the consulting environmental firms in the United States.

> **Exhibit 7.3** Note the detail and thoroughness with which this plan was prepared.

3. It attempts to provide "one-stop" total environmental services.

4. It has X% repeat business.

5. The firm has been profitable for the past years although margins have been thin.

6. It has been successful in penetrating both private and public markets.

7. It has been successful in establishing other offices, although their role, reporting relationships, and ultimate contribution to profits have not been completely determined.

8. It has some capabilities, such as X, which, while they are not unique, do not have as much competition as other units.

9. It has attracted and retained a significant number of highly qualified and motivated people.

10. It has a young, friendly staff and, for the most part, a pleasant work environment.

11. It has successfully marketed large multidisciplinary projects.

Weaknesses

1. The firm is in a process of significant change in marketing, line, and project management methods and techniques.

2. Its resources are stretched with the recent active program of geographic expansion, significant percentage of unprofitable projects, and rising overhead costs.

3. It has limited ability to grow and to attract qualified individuals in quantity from outside the immediate area because of noncompetitive salary structures.

4. "Charters" between divisions/offices overlap and/or remain undefined.

5. Line management is viewed as the only route to the top by most of the professional staff, yet management education is not required, perhaps not really encouraged.

6. Affirmative Action/Equal Opportunity programs are ineffective.

7. Space problems hamper growth.

8. Staff turnover is high.

9. Systematic, successful efforts have not been made to answer basic questions such as: (1) Why are we in business? (2) Do we wish to be specialists or generalists? (3) Why have we been successful/unsuccessful in the past? (4) What do we want to be?

10. It has inconsistent attitudes toward profits, billable time, and overhead.

11. It has not learned to successfully manage large multidisciplinary projects and to generate the requisite division/office cooperation.

II. CORPORATE GOALS

A. To continue to build a state-of-the-art professional engineering organization.

Exhibit 7.3   Continued.

B. To foster interdependence with checks and balances on professional performance through:
1. Teamwork.
2. Careful planning.
3. Quality work.
4. Persistent follow-through.
5. Good business practices.

C. To provide the proper working environment and tools to permit the staff to achieve satisfying and stimulating professional careers.

D. To make a major contribution to the national goal of restoring and maintaining the quality of our environment without sacrificing social or economic gains.

E. To build a staff of the most highly qualified and recognized professionals and to encourage all staff members to seek registration and/or certification by their peer professionals.

F. To maintain a commitment to research and development in order to anticipate emerging needs for consulting services.

G. To maintain adequate profit from our activities to ensure sound growth and development.

H. To contribute our efforts and energies to bettering our own communities and to encourage our staff to participate in such activities.

III. CORPORATE OBJECTIVES

A. Organization and Management
1. To further develop the role and effectiveness of the executive committee as a policy review and advisory group.
2. To complete the reassignment of the responsibility for technical achievement, schedules, and budgets of both projects and proposals to operating divisions.
3. To further develop the role and effectiveness of the corporate marketing committee.
4. To assign all branch offices to division directors.
5. To further define the role, composition, and reporting relationships of branch offices.
6. To continue and further develop quarterly evaluations of all organizational units reporting to the president.
7. To hire an outstanding person to head up the environmental division.
8. To eliminate obvious overlaps in "charters" between offices and organizational units.
9. To examine, further define, and strengthen the role, authority, responsibility, accountability, and rewards to both division and project managers.
10. To develop a long range (three- to five-year) corporate business plan.

B. Physical Facilities and Equipment
1. To break ground on a new building.
2. To organize and develop a central shipping, receiving, storage, and maintenance activity and facility.
3. To investigate, evaluate, purchase, and install a modern data processing and computer system.
4. To experiment with shifts in overcrowded, particularly capital intensive, areas.

Exhibit 7.3 Continued.

C. Marketing

1. To evaluate our corporate marketing successes, failures, philosophy, and goals so that long-range plans can be developed. For example, are we to be specialists or generalists or both?
2. To study and determine feasibility of a formal research and development effort as part of an overall marketing program.
3. To identify individuals in each division who are interested and capable of being further developed in client contact and proposal preparation skills and to provide some formal development of these individuals.
4. To develop and install a system for forecasting, budgeting, and controlling marketing costs and benefits.
5. To develop a plan for systematic market research so that future markets can be identified.
6. To refine concept and reporting relationships of marketing managers.

D. Human Resources

1. To intensify efforts and set up formal programs to train and develop current staff in technical, marketing, and management areas.
2. To improve Affirmative Action/Equal Opportunity Employment programs and to conduct at least one formal training program in management staff sensitivity on this issue.
3. To formulate and install a cost-effective orientation program for new employees.
4. To further train managers in the processes of motivating and evaluating employees.
5. To reevaluate profit sharing and retirement options and programs and to propose changes if required.

E. Profitability

1. To establish reasonable long-term project profitability, billable time, and overhead goals and to require accountability by managers at all levels throughout the year.
2. To complete the process of assigning project profitability responsibility to operating division directors.
3. To develop and install an improved project cost control system.
4. To require each division to cross train at least 25% of its technical staff in one other division.
5. To require a pragmatic compensation system that rewards interdivisional cooperation.
6. To establish divisional cost and/or profit centers.
7. To achieve sales of _____ and profits of _____ .

Exhibit 7.3 Continued.

CHECKLIST OF KEY STRATEGIC PLANNING QUESTIONS

A. Firm Strategy
1. What is your definition of growth?
2. How does your form of organization affect growth?
3. Form a mental picture of what the practice should be like in three years.
4. How many people can you personally manage?
5. What effect does your ownership transition plan have on growth?
6. What role will you play in your visionary practice?
7. What talent will you need that is not now present in the firm?
8. Why is growth important to you?
9. What impact does your management of time have on growth?
10. List three external factors that can help you grow and then three that will hinder growth.
11. Define change.
12. How do you implement change?
13. What conflicts do you perceive between your visionary firm and the present situation?
14. Why do these conflicts exist?
15. What can you do to resolve the conflicts?
16. Define the kind of leader you are.
17. What impact does your leadership style have on growth?
18. How do your clients perceive the firm?
19. Is their perception in line with goals for your visionary firm?
20. Crystallize your thoughts into a one-statement strategic goal for the firm in specific terms.

B. Marketing
1. What are the three primary strengths of the firm?
2. Do your clients perceive these as your strengths?
3. Why do you call them strengths?
4. List three types of work in which the strengths can be maximized.
5. List three more peripheral markets that you are not now serving that could be entered using your strengths.
6. What kind of work should the firm do in order of priority?
7. What geographic area should be covered?
8. Who should be responsible for marketing performance in the firm? Why?
9. Define marketing.
10. Define selling.
11. What is the difference?
12. What image does your firm project? How do you know?
13. What image will your visionary firm project?
14. How do the images differ?
15. Is there a project too large for the firm? Too small? Why?
16. Do you like to sell? List why/why not?
17. Do you have fear of sales failure?
18. List the three things that you personally do best.
19. In one paragraph convince me that you are best for each of the strengths listed above.
20. Write a specific marketing goal statement for the firm.

> **Exhibit 7.4** The answers to these questions require deep insight and considerable thought, which are essential to the planning process.

C. Finance

1. Define profit.
2. How much money should you earn?
3. How much gross income will your visionary firm earn?
4. How does this compare with today?
5. Where will additional fees come from?
6. How much investment will it take to grow?
7. Are your sources of borrowing sufficient to fund the growth?
8. What is your profit goal for next year?
9. How does your profit goal tie in with your personal goal for income?
10. Do you want to communicate the financial status of the firm to the staff?
11. How often do you want to know how well or how poorly the firm is doing? Why?
12. How much should you spend to get the information you want?
13. Should all owners have 100% access to all financial data?
14. Should there be a difference between function and ownership? Should all owners manage?
15. How much capital do you want to invest in the operations of the firm?
16. Is return on your investment important to you, and if so, how should it be measured in terms of dollars and cents or in terms of your other goals?
17. List three financial factors affecting growth.
18. What control do you have over each factor?
19. What impact does the economy have on your finances?
20. List three things you can do today to improve the finances of the firm.
21. How can you enlist the help of the entire staff to improve profits?

D. Human Resources

1. What is your primary goal in life?
2. Where do you want to live?
3. How long do you want to work?
4. What is your favorite hobby?
5. What is your favorite work?
6. If you had all the money in the world, what would you do today?
7. What is your family's goal?
8. Do your spouse's goals match yours?
9. Do you know the answers to the above eight questions for each member of your staff?
10. How can you find out more about your people?
11. Define motivation.
12. Define communication.
13. How do you communicate with your staff?
14. How does the staff perceive you? How do you know?
15. List ten traits you look for in any person you hire. Rank them from 1 to 10 in importance.
16. How do the traits compare with what you listed as your three primary strengths?
17. Identify specific roles needed in your visionary firm that are not now present.
18. What traits should people in those roles have? Why?
19. What is the goal of your recruiting effort?
20. How do you reinforce that goal once an individual is hired?
21. List all benefit programs you now provide your staff.

Exhibit 7.4 Continued.

D. Human Resources (Continued)

22. Next to each benefit, list how it affects your profit and how it helps you get more work.
23. How do your benefits compare with other architectual, engineering, or planning firms? To other professional firms?
24. Define recognition.
25. List five kinds of recognition you have power to give to each employee.
26. How good a listener are you?
27. In an eight-hour day, how much time do you spend listening? Talking?
28. How does human resources planning affect market and financial planning?
29. Identify one thing you can do better today to improve the human resources effort in the firm.

Exhibit 7.4   Continued.

4. A business plan becomes meaningful when it
   a. fits with profit goals.
   b. establishes a bench mark.
   c. fits in with goals established at the beginning of the planning process by the principal.

5. The business plan is a planning document that
   a. allows everyone to work toward the same goals.
   b. allows the principal more control.
   c. lets everyone know the firm's goals.

6. Tracking actual performance
   a. is impossible without a proper business plan.
   b. is not possible at all.
   c. becomes meaningful when you obtain input from everyone on the team.

7.4   STEPS IN PLANNING

Planning is often thought of as an activity that only larger firms have time to do. It is not. All firms can and should develop long-range plans. Since each firm is unique, its planning process and the final plan must take into consideration individual characteristics of a particular firm. However, the cornerstone of all successful plans is that they are simple, extremely realistic, and easily communicated to others.

Although it takes very little time to plan, it can make a substantial difference in the success or failure of a firm. The following points should be considered in the planning process:

1. *Start with Yourself.* Make a list of those things you personally want to happen over the next few years. Do you want more income? More challenging projects? A sabbatical? Or a different role? Write down a description of your personal vision of what the firm will look like in three to five years if all goes as you wish.

2. *Establish Time Parameters.* Think in terms of a three- to five-year planning parameter that will help make your plan realistic, and keep it simple.

3. *Get Others Involved Early.* Identify those in your firm who have the most impact on its future and ask each to write down his or her personal ambitions and desires and then a description of the firm three to five years from now. It is important not to ask that these written statements be submitted, but that they be used to direct the thinking of the individuals in anticipation of a group planning session.

4. *Pick a Planning Leader.* Identify an individual in your firm who is good at conducting brainstorming sessions. The role of this individual is to coordinate and conduct a planning session among top management to synthesize personal goals and desires of the individuals into a concise long-range plan. If such a person is not available in-house, choose a consultant as a catalyst to help you with your planning meeting.

5. *Set a Date.* Schedule a full-day planning session for all individuals asked to write down goals in step 3 above. The session must be held outside your facility so that interruptions will be eliminated and so that your commitment to the planning process can be emphasized. The room should be comfortable and provision made for a flip chart, markers, and masking tape. No more than 10 to 12 individuals should ever be invited to the session even in the largest firms.

6. *Don't Do Extensive Research.* The purpose of the planning session is to clarify goals and direction. Subsequent to the session, assignments can be made to research specific aspects for validity of your plan, but your experience and that of your colleagues collectively minimizes the need for extensive preplanning research.

7. *Establish Your Own Yardstick.* Using the flip chart and markers, begin your planning session by asking all individuals to describe verbally what the firm will look like in three, four, or five years. Pick a year (say,

three), and list very specific items such as 200 projects, 55 people, $3 million gross fees, two new markets. Be certain to discuss all aspects of the resources, finance, and management in terms of goals and targets. Be realistic, yet stretch your expectations a bit. Also, don't be trapped into clichés such as a goal of continuous growth if the principals of the firm have decided not to grow. The importance of this step is to actively seek and draw out the most realistic picture of what the firm will be like in three to five years from those who will create it.

8. *Set One-Year Expectations.* After agreeing on three- to five-year goals, the leader asks each individual where the firm will be in one year to be on track for achieving the three-year goals. Use the flip chart again, and list in more specific terms exactly where the practice should be in one year.

9. *Give Individual Six-Month Assignments.* Identify specific individuals within the session who agree and commit to the group to carry out specific assignments in order to begin working toward the goals. Set target calendar dates, not elapsed time dates, and establish specifically what is to be done, by whom, and who else will assure that it is done. For example, your three-year goal is to be a recognized expert in a new building type for your firm. In one year, you will have three projects in that building type. By January 1 (30 days) John Smith will develop a written marketing plan to get three projects, and Al Jones will verify that John has carried out the assignment.

10. *Communicate All You've Written.* At the end of your session, summarize in outline form on your flip chart your three-year, one-year, and six-month plans. Using the flip chart forces you to minimize words and to clarify decisions. Take the sheets back to the firm and have them typed. Using this method assures that your written plan will be no more than three to six pages long. It will be simple, clear, and easily understood. Assign each individual in the group session the responsibility to talk personally with four to eight people from the staff about the planning session and personally hand out copies of your typewritten plan to those people. Do not bind your plan in fancy covers or permanent binders. Instead, mark it as a draft: to be updated in June (six months from now). Doing so tells the staff that their input can still have an impact on the

firm's direction. When the plan is discussed with the staff, the primary objective is to get their feedback.

11. *Schedule Your Next Planning Session.* Before leaving your one-day meeting, pick a specific calendar date, a specific location, and specific people in order to hold another all-day planning session in six months and repeat the entire process. Following this rule means that you will be devoting two days (sixteen hours) of your staff time per year to planning, which is a price you can afford. It also means that you will respond to the input you receive over the next six months from others in your staff.

By following the planning process, you will see that long-range planning is nothing more than setting goals, establishing one-year objectives, and assigning six-month strategies and action plans on how to achieve your goals. You will determine where your firm is going and when it will get there.

EXERCISE 7.4

Finding the Time to Plan

True or False

T F   Most small firms cannot prepare annual plans because they can't afford to take the time.

T F   Since each firm is unique, its planning process, and the final plan, must take into consideration the firm's individual characteristics.

T F   The first person to start with in preparing a financial plan is yourself.

T F   The worst thing you can do is get others involved early.

Planning Your Steps

1. Make a list of milestones you'd like to see reached within the firm over the next few years.

_____

_____

_____

2. What do you want? More income? More challenging projects?

_____

_____

3. Write out your personal vision of where the firm is going.

_____

_____

_____

4. What are the time parameters for each of your goals?

_____

_____

5. Identify the key players in the firm who greatly impact its future. Ask each of them to write down his or her personal ambitions and desires.

6. Have each of the key players write down their vision of the firm three to five years from now.

Taking the Steps

1. Pick a planning leader.

2. Gather your goal statements and those of your firm's key players.

3. What is the earliest date to hold a full-day brainstorming session, preferably outside your facility?

_____

4. In the planning session, what will you clarify?

_____

_____

_____

7.5 LONG-TERM PLANNING

After a firm has had some experience with annual planning, the next step is to develop a three-year plan and eventually a five-year plan. These longer-range plans are obviously very sketchy, but uncertainty of planning in the longer range should not be a hindrance. The importance of long-range

CHECKLIST OF SIGNIFICANT STEPS IN
PREPARING A STRATEGIC FINANCIAL PLAN

1. Identification of financial goals of ownership.
2. List of the management team (personnel) necessary to carry out the financial goals of ownership.
3. Effective communication of ownership goals to the management team.
4. Integrated budget preparation.
5. Execution of the plan.
6. Critical review and update process.

Exhibit 7.5 *Each of these steps must be addressed in a carefully thought-out plan.*

planning is not in its accuracy or how closely an individual can guess the future, but in the *discipline* of the planning process. It forces the firm management to think about its future direction and to answer questions about growth and diversification, geographical expansion or contraction, new markets, and similar questions. Exhibits 7.5 and 7.6. are checklists to review when preparing plans.

EXERCISE 7.5 ■■■■■■■■■■■■■■■■■■■■■■■■■

Looking at Your Long-Range Plans

1. Identify your firm's financial goals.

   _____

   _____

   _____

2. List the management team (personnel) necessary to carry out the financial goals.

   _____

   _____

   _____

3. How will you communicate those goals to the management team?

   _____

   _____

   _____

CHECKLIST OF GOALS AFFECTING THE PROFIT BUDGET

1. Capital expenditures (rent versus buy).
2. Investment in other ventures.
3. Estate settlements with decreased partners.
4. Lease/purchase equipment.
5. Market diversity.
6. Economic climate.
7. Merger versus acquisitions.

Exhibit 7.6 Review this checklist for applicability when finalizing profit plans.

4. Have you prepared an integrated budget for the long-range plan? If not, what is a realistic timetable for accomplishing this goal?

_____

_____

5. How and when will this plan be executed?

_____

_____

6. When will you review and update the long-range plan?

_____

_____

7.6 PERFORMANCE MONITORING

Monitoring financial performance is a basic activity of management, and it is performed at various levels in a firm. For example, the project manager monitors the performance of particular projects, and his or her interest is generally confined to these projects. The department head's responsibilities in monitoring performance, like those of the project manager, are generally confined to the overall performance of his or her department. The financial manager monitors the overall financial condition of the firm, and generally his or her responsibilities are to bring to the attention of others in management any discrepancies that are discovered. Finally, the principals in a smaller firm and the senior management in a larger firm have the responsibility to keep informed of the overall condition of the firm and to take the necessary action to correct problems as quickly as they are discovered and before it is too late to remedy the situation.

EXERCISE 7.6 ■

Checklist for Monitoring Performance

Use this checklist as a guide for considering items that might not be covered under normal operating procedures.

YES	NO	
☐	☐	Are manpower forecasts prepared on a routine basis?
☐	☐	Do project managers and department heads meet on a periodic basis to plan the utilization of personnel?
☐	☐	Does the firm have adequate accounting procedures to prevent late charges that cannot be billed to clients?
☐	☐	Are project managers evaluated on their performance quarterly or at least twice yearly?
☐	☐	Has the firm prepared a project managers' manual?
☐	☐	Is there a training program for new project managers?
☐	☐	Do project managers carefully monitor consultants' costs as well as performance?
☐	☐	Are reimbursable expenses controlled by including them in the project budget and making the project manager responsible for them?
☐	☐	Are profit margins on projects examined at the close of each project and explanations requested whenever the profit is below budget?
☐	☐	Do project managers understand accrual accounting and how costs are recorded against their projects?

☐ ☐ Is work in progress recorded on the basis of selling price? (That is, the value of work in progress should be the same as the amount that will eventually be invoiced to the client)

7.7 WHAT IS BEING MONITORED?

Labor costs are obviously the most important item to monitor, and there are a number of ways to accomplish this important task. Manpower utilization forecasts are a useful tool to determine in advance what people are scheduled to do in the weeks and months ahead. In larger firms they are prepared by the department heads in consultation with project managers. The manpower forecasts list each individual and the time on each project he or she is expected to spend in the weeks and months ahead, depending on the time frame of the projection. In larger firms with longer-term projects, a three-month projection is often prepared, but other firms may have to use a shorter period. Forecasts can and should be revised and updated to achieve maximum use of personnel and a minimum of unutilized or unproductive time. Manpower forecasts may show an overloaded situation with more work to accomplish than people available and vice versa, but their importance is that they give management time to make adjustments. Examples of simple utilization forms are shown in Exhibits 7.7 and 7.8. Remember that once time has been charged on a time sheet, it is too late for corrective action.

For control purposes it is important to have all time charges approved by the appropriate project manager or department head (in the case of time not charged to a project by an individual in that department). Labor hours should be reported after the close of each time sheet period; reports should include what projects each individual worked on and what hours were charged to overhead accounts. These reports should go to the project managers and department heads concerned and comparisons should be made against the manpower forecasts and budgeted project hours.

In addition to monitoring hourly charges it is necessary to monitor dollars. Revenue and profit forecasts by profit center should be compared with actual figures, as shown in the example in Exhibit 7.9, and project costs should be monitored on a profit-and-loss basis, as shown in Exhibits 7.10 and 7.11. While there are several ways to monitor performance on a

EXAMPLE OF MANPOWER UTILIZATION FORECAST
PREPARED BY DEPARTMENT HEAD (Prepared in Hours)

Department: *Structural*

Period: *Week Ending 7/31*

List Employees by Name	Total Hours	Holidays/ Vacations	Avail. Hours	PROJECTS A		B, etc.		OVERHEAD Business Development		Administration		Unutilized
				Time Needed	Time Avail.	Time Needed	Time Avail.	Time Needed	Time Avail.	Time Needed	Time Avail.	
J Smith	80	0	80	40	40	40	40			5*		
M. Jones	80	8	72	60	60	20†	12					
B Henry	40	0	40	30	30							10‡
A. Aron	80	20	60	40	40	20	20					
T King	80	0	80	80	80							
R. Keith	80	0	80					80	80			
Total	1,460	240	1,220	540	580	200	180	150	200	100	120	180

*Cannot be accommodated in normal week—consider use of overtime
†Cannot be accommodated in normal week—consider use of contract labor, other employee
‡Consider asking employee to take vacation if productive work cannot be scheduled

Exhibit 7.7 This report gives the department head a complete picture of the projected utilization status of all members of his or her department. Trade-offs and adjustments in assignments can then be made for the most effective use of personnel.

project, the profit-and-loss approach is very clear and direct, and it leaves no room for doubt as to the status of the project. Another type of report for monitoring status on the basis of percentage of completion is shown in Exhibit 7.12.

In addition to labor charges, reimbursable expenses, including consultants' costs, must be closely monitored. One of the most troublesome aspects of monitoring reimbursable expenses is in closing out a project before all the costs are in. On other than lump sum projects, these late charges come directly out of profits if they cannot be recovered from the

EXAMPLE OF MANPOWER BUDGET PREPARED BY PROJECT MANAGER
(Prepared in Hours)

Project Name _____A_____

Project Number _____83-15_____

Project Manager _____L. Brown_____

Budget Period _____4/30_____

Project Starting Date _____1/15_____

Project Ending Date _____5/30_____

List Requirements by Department and Staffing Levels within Departments	Total Project Estimate	Hours Spent to Date	Balance	Projected by Month					Six Months Total Estimate
				Jan.	Feb.	Mar.	Apr.	May	
Structural Dept.									
S. Smith	230	200	30				15	15	30
M. Jones	120	120	0						
B. Henry	80	45	35				30	5	35
Total	980	900	80				50	30	80

Note: Project expenses may be listed below and projected on this same report.

Exhibit 7.8 This report converts the budgeted hours on a project to a time sequence for planning purposes. In cases where many projects are being scheduled, a chart or graphic presentation is even more effective.

client. Therefore, it is important for the financial manager to coordinate closely with the project manager so that a final invoice is not sent until all costs are known. Another important aspect in monitoring consultants' costs is to try to get consultants onto your invoicing cycle so that they do not have to wait an extra 30 days to be paid. To accomplish this, the project manager should discuss the firm's invoicing dates

EXAMPLE OF MONTHLY PERFORMANCE REPORT
(Prepared in Dollars)

List Months Beginning with First One in Fiscal Year	Revenue			Profit/Loss*		
	Original Budget	Revised Budget	Actual	Original Budget	Revised Budget	Actual
January	$100,000	$90,000	$96,000	$15,000	$14,000	$12,000
February	120,000	No Change	115,000	18,000	No change	20,000
December	140,000	No Change	140,000	(2,000	No Change	8,000
TOTALS	$1,600,000	$1,400,000	$1,350,000	$120,000	$110,000	$95,000

*List total dollars of revenue and profit expected to be earned by the profit center each month under various budgets prepared and compare with actual.

Exhibit 7.9 This report is prepared by a profit centre manager, that is, the head of an individual office or division or anyone who has profit responsibility for a segment of a larger firm. In smaller firms this report would be prepared for the firm as a whole.

with the consultant so that the consultant can arrange to get his or her invoice in on time. It is simply good business practice to treat consultants as you would wish to be treated. In a few cases the roles may be reversed and the consultant may sometimes be acting as the prime professional. In any event, you want the best service from the consultant so you should give him or her good service in return.

Another area of concern in accounting for consultants' costs is in the proper matching of income and expenses. In the case of lump sum projects, for example, where project managers are calculating revenue on a percentage completion basis, it is very important that they and the financial manager communicate properly. If the percentage completion includes work done by a consultant, then the financial manager must be certain that the expenses include the consultant's costs; otherwise there will be a distortion in the profit on the project.

EXAMPLE OF OF PROJECT FINANCIAL REPORT

Prepared in Dollars by Accounting Department for Project Managers

Project Name _____A_____   Project Number _83-15_   Project Manager _L Brown_

Report Period _3/31,_____

	Current Month		Actual Project To Date	Total Budget	Balance Remaining
	Actual	Budget			
Project Revenue	$15,000	$20,000	$120,000	$150,000	$30,000
Project Expenses					
Direct salaries	5,000	8,000	42,000	60,000	18,000
Overhead	8,000	11,000	70,000	82,000	12,000
Other direct costs					
Consultants	0	0	1,000	1,000	0
Other	500	0	5,000	4,000	<1,000>
Subtotal for Other Direct Costs	500	0	6,000	5,000	<1,000>
Total project costs	13,500	19,000	118,000	147,000	29,000
Profit/Loss	$1,500	$1,000	$2,000	$3,000	$1,000

Exhibit 7.10 This report summarizes the status of a project in profit-and-loss format, giving the project manager the essential ingredients he or she needs to know. In this illustration the project manager has overspent the budget on expenses but may be able to recover through a lesser expenditure on labour.

Profit must also be carefully monitored. It is the ultimate test of financial performance, and if it is lower than the amount budgeted or if the profit turns into a loss, there must be an explanation so that the same mistakes are not repeated. It is emphasized throughout this text that knowing beforehand when losses are likely to occur, and informing senior officials so that corrective action can be taken in time are the mark of good management. The project manager must not attempt to cover up an unfavorable situation, because it will usually only get worse if unreported. The urge to cover up will disappear if senior management encourages an open attitude by minimizing criticism of mistakes and emphasizing a helping hand that encourages everyone to assist in solving the problem.

EXAMPLE OF SUMMARY PROFIT AND LOSS BY PROJECT
FOR EACH COST CENTER

Prepared in Dollars by Accounting Department for
Senior Management in a Larger Firm

	Project Revenue	Project Costs	Profit/ Loss	Profit as % of Project Revenue
Silver City Office				
001 Project A	$402,000	$398,000	$4,000	1%
002 Project B	116,000	120,000	⟨4,000⟩	—
003 Project C	500,000	425,000	75,000	15
008 Project K	950,000	900,000	50,000	5
Total Projects (Silver City Office)	$2,000,000	$1,900,000	$100,000	5%
Total Projects (All offices)	$4,000,000	$3,800,000	$200,000	5%

Exhibit 7.11 This report shows the status of each project in a one-line summary of profit or loss. In a larger firm with many projects to review this is useful to senior management. Projects that are incurring losses or not meeting budget expectations should be earmarked for further investigation.

EXERCISE 7.7

Monitoring Manpower

1. Manpower utilization forecasts determine

_____

_____

2. The manpower forecasts list each individual and

_____

3. A typical projection schedule is _____ months.

FIRMWIDE PROJECT BUDGET STATUS REPORT

Date __/ /__

Project Number	Project Name	Project Mgr.	Est. Date Completed	Budget		Totals to Date		% Hr Spent
				Hours	Fee ($)	Hours	Charges ($)	
1000	Hospital	Baker	10/31	30	$1000	19	$1,933	63%
1010	Office	Jones	10/30	55	846,833	45	830,339	82
1015	Garage	Smith	1/1	150	6,780	33	8,363	22
1020	Warehouse	Thomas	10/16	76	480,000	74	484,329	97
1023	Renovation	Edwards	1/1	5,000	2,000,000	432	9,561	8
1030	Church	Apple	1/1	5,000	846,833	530	91,110	10

Exhibit 7.12 This project budget status report shows the percentage of hours spent (actual versus budget) in the last column. This percentage is compared with the actual percentage completion determined by the project manager in order to know whether the project is within budget. For example, if Baker estimates that the hospital is only 50 percent complete based on the work yet to accomplish, this project is over-budget with 63 percent of the hours already used.

4. Manpower forecasts may reveal

_____

_____

5. Time charged to a time card is

_____

6. All time charges should be approved by _____

or _____

7. After the close of each time sheet period, _____
are reported.

8. Comparisons are made with these reports to

_____

_____

_____

9. It is necessary to monitor both _____ and _____ .

7.8 ACCRUAL VERSUS CASH ACCOUNTING

It is important to understand the difference between cash and
accrual accounting when monitoring performance on
projects. This difference has often been described in accountant's technical jargon that is difficult for the design professional to comprehend. Exhibit 6.1 is a visual explanation that
makes it easier to understand and also clearly demonstrates
the accounting cycle. Beginning with the time sheets and reimbursable expenses, these items go into a category referred
to as "unbilled work in progress." Work in progress can be
written off, it can remain work in progress indefinitely, or as is
usually the case, it can be billed to the client and become an
account receivable. Accounts receivable can also remain indefinitely in that account, they can be written off as a bad
debt, or they can be collected as cash.

The difference in time of when revenue is recognized in
the firm determines whether the firm is on a cash or accrual
basis. If revenue is not recognized until cash is received, the
firm is on a cash basis. Cash expenses are applied against this
revenue to determine cash excess or deficiency. If the firm
recognizes income at the time the work is performed and it
becomes work in progress, then the firm is on the accrual
system. Accrual expenses—that is, expenses incurred regardless of when they are paid—are applied against this income to
arrive at accrual profit or loss.

When the value of work in progress is determined for revenue purposes, the most generally accepted method is to
evaluate it at full value to the client rather than at cost. This

means that profit should be added to cost so that the amount of work in progress is the same as the amount that will eventually be invoiced to the client. This is what is recorded as revenue. If work in progress is evaluated at cost only, then revenue will be understated.

Another method of recognizing revenue is at the time the work in progress is invoiced. This is generally not satisfactory because if for some reason invoices were not prepared for several projects during the month, then the revenue picture would be distorted.

Under the accrual system we are recording revenue that has not yet been received as cash. This means that we run the risk of having to write off or eliminate that revenue if, for whatever reason, the client does not pay. In effect, we are "counting our chickens." However, the accrual method is still effective because it forces management to focus its attention on the size of the accounts receivable and work in progress and to do something to enforce collections.

Most larger firms keep their accounting on the accrual basis for internal management reporting purposes. They recognize it as the only way to effectively manage their operations. However, many smaller firms remain on the cash basis because it is easier for their accountants to prepare tax returns. Smaller firms should adopt the accrual method as well. The extra accounting effort is repaid many times by having financial statements that truly reflect the status of operations and tell the principals if the firm is in a profit or loss position. The principals then have information on which to base management decisions. Exhibit 7.14 is an example of cash versus accrual financial statements.

EXERCISE 7.8 ■■■■■■■■■■■■■■■■■■■■■

Cash Versus Accrual Accounting

1. The difference in time of when revenue is recognized determines

_____

_____

2. If revenue is not recognized until cash is received, the firm operates on a(n) _____ basis.

DIFFERENCE IN INCOME STATEMENTS BETWEEN
CASH AND ACCRUAL BASIS ACCOUNTING

ABC Architects, Inc.
Accrual Basis Income Statement for Year Ending 12/31
Annotated for Adjustments to the Cash Basis
(In Thousands)

		To adjust the accrual basis income statement shown to a cash basis, enter the following:
Revenue		
Fee income	$2,000	Record as revenue only amounts received in cash from clients/others.
Other income	12	
Total Revenue	$2,012	
Expenses		
Direct labor	701	Record as expenses only those amounts actually paid out in cash. The only exception is the expense of depreciation, a noncash item that is usually also recorded in cash statements.
Indirect labor	265	
Payroll burden	203	
Rent	318	
Office supplies and equipment	40	
Insurance	18	
Business development	21	
Telephone	37	
Miscellaneous	33	
After direct costs (including consultants)	344	
Total Expenses	$1,980	
Net Profit Before Taxes	$32	"Profit" is not proper terminology in cash statements. This figure is actually the excess or deficit of cash receipts over disbursements.

Exhibit 7.14 Note that the bottom line of a cash basis income statement is the excess of cash receipts versus disbursements—a meaningless figure as far as management of the firm is concerned. (A client might pay the day after the statement is prepared and it would not be recorded.)

3. If a firm recognizes income at the time the work is performed, and it becomes work in progress, then the firm operates on a(n) _____ basis.

4. Accrual expenses are applied against accrued income to arrive at

_____

_____

5. The accrual system records revenue that has not yet been received as

_____

6. The accrual method is effective because it forces management to

_____

_____

7. The risk of using an accrual system is that you must

_____

if the client does not pay.

8. Large firms operate on a(n) _____ basis because

_____

9. Small firms operate on a(n) _____ basis because

_____

7.9 MORE IMPORTANT CONCEPTS IN BUDGETING

Before we leave the subject of planning and monitoring performance, it is important to recognize several budgeting techniques that have been used in other fields of business and that have applicability to professional services. In this case it is important to understand which concepts can be borrowed and used, rather than the actual budgeting techniques themselves.

   1. *Zero-Based Budgeting.* In this system each unit in the organization starts with a zero budget for the new year and then must justify its existence, and therefore the right to a budget, by demonstrating how it can accomplish its tasks and mission in the most economical way. This procedure contrasts with the usual budgeting method of examining last year's budget and making any necessary changes for the new year, which automatically assumes that last year's budget was correct. Zero-based budgeting is actually more complex than what has been described, and it is more suitable to very large organizations and governmental agencies that have certain missions to accomplish. However, the concept of not using last year's budget as a guide for this year and making each overhead cost center prove that it is operating in the most efficient manner is useful and can easily be adapted in almost any firm.

2. *Flexible Budgeting.* This is a system used in many manufacturing organizations. Instead of using fixed budgeted amounts, the elements of overhead are converted to unit costs that vary according to the rate of production. That is, when fewer items are produced than anticipated, the cost per unit is higher and vice versa. While the techniques of flexible budgeting relate primarily to a manufacturing operation, the concept that budgets are not fixed and should be changed to reflect the overall level of a firm's operations can be adapted to any organization. For example, midway through the year the firm may realize that it is not going to come close to reaching its budgeted goals because several large anticipated projects were lost to other firms. A new budget should be prepared for the last half of the year to reflect the lower revenue. Expenses have to be reduced to conform with the lower revenue figure, and in some cases the budget may indicate a break-even or loss position, depending on how quickly expenses can be cut. It is better to recognize the situation early and plan for lower expectations than to compare current performance with a budget that is out of date and meaningless.

3. *Capital Budgets.* Most firms, particularly those with heavy capital equipment requirements, use very sophisticated techniques to develop capital budgets that include return on investment calculations, make or buy justifications, and forecasts of obsolescence. Most design professionals do not require such detailed capital budgets, but they all buy capital equipment, including office furniture, automobiles, and computers. The capital budgeting process need not be complex, but as a minimum, it should include a listing of all capital expenditures expected during the year and an approximation of the month when the equipment will be purchased. Having a prioritized list will ensure that no purchases are overlooked, and it will enable management to make better decisions when allocating resources to these expenditures.

4. *Contributions Budgets.* Charitable contributions are not a significant item of expense, but a firm should decide at the beginning of the year how it wants to budget for donations. Otherwise the question of whether to support a particular charity and how much to give will keep coming up throughout the year as fund drives are carried out. These decisions tend to take an inordinate amount of management time, and a budget will enable a firm to channel its contributions in the most meaningful manner.

Examples of some of these budgeting concepts are shown below:

1. *Zero-Based Budgeting.* Marketing costs in a 915-person architectural firm have averaged 8–10% of gross revenues. These costs include both the time of marketing personnel as well as expenses. The person in charge of the marketing effort expects to spend $50,000 next year and is the first to submit a budget. The managing principal has read that marketing costs average about 60% of revenues in firms of this size according to a recent survey. The managing principal asks for a detailed explanation of the number of calls to be made, new markets reached, schedule of out-of-town trips, types of prospective clients to be called upon, estimated success rate based on the firm's past experience, and a plan for calling on each of the firm's past clients. The marketing director is surprised by this request, but he begins working to comply.

2. *Flexible Budgeting.* A 25-person architecture and interior design firm has budgeted gross revenues of $800,000 in the new year and a net profit of $120,000 (15%). One-quarter of the revenue was expected to be earned from two large apartment complexes scheduled for design early in the budget year, but because a major employer in the city expects to shut down operations and move to the West Coast, plans for the apartment complexes have been delayed. There is even a possibility they may be cancelled. Although the firm is two months into the budget year, the managing principal has asked for a revised budget. Additional hiring has been postponed and expected salary increases deferred. A move to larger quarters has also been cancelled. With some anticipated cost savings a new budget is prepared with revenues estimated at $600,000, and the firm is expected to break even if it can achieve this new revenue figure.

3. *Capital Budget.* A ten-person architectural firm recognizes that it needs to acquire a computer-aided drafting (CAD) system in order to compete effectively for the design of multistory office buildings. Previously, the firm has done mostly low-rise buildings and apartments. A cost study indicates that total hardware and software costs plus installation will amount to about $250,000. In addition, office furniture in the reception area needs to be replaced (cost $3,000) and the managing principal needs a new automobile (cost $20,000). To arrive at a capital budget for planning purposes, the managing principal lists the items of equipment needed and the approximate quarter when they are expected to be purchased.

| | Budget Quarter | | | |
	1st	2nd	3rd	4th
CAD system	$250,000			
Furniture	3,000			
Automobile			$20,000	
Other		$1,000		$1,000
Total	$253,000	$1,000	$20,000	$1,000

After examining alternatives, it is decided to use a CAD service bureau for the first half of the budget year and then re-examine the purchase option in the third quarter. All other capital equipment purchases are expected to be made during quarters listed in budget.

4. *Contributions Budget.* After contributing about $5,000 per year to various charities, a five-person architectural firm decides to establish a budget for this item. The principal starts by examining the list of charitable contributions from last year and makes the following comments:

United Way	$ 500	Should be the major recipient of contributions; increase to $2,500.
Children's Home	$1,500	Part of United Way; discontinue.
National Hospital	$1,000	This hospital is in another state and was a favorite charity of a former associate; discontinue.
Red Cross	$1,000	Increase to $2,500.
Aid to Refugees	$1,000	This got on the list several years ago; no one knows why; discontinue.

By directing its charitable contributions to a few well-known causes, the firm can decline other inquiries during the year simply because they were not included in the budget.

EXERCISE 7.9 ■

Preparing a Meaningful Budget and Annual Business Plan

Multiple Choice

1. In zero-based budgeting
   a. each organization unit starts with $10,000.
   b. each organization unit starts with a zero budget for the year.
   c. each individual starts with his or her own budget.

2. Zero-based budgeting means
   a. you must have nothing in your budget.
   b. you start with zero, and accrue your budget.
   c. each unit must justify its right to a budget.

3. Zero-based budgets require that you
   a. demonstrate proficiency in your unit.
   b. demonstrate how each unit can accomplish its tasks and mission in the most economical way.
   c. look at last year's budget.

4. Zero-based budgeting is most suitable for
   a. small firms.
   b. medium-size firms.
   c. large firms.

5. The advantage of using a zero-based budget is
   a. it is not complex.
   b. it gets you away from using last year's budget.
   c. it makes each unit prove its efficiency.
   d. a and b.
   e. b and c.

6. Flexible budgeting is used by
   a. operations plants.
   b. manufacturing organizations.
   c. facilities management firms.
   d. none of the above.

7. Flexible budgeting uses
   a. square foot costs.
   b. per person costs.
   c. unit costs.
   d. all of the above.

8. The advantage of flexible budgeting is
   a. its adaptability to any organization.
   b. unit costs are adjustable depending on rate of production.
   c. it can be adjusted halfway through the year.
   d. all of the above.
   e. none of the above.

9. It is better to
   a. recognize your mistakes and go along from there.
   b. cut expenses quickly.
   c. recognize a reduced revenue situation early and plan for lower revenues.
   d. none of the above.

10. Capital budgets are
    a. not necessary.
    b. minimal for large firms.
    c. not necessarily complex.
    d. necessary.
    e. a and b only.
    f. c and d only.

11. Contribution budgets are necessary only if you
    a. plan to budget for charitable donations.
    b. require justification from executives.
    c. look for more write-offs.

7.10 FIRMWIDE REALIZATION BUDGETING

Firmwide realization budgeting is a technique that is used in other professional services, such as accounting and law, but is not widely used by design firms. It basically is a budget based on the earning power of the firm. Realization budgeting starts with a compilation of potential revenue that can be generated by the firm, as shown in Exhibit 7.15. All individuals in the firm are listed and a percentage utilization is determined for everyone, from zero for such supporting staff as accounting

EXAMPLE OF FIRMWIDE REALIZATION BUDGETING

List Individuals (Group by Dep'ts)	Percent Utilization	Hours per Year	Chargeable Hours	Billing Rate ($)	Gross Revenue ($)	Percent Availability	Potential Revenue ($)
Graphics Dep't							
John Smith	60%	2,080	1,248	$15.00	$18,720	100%	$18,720
Mary Jones	80	2,080	1,664	12.50	20,800	100	20,800
Bill Henry	80	1,040	832	15.00	12,480	50	6,240

Total potential revenue $10,000,000

Exhibit 7.15   Using existing manpower and expected utilization, calculate expected net revenue as shown above. Then insert net revenue amount on the top line in Exhibit 7.17.

personnel to, say, 85% for a draftsman who is expected to be fully occupied on projects. The 85% is to allow for vacations, holidays, and sick days. A standard year of 2,080 hours is used and the percentage is multiplied by this standard to arrive at chargeable hours. Multiplying the chargeable hours by a billing rate for each individual gives a gross revenue figure that is multiplied by the percentage the individual is expected to be available, which is generally 100% for a full-time individual who is expected to be with the firm for the entire year. The final figure is the potential revenue that can be generated by the individual. Summarizing this for all individuals results in the firmwide revenue potential. Anticipated write-offs of bad debts and work in progress not invoiced must be subtracted based on past history, to arrive at the net revenue potential. Net revenue potential is then added to miscellaneous income and the markup earned on reimbursable expenses to arrive at

EXAMPLE OF FIRMWIDE REALIZATION BUDGETING

	Annual	Per Month
Total Potential Revenue (Net fees)		
Net fees	$10,000,000	$833,000
Expense realization income from markup on consultants' costs	100,000	8,334
Other income		
Bad debts recovered	0	0
Interest income	2,000	170
Total Income	$10,102,000	$841,504
Budgeted Expenses		
Professional salaries and wages	$ 7,000,000	$580,000
Management salaries and wages	800,000	66,000
Management expense		
Rent and utilities	65,000	5,417
Equipment rental	8,700	725
Equipment supplies	0	0
Professional liability insurance	30,000	2,500
Office management travel	1,900	150
Marketing salaries and wages	120,000	10,000
Marketing expenses		
Graphics	8,000	667
Publications	1,000	84
Conventions	2,400	200
Travel expenses	5,000	417
Public relations	2,600	217
Miscellaneous	2,000	167
Total Expense	$ 9,737,000	$810,000
Budgeted Profit	$ 365,000	$ 30,000

Exhibit 7.16 Budgeted expenses are developed from the potential revenue figure by using estimates based on past experience and projected costs expected to be incurred during the budgeted period.

net firmwide revenue. Subtracting anticipated expenses from this figure will give the firm an approximation of the profit potential that can be earned, as shown in Exhibit 7.16.

Realization budgeting is a way of looking at the budgeting process from another angle. That is, it's a means of assessing what is capable of being accomplished by the firm rather than what is likely to be accomplished based on the economic outlook. Adjustments to the standard formula may have to be made depending on the firm's operation. For example, if a consistent amount of overtime is worked throughout the year, a factor can be added to the standard number of hours. If, through good management, the firm is able to earn a higher profit on lump sum work than what is generated by using standard billing rates, then the rates should be adjusted to account for that fact. In any event, the calculation of revenue potential gives the firm another method of looking at budgeting.

EXERCISE 7.10

Discussion Problem

Background. A ten-person architectural firm is interested in expanding by opening an office in a nearby state. The firm has been very successful in its three-year history of operation by concentrating on the design of prison facilities. Profits have averaged XX% of revenues after suitable bonuses to the two principals and staff members. However, the market is becoming saturated in the state where the firm is located, since adequate prison facilities have now been built in most areas. The state's budget for new construction has been drastically reduced this year.

The two principals have been considering a geographic expansion for a long time. Another alternative is to expand into different types of work, but they recognize that prison facilities are what they do best and they want to continue to excel in this area. They have recently been approached by a large architectural firm interested in acquiring their specialty.

Assignment. Consider the alternatives available to this firm, and develop a business and financial plan. Begin by preparing a series of goals and objectives for the firm. Carefully think through the various options and examine the advantages/disadvantages of each. As part of the assignment develop a complete realization budget for the ten-person firm.

Alternatives available:

Goals and objectives:

_____

_____

Options	Advantages	Disadvantages

FINAL EXAMINATION — CHAPTER 7

Multiple Choice

1. Budgets are often prepared from the top and not from the bottom because
   a. the press of current business leaves little time for planning.
   b. growth is not expected.
   c. staff is not trained to prepare budgets.
   d. none of the above.

2. The single largest factor in causing budgets to get out of line is
   a. management.
   b. staff's noninvolvement and therefore lack of responsibility toward the budget.
   c. unrealistic spending.
   d. all of the above.

3. An annual business plan must tie
   a. profits to revenue.
   b. expenses to revenue projections.
   c. knowledgeable experts to budget control.
   d. none of the above.

4. Tracking actual performance
   a. is impossible without a proper business plan.
   b. is not possible at all.
   c. becomes meaningful when you obtain input from everyone on the team.
   d. a and b only.

5. What is the significance of defining milestones for your firm to reach?
   a. It allows you to plan better financially.
   b. It sets in motion your firm's strategic plan.
   c. The milestones become cornerstones in your plan.
   d. All of the above.

6. Which of the following statements is not true with regards to financial planning?
   a. Most small firms don't prepare annual business plans because they don't have time.
   b. Each financial plan must take into account the firm's individual characteristics.
   c. Every financial plan is the same.
   d. The first person to look at in preparing a financial plan is yourself.

7. What's the first step in looking at your long range goals?
   a. Identifying your team.
   b. Identifying your firm's financial goals.
   c. Preparing an integrated budget.
   d. None of the above.

8. A man-hour forecast is a projection showing
   a. total hours.
   b. holidays/vacations.
   c. time needed for projects.
   d. all of the above.
   e. none of the above.

9. Cash accounting is best for
   a. large firms.
   b. medium-sized firms.
   c. small firms.
   d. none of the above.

10. Accrual accounting bases income on
    a. receivables.
    b. anticipated income from work in progress.
    c. anticipated income from future projects.
    d. all of the above.
    e. none of the above.

11. Zero-based budgeting means
    a. you must have nothing in your budget.
    b. you start with zero and accrue your budget.
    c. each unit must justify its right to a budget.
    d. none of the above.

12. The advantage of using the flexible budgeting method is
   a. its adaptability.
   b. that unit costs are adjustable depending on rate of production.
   c. that it can be adjusted halfway through the year.
   d. all of the above.
   e. none of the above.

8

CONTRACT NEGOTIATIONS

Chapter Summary

- Most profitable contract types
- Drawbacks to using published standard billing rates
- When to use retainer-type contracts
- When to consult an attorney
- When to have an insurance broker review contract insurance provisions
- Letters of agreement
- Twenty-nine terms to include in a contract

Financial Manager As Negotiator

Financial managers often assume responsibilities in areas closely related to the financial function. This is particularly true in smaller firms where specialists in these areas cannot be hired. For example, the financial manager is often closely involved in contract negotiation procedures when he or she is asked to review contracts prior to signing. Then the financial manager sees that the contract is properly administered in accordance with the project terms, particularly when invoices are prepared. The financial manager is also responsible for executing any documents required by governmental agencies at the close of a project. Therefore he or she needs to have familiarity with the financial aspects of contracting.

8.1 THE IMPACT OF CONTRACT TYPE ON PROFITABILITY

Design professionals work under various types of contract arrangements, which largely determine the level of profit on a project.

Cost Plus Fixed Fee. This is one of the most common types and in theory it should guarantee a profit of the fixed fee. In reality, overhead costs are not known for certain until after the project is completed, and in many cases, there is a stated or implied limitation on the total amount of the contract established at the beginning. When a total limit is established, cost plus fixed fee contracts become one of the most limiting in terms of profit. This is because the fixed fee is the maximum that can be earned, but any costs incurred beyond the contract limit must be absorbed in the fee. Cost plus fixed fee also exposes the firm's costs to the client and are subject to downward adjustments in case an audit discloses any unallowable costs in overhead.

Lump Sum. These contracts are widely used and are effective when the scope of work is well defined. Unlike cost plus fixed fee contracts, there is no limitation on the profit for these projects, and conversely there is no limitation on the loss. To use a lump sum agreement also requires close scrutiny to be certain that legitimate changes to the original scope are paid for above the lump sum as an extra service.

Percentage of Construction. These contracts used to be more widely accepted, but they are not used as much currently because both parties recognize that they bear no relationship to the cost of the work. While there is no limitation on profits or losses in percentage contracts, the risk is neither in the hands nor under the control of the design professional. Instead, the design professional's fee depends on the contractor's bid. In a poor economic climate, this can be disastrous, when contractors are anxious to cut prices in order to obtain work.

Standard Billing Rates. As the basis for contracts standard billing rates have received greater acceptance in recent years. To determine standard billing rates, overhead and profit are added to base salary rates to arrive at a flat hourly rate for each individual or classification (such as junior or senior engineer) within the firm. The problem with using billing rates based on classifications is that the rates for the classifications are generally averaged. As people move up the salary scale with periodic increases during the year, the average rates for the classifications must be revised before they are outdated. Generally, standard billing rates should be reviewed and revised, if necessary, on a quarterly basis.

Multiplier Times Salary. This is another common method for pricing services. This method overcomes the objections raised with standard billing rates that have to be constantly revised, but the multiplier contract has the drawback of revealing salary rates to the client and staff who see the invoices. The invoicing procedure also takes longer to complete. An effective way of not revealing salary information on each invoice and yet giving the client the information needed to check the computations is to send the client the individuals' salaries once in a sealed envelope and update changes as they occur. Then the invoices need only show the hours by individual and a total dollar amount for all labor, which the client can check privately.

Exhibit 8.1 shows a numerical example of the major types of contracts.

In addition, two other types of contract arrangements are sometimes used.

Level of Effort. Generally found in research projects, these contracts require the design professional to perform a service without necessarily completing a finished product. They are generally used where a problem must be studied, but there is no indication of what amount of work may be required. Generally, the consultant is given a dollar limitation and told to work at standard rates until there is a resolution or until the money is spent. These kinds of projects are generally profitable since there is little risk of overrun.

Retainers. These contracts are another type of arrangement that generally is satisfactory. In this case the client wants to use the services of one design professional for a number of projects or else keep the professional available or "on call" as problems develop. Payment of a flat monthly fee based on an estimated value of work that is adjusted periodically is one method of retainer. Another is the use of a base figure plus standard hourly rates for work over a certain level. Either arrangement can be worked out to the satisfaction of both parties.

NUMERICAL EXAMPLES OF BASIC CONTRACT TYPES

1. Lump Sum

Architect agrees to do a certain project for a total price of $75,000. Regardless of whether the work takes longer or shorter than estimated, the architect receives $75,000 as full compensation. He or she bears the full risk and may recoup an extra reward if efficient or lose money on the project if the estimate is too low to cover the scope of work as defined.

2. Percentage of Construction

The terms of agreement provide for the engineer to receive 7% of the cost of construction. For estimating purposes the construction cost is fixed at $2,000,000. The engineer invoices his client monthly based upon his percentage of completion against a project revenue estimate of $140,000. When bids are received and the construction contract is awarded for, say, $1,900,000, the engineer must adjust the latest invoice to reflect a project price reduced to $133,000.

3. Standard Billing Rates

All personnel in the firm are classified into groups according to their levels of skill, and an hourly rate that includes overhead and profit is established as follows: principal engineer $55/hour, senior engineer $45/hour, intermediate engineer $30/hour, and junior engineer $25/hour. Project work is invoiced at these rates plus reimbursable expenses.

4. Multiplier Times Salary

An interior design firm marks up base hourly salary rates by a factor of 1.40 to cover fringe benefits and 2.25 to cover general and administrative expenses. In effect, base salary is multiplied by 3.15 (1.40 times 2.25) to arrive at the billing rate to the client, which includes overhead and profit. Reimbursable expenses are invoiced separately.

5. Cost Plus Fixed Fee

Architect agrees to perform work at a rate to cover direct labor costs, overhead, and reimbursable expenses plus consultant's costs. For estimating purposes this amount is expected to be $50,000. In addition, the architect will receive a fee or profit of $5,000 on the project. In a true cost plus fixed fee arrangement the architect receives all costs whether they were above or below the $50,000. Salaries are the actual amounts paid, and overhead is determined on a provisional basis and then adjusted at the conclusion of the project. In any event the architect would only receive $5,000 as profit. There is little risk in the pure cost plus fixed fee contract since all costs are supposed to be recoverable. Therefore, the profit can be fixed at a relatively low amount.

Exhibit 8.1 Most firms have a preferred type of contract, depending on the kind of work they perform and their mix of clients.

EXERCISE 8.1 ■

Contract Types

1. Why is cost plus fixed fee a risky contract type?

_____

_____

2. What is the limitation on profit for lump sum contracts?

_____

_____

3. Why do percentage of construction contracts bear no relationship to the cost of the work?

_____

_____

4. How do you determine standard billing rates?

_____

_____

5. Why is the difference between level of effort contracts and multiplier contracts?

_____

_____

6. What contract type requires payment of a flat monthly fee?

_____

_____

8.2   CONTRACT NEGOTIATIONS

The financial terms of a contract are usually negotiated at the same time as the scope of work. This means that financial considerations may be sacrificed by the project manager who is all-too-eager to get the contract signed and the work underway. Some firms overcome this problem, particularly in negotiating large contracts or contracts with governmental agencies, by designating the financial manager as leader of the negotiating team. The design professional's negotiating team must include the technical specialists, but in many cases, they negotiate through their spokesman, the financial manager. This requires the team to break off the discussions periodically in order to caucus privately to discuss the handling of technical matters. This is a good tactic because it gives the team an opportunity to discuss matters alone and reach a consensus on strategy. With the financial manager in charge, important negotiations on contract price and payment terms will be carried on as equal to equal. This prevents an overly anxious project manager from "giving away the store" during negotiations.

Contract Negotiations in Smaller Firms

While smaller firms cannot afford attorneys and other specialists on their full-time staff, they are not without resources in this area. Although contract negotiation is a very specialized function requiring the assistance of experienced personnel, assistance is available to the small practitioner. Therefore it is important to know when to call in an attorney. If the firm does not use the standardized contracts approved by the professional societies, an attorney should prepare a standard form for the firm to use with variations, depending on the types of contracts.

In cases where the firm must use a contract prepared by the client, an attorney should review it, particularly if this is the first time the firm has worked for that client. Another good practice is to have your insurance broker review insurance clauses of any detailed contracts, to make certain that you are fully protected. The insurance company should do this for you at no charge and without any hesitation.

Many firms, particularly smaller ones, work without contracts for some clients or do not have strict procedures that require a contract in hand before the work progresses. A contract need not be a formal document—in many cases a simple one-page letter of agreement will do—but the important point to remember is that some form of agreement is necessary in writing. See Exhibits 8.2 and 8.3 for examples of agreement letters. If the work must proceed without a contract in hand, the next best procedure is for the design professional to write a letter of confirmation to the client outlining the steps taken to proceed with the work and briefly referring to the terms that will be formalized later in the agreement.

EXAMPLE OF A LETTER OF AGREEMENT FOR ARCHITECTURAL WORK

Dear Client:

As discussed, we are pleased to outline the scope of architectural services to be provided for you on the subject project. This project will be an office building of a size and scope to be determined by our mutual efforts.

Site Planning and Schematic Design

Initially we will conceptualize a series of alternative site plans that will clearly illustrate the size and scope of the basic project. We can also provide pro format that will indicate the financial aspects of various alternatives, based upon our recent experience with similar buildings. Once a concept is agreed upon, we will develop the exterior design of the building as well as refine the floor plans in compliance with the program established by you.

After meeting with you, we will provide sketches that will illustrate the proportion and final configuration of the building. At the end of this phase of work, we will also furnish you an ink line presentation loan package.

Design Development

Upon approval of the schematic design work, and with your authorization, we will enter into the design development phase. In this phase, we will more precisely define the concept of the project and prepare preliminary working drawings for your approval. This phase of the work will include initial engineering recommendations for the structural and air conditioning systems.

Construction Documents

The construction document phase will consist of working drawing and specifications that will detail the requirements for the construction of the entire project, including all necessary bidding information. Toward the end of this phase, we will file the required documents for approval by governmental agencies having jurisdiction over the project.

Bidding and Negotiation

During the approval stage of the construction documents, we will assist you in obtaining bids or negotiated proposals. We will also assist you in awarding construction contracts.

Construction Phase

The construction phase will include our work in relation to the construction contract. In this phase, we will issue change orders as required, make periodic site visits to observe the progress and quality of the work, review shop drawings, and review samples and other submissions to see they conform to the design concepts of the project. We will not make exhaustive or continuous on-site inspections; however, we will endeavor to determine, in general, whether the quality of the work is in accordance with the contract documents.

> **Exhibit 8.2** A basic letter such as this should be developed with the assistance of an attorney. Then clauses that are not acceptable in certain circumstances can be eliminated.

Engineering and Landscape Design

Structural, electrical, and plumbing engineering, as well as landscape and landscape irrigation design, will be included as part of our basic services. Air conditioning will be executed on a design and construct basis, whereby criteria for this work will be established by our consultant, and as such, may be bid on a competitive basis. Upon submittal of the bids, our consultant will assist in the selection of a heating, ventilation, air conditioning (HVAC) contractor, who will then prepare air conditioning drawings to be submitted to our consultant for review.

A fire sprinkler system, if required, will be executed on a design and construct basis in accordance with architect's specifications.

Compensation

Initially, our work on conceptual studies will be billed on the basis of $25 per hour merely to cover our expenses.

When we are all well satisfied with the direction of the project, the professional service fee will be converted to a fixed lump sum amount, based upon a percentage of an agreed-upon budget for the total construction cost of the building shell, structured parking, and on-site improvements. Tenant improvement work is excluded from this amount. This will enable you to know the exact amount of professional service fees, prior to construction, and will serve as your guide in calculating total development costs.

Percentages for the total cost of construction vary in accordance with the size of the office building shell as follows:

40,000 + sq ft	5%
75,000 + sq ft	4.50%
100,000 + sq ft	4.25%
150,000 + sq ft	4%

Fees paid on an hourly basis that are directly related to the final project will be deducted from the lump sum amount.

The American Institute of Architects (AIA) of the United States uses a Standard Form of Agreement between Owner and Architect. This document more precisely defines the architect's professional services and the responsibilities of the owner.

Payments of the fees in the AIA agreement are customarily made on a monthly basis, in proportion to services performed. The total payments at the completion of each phase of our work correspond to the following percentages of the basic fee:

Schematic design phase	15%
Design development phase	85%
Construction document phase	85%
Bidding or negotiation phase	90%
Construction phase	100%

(*source: AIA Standard of Agreements, U.S. Version*)

Reimbursable Expenses

Reimbursable expenses, for which you will be billed at cost, include blueprints and reproductions, the cost of all fees for government agencies, travel and long distance telephone calls, if required.

Exhibit 8.2 Continued.

Additional Services

Additional work that is over and above our normal services, as described above, and for which we shall be entitled to extra fees, include the following:

1. Providing space planning, interior design, or decorating services for the lease space.
2. Preparing extensive drawings for alternative bids.
3. Making major revisions to contract documents that are at variance with your previous approvals or instructions.
4. Providing professional services made necessary by the default of a contractor or by major defects in the contractor's work.
5. Contracting the service of a professional artist for an architectural rendering.

None of the above will be undertaken without your full authorization.

Items that are specifically excluded from the scope of our services are as follows:

1. The cost of special testing and inspections required by governing agencies.
2. The cost of a survey of the property and a soils investigation report.

For additional services, authorized by you, the fee will be as follows:

Principal's time	$150 per hour
Partner's time	$100 per hour
Employee's time	$75 per hour

In the event there are additional services by our consulting engineers, their services will be charged as a multiple of one and one-tenth (1.10) times the amount billed to us for such services.

Should either party to this agreement institute legal proceedings on account of alleged failure by the other to perform in accordance with its terms, the party against whom judgment is rendered in a court of law or court of arbitration shall pay for all costs, both legal and otherwise, incurred by the other in the course of said action.

We truly appreciate the opportunity to work with you and believe the results of our joint effort will satisfy your needs in a successful and creative manner.

If the foregoing meets with your approval, please sign and return one copy of this agreement as our authorization to proceed with the work.

Very truly yours,

Principal-in-Charge

Confirmed and accepted

By _____

Date _____

Exhibit 8.2   Continued.

EXAMPLE OF A LETTER OF AGREEMENT FOR INTERIORS WORK

Dear Client:

Thank you for this opportunity to submit this agreement for interior architecture services provided by our firm.

We will consider your signature below as our authorization to proceed with the work.

ARTICLE 1—Scope of Work

To provide space planning and tenant construction documents for your building complex.

Our firm will provide preliminary services prior to space planning that include preparation of backgrounds, master inventory control book, a check of applicable code requirements, and development of standard wall and millwork details.

Our firm will provide programming services that involve interviewing prospective tenants to determine their space requirements and space planning services that include preparing one-line space plans for review by you or your representative and prospective tenant. A revision to the plan will be submitted if required.

Our firm will provide construction documents for the build-out of the space, including a floor plan, reflected ceiling plan, telephone and electrical outlet plan. Mechanical, electrical, and plumbing design and documentation are to be provided by others. All details and finishes are to be building standard.

ARTICLE 2—Compensation to Our Firm

You will compensate our firm for services provided in Article 1 as follows:

Preliminary services	$85/hr up to $1,400
Programming and space planning	$.15 per rentable sq ft
Tenant construction documents	$.45 per rentable sq ft

Additional services that are authorized by you will be billed at the rate of $150 per hour for principals and $100 per hour for others. Examples of additional services that you may desire are additional revisions or further development to the space plans, design of special millwork, design of renderings or models, graphic design.

Reimbursable expenses are in addition to the compensation listed above and include expenditures made by our firm in the interests of the project. Examples are automobile mileage at $.35 per mile, messenger service at standard commercial rates, reproduction, graphic materials connected with the execution of the work, and long distance phone calls. Reimbursable expenses incurred in performance of additional services shall be invoiced along with additional services. Billing will be on a monthly basis for work accomplished during the preceding month. Invoices submitted by the 20th of the month will be due the first day of the next month. Interest for late payment will be charged and applied to subsequent billings at a rate of 1.75% per month on the outstanding total.

Exhibit 8.3 Note the clear scope of work and specific payment terms outlined that can eliminate misunderstandings later on.

Failure to pay within 45 days from date of receipt of statement shall grant our firm the right to refuse to render further services and such acts shall not be deemed a breach of this agreement.

ARTICLE 3—General Provisions

You will provide information on wall systems, millwork, etc., which is preferred for the project.

You authorize our firm to contract separately with tenants of the project for interior design, move coordination, or other professional services.

This agreement is re-negotiable within one year from date of execution.

This agreement may be terminated by either party upon seven days written notice should the other party fail substantially to perform in accordance with its terms through no fault of the other. In the event of termination, our firm will be paid compensation for services performed and reimbursables incurred to termination date.

This agreement shall be governed by the laws of the State of _____ .

OUR FIRM   **CLIENT**

_____   _____
By   *By*

_____   _____
Date   *Date*

Exhibit 8.3   Continued.

While it is possible to collect under a verbal agreement in some cases, it is difficult and expensive, particularly when the client's personnel change and memories fade.

EXERCISE 8.2

The Financial Manager's Role in Contract Negotiations

1. List three reasons why you might hire outside personnel to assist with contract negotiations.

   1. _____

   2. _____

   3. _____

2. What type of contract document does your firm use?

   _____

3. How could you improve your contract?

_____

_____

_____

8.3 PROFITABLE CONTRACT TERMS

With the economic climate continually uncertain, the emphasis on solid contract terms is increasingly vital to a firm's financial success. Most clients are demanding more work for lower fees, and firms that do not reexamine the terms of their contracts often find themselves without enough income to break even, let alone make a profit.

When negotiating a contract, first remember to negotiate scope, not price, because the scope of the work should control the price. Next, break down your price into many small pieces that relate to specific scope items so that portions of the work can be eliminated if a prospective client thinks the price is too high and, more importantly, so that it will become difficult for a client to argue with any small piece of the work when negotiating. Finally, insert as many of the following terms into the contract as possible:

1. Get partial or full payment of fees before starting. It is appropriate and a good negotiating tactic to ask for money up front. The client may not agree, but will understand because many firms are doing the same thing. Also, getting money up front, depositing it, and not crediting it to the client until the last invoice allows you to avoid a bad debt and also earn maximum interest on the desposit.

2. Dare to require the client to pay unusual reimbursable costs. In addition to normal reimbursables, ask for reimbursement for items such as liability insurance premiums, computer time, messenger service, and outside project accounting. With government clients this term may reduce overhead, making your contract price more attractive. With private sector clients, it can dramatically increase profits.

3. Include a streamlined form of billing and payment. Have the client agree to a simple monthly payment schedule tied to the scope and schedule of work. This avoids time-consuming breakdowns of hours and expenses as well as pages of backup. Then at the end of the project, make any appropriate adjustments.

4. Have the client's in-house staff do some of the work. For example, instead of delivering prints to the client using your messenger, specify that the client's messengers will pick up and delivery all correspondence. If this term were in all contracts, it might be possible to eliminate one messenger from the staff.

5. Shorten the client's schedule and then work overtime. In general, shorter schedules produce more profitable projects by reducing excessive perfectionism. Also by working overtime for private sector clients, you may be able to charge clients at your normal billing rate without incurring additional salary or overhead costs.

6. Shorten the billing/payment cycle. To improve cash flow, ask the client to pay twice a month in accordance with a predetermined payment schedule. Shortening the cycle reduces borrowing, thus saving interest expense, and also indicates sooner whether there is a potential bad debt situation.

7. Agree to split savings on underbid construction amounts. This term requires an independent estimator, but it could save the project's profitability. If you agree to a design fee lower than the original fee estimate without a corresponding scope reduction, you should also not share in losses if the project comes in under bid.

8. Agree to guaranteed interest on late payments. Discuss interest terms with the client and make certain to include a guarantee of interest on late payments. If the client does not agree, negotiate for an advance payment instead.

9. Insert a limit of liability clause. This term can save considerable amounts on professional liability insurance. Limit liability to net fees, rather than gross fees.

10. Insert a provision that measures scope changes precisely. For instance, arrange for the client to sign a record copy of the drawings at specified calendar dates, indicating that decisions made as of that date are known and accepted. Do not tie the signature to completion of a phrase, since that is difficult to ascertain.

Few of the above terms taken alone will produce significant

improvements in project profitability. However, by adopting as many of these terms as possible, you should see an improvement in project profitability.

Another term now used by many design firms is to have the client make payments directly to consultants instead of through the prime professional. This eliminates the problem of one design firm holding funds for another. Also, all design contracts should stipulate a date after which all monetary terms of the contract are subject to renegotiation. This allows for an increase in fees if, for instance, the project is shelved.

Finally, since many projects are based on a letter of agreement, be sure to incorporate these terms plus any additional terms you may have into a one-page typeset sheet that can be attached to all agreements.

EXERCISE 8.3

Discussion Problem

Background: Your architectural firm is located in the downtown area of a moderate-size midwestern city. Recently there has been a resurgence of interest in many buildings located near your firm, and you have been asked if you would be interested in some large renovation projects. You have done only small renovation projects in the past and are not sure whether this work is a type you want to pursue.

Several younger principals and associates are very interested in pursuing this work. You hesitate because of the many uncertainties associated with renovation projects and what conditions are likely to be encountered during construction. Most of your work has been accomplished on a lump sum basis in the past, but you know that this is risky in projects filled with uncertainty.

You ask your attorney and professional liability insurance adviser to meet with you to discuss the various contracting options available.

Assignment: Prepare a listing of the advantages and disadvantages of the various contract types to present at this meeting. Which type would be most advantageous, and what specific terms would be most important to include?

_____

_____

_____

_____

_____

_____

_____

_____

_____

_____

_____

_____

_____

_____

8.4 TWENTY-NINE TERMS TO INCLUDE IN A CONTRACT

The contract is a design firm's only ammunition against liability and out-of-control job costs. However, design firm owners do not use this tool often enough to protect themselves. Following are 29 terms to be studied, considered, and incorporated into the contract. You may not agree with every one of these terms, but each one you add will improve your approach to the "business of design." Of course, be sure to check with your attorney before finalizing any contractual change.

1. *Prepayment.* "Upon acceptance of this contract by the client to provide professional design services, a prepayment of $ ____ will be required to initialize the project."

2. *Fee in Escrow.* "Upon acceptance of this contract by the client to provide professional services, a deposit of $ ____ will be placed in an interest-bearing escrow account in the name of XYZ Associates. These funds, including interest, will be released to XYZ on ____ , 1994, or upon completion of the contract, whichever comes first."

3. *Job Cancellation Fee.* "Because of potentially significant revenues from other projects foregone by XYZ Associates to take on this project, if this project is cancelled by the client within X days of starting, a cancellation fee of $ _____ will be immediately due and payable according to the following schedule: 0 to 30 days, $ _____ ; 31 to 60 days, $ _____ ; and so on."

4. *Project Restart Fee.* "Because of substantial costs incurred by XYZ Associates in stopping and restarting a project once it is under way, should this project's progress be halted at any time for 30 or more days by the client, for any reason, a project restart fee of $ _____ or 10% of the total fee earned to date, whichever is greater, will be due and payable immediately."

5. *Construction Contingency.* "A contingency fund of % _____ (usually 3–5%) of the total estimated construction cost of this project will be established by the client. The purpose of this fund will be to pay for any unanticipated changes that occur during the course of the design and construction of the project."

6. *Automatic Escalator.* "After _____ , 1994, all fees and hourly rates quoted within this contract may increase by _____ %, at the determination of the design firm, and may increase by _____ % annually thereafter."

7. *Limit of Liability.* "It is understood that any and all professional liabilities incurred by XYZ Associates throughout the course of rendering professional services on this project shall be limited to a maximum of the net fee plus reimbursable expenses and subconsultants' fees, for all services rendered on the project."

8. *Late Penalty Schedule.* "All invoices not paid promptly will be subject to an additional administrative fee according to the following schedule: 30–59 days overdue, $500.00; 60–89 days overdue, $750.00, and so on."

9. *Sample Invoice Format.* "All invoices will be formatted as in the attached example provided in Appendix A."

10. *Certification Indemnification.* "XYZ Associates will be totally indemnified on all certifications which are required to be signed on behalf of the client during the course of the project."

11. *Certification Fees.* "Understanding the significant liabilities incurred by XYZ Associates when signing certifications, a certification fee of $5,000 will be due and payable for the first certification required on this project, $4,000 for the second certification, and so on."

12. *Limitation on Design Alternatives.* "XYZ Associates will (choose one of the following): (1) limit the number of design alterations provided under this contract to three; (2) limit to ____ hours the time expended by design; or (3) stop developing project design by ____ , 1994, upon which design will be considered complete."

13. *Premium for Client Team Member Reorientation.* "There will be a client team member reorientation fee of $10,000 paid for each project team member from the client who is added or replaced prior to 25% completion of the project, $20,000 for each team member added or replaced prior to 50% completion, and so on."

14. *Job Site Signage.* "Because of its standing as a professional firm, XYZ Associates has complete authority over all content, graphics, and placement of all job site signs with the exception of those required in the interest of maintaining worker safety and the security of the facility."

15. *Graphics Control.* "Because of its standing as a professional design firm, XYZ Associates has complete control over the graphic content and presentation of all studies, reports, and other documents produced under this agreement."

16. *Lien Provisions.* "The client acknowledges that it has secured legal rights to the property upon which the project will be built or that such right will be secured by ____ , 1994. The client further acknowledges that nonpayment of fees owed under this agreement will result in a mechanics lien being placed on the property upon which the project is/will be located."

17. *No Backup for Reimbursables.* "No backup data or copies of bills will be provided for reimbursable expenses invoiced under this agreement. Should backup data be requested, it will be provided for an administrative fee of $100 per monthly invoice requiring verification, and $1.00 per copy of backup data supplied."

18. *No Exact Reimbursables.* "The client will pay 15% of each total monthly invoice for professional services submitted by XYZ Associates as a reimbursable fee to cover all typical reimbursable expenses."

19. *Client Signatures at Various Stages in the Project.* Beginning with the date of project initiation, all drawings produced under this agreement will be signed by an authorized representative of the client each 60 days during the project."

20. *Ownership and Copyright of Documents.* "All drawings and documents produced under the terms of this agreement are the property of XYZ Associates, and cannot be used for any reason other than to bid and construct the above-named product."

21. *Fee for Prints After Five Years.* "After five years from the date of project completion, or on _____ , 1998, a document reproduction fee of $ _____ (typically $500 to $100) per sheet will be charged."

22. *Higher Fees Paid for Changes.* Any changes requested in the attached scope of services provided under this agreement will be billed at a multiplier of 1.25 times customary hourly billing rates."

23. *Stamp Only After Payment.* "XYZ Associates will not stamp drawings produced for any phase of this project under the terms of this agreement until all invoices billed up to that point in the project have been paid in full."

24. *Stamp on Drawings.* "XYZ Associates accepts no liability for any plans or specifications produced under this agreement until such drawings are stamped as approved by all relevant building department officials."

25. *Contract Validity.* "This contract is valid only if signed on or before _____ , 1993, unless officially extended by both parties."

26. *Free Publicity.* "XYZ Associates has the right to photograph the above-named project and to use the photos in the promotion of the professional practice through advertising, public relations, brochures, or other marketing materials. Should additional photos be needed in the future, the client agrees to provide reasonable access to the facility. The client also agrees to cite the name of XYZ Associates as the _____ designer on all publicity, presentations, and public relations activities that mention the name of the facility."

27. *Third Party Legal Defense After a Specified Period.* "After September 1, 1998, any legal costs arising to defend third party claims made against the XYZ Associates in connection with the above-named project will be paid for in full by the client."

28. *Royalty Clause.* "Acknowledging that XYZ Associates has significantly contributed to the long-term real value of the above-named project and property through the rendering of unique design services, a term will be added to the legal deed on the property by the client at time of closing providing XYZ Associates a royalty of $ _____ each and every time the property is sold subsequent to the initial closing for a period of 99 years."

29. *Hazardous Waste.* "Any hazardous waste or asbestos required to be removed, encapsulated or otherwise contained during the course of this project will result in compensation of XYZ Associates equalling 3.0 times above normal customary hourly billing rates for any plans, specifications, or construction observation services provided. XYZ Associates will additionally be indemnified from any and all liability associated with the removal, encapsulation or containment of hazardous waste or asbestos."

Note: The above listed contract terms and conditions are to be used only after consultation with a competent attorney knowledgeable in contract law in your area of professional practice and in your locale.

FINAL EXAMINATION—CHAPTER 8

Multiple Choice

1. The contract type with the highest potential for profit is
   a. cost plus fixed fee.
   b. percentage of construction.
   c. standard billing rates.
   d. lump sum.
   e. none of the above.

2. Which contract requires payment of a flat monthly fee?
   a. lump sum.
   b. cost plus fixed fee.
   c. standard billing rates.
   d. level of effort.
   e. retainer.

3. Contract negotiations for the smaller firm require
   a. a full-time staff person.
   b. efforts of the financial manager.
   c. one or more outside consultants.
   d. none of the above.
   e. a and b only.

4. Many firms work without contracts because

a. they use a simple one-page letter instead.
b. they use a verbal agreement.
c. because they assumed a contract was not necessary.
d. a and b only.

True or False

The following statements are either cost-effective or not. Please circle T for those that are cost-effective and F for those that are not.

T F   Get partial payment before starting the work.

T F   Do not require the client to pay for unusual reimbursement items.

T F   Have the client agree to a simply monthly payment schedule tied to scope and schedule of work.

T F   Get the client's messenger to pick up all the work.

T F   Lengthen the billing/payment cycle.

T F   Do not agree to split savings on underbid construction amounts.

T F   Shorten the client's schedule, then work overtime.

T F   Do not insert a limitation of liability clause.

T F   Insert a provision that measures scope changes precisely.

9 FINANCIAL REPORTING SYSTEMS

Chapter Summary

- How to improve performance
- How to evaluate your present reporting system
- Four characteristics of an effective reporting system
- Why "information only" reports should be minimized
- "Exception reporting" and why it is important
- Reports and the decision-making process
- Variance reports

Achieving Results

A good financial reporting system can have a significant impact on overall financial results. Firms with good reporting systems generally are the most profitable and also do the best work for clients.

9.1 IMPACT ON OVERALL FINANCIAL PERFORMANCE

A good reporting system focuses on results and measures these results against goals that were established in advance. How well these results measure up is a key element in evaluating staff. Project managers and department heads will soon discover that it is easier to perform well than to make excuses about why they fell short of expectations. A good financial reporting system will have everyone pulling in the same direction, since they are all working toward the same set of goals.

It should be recognized, however, that a good reporting system will not turn a poor performer into a good performer.

A poor performer may have problems unrelated to overall performance, and these need to be discovered through discussion and counseling. However, good reporting will turn a good performer into an even better performer. This is because the reports encourage people to do well, since they are a way to gain recognition in management's eyes. People's abilities are brought to the forefront, and periodic reporting of results sparks healthy competition among high achievers.

Evaluation of a Reporting System

To discover whether a firm has a good financial reporting system, a number of questions need to be asked.

First, are the reports being read and acted upon? Reports distributed without any feedback are an indication that the system is not highly effective. Project managers and department heads should be asking questions about the numbers and the derivation of certain allocation methods for the financial manager to know for certain that the reports are being read and understood.

Second, do the reports give warnings in time for management to take corrective action where necessary? The main purpose of reporting is not simply to tell the firm where it has been but, more importantly, where it is going. If this kind of information cannot be gleaned from the reports, then they are simply not doing their job.

Third, can the reports be prepared routinely with the financial staff available? Most financial staffs are stretched thin at the time financial statements are being prepared, but they should be able to handle the regular workload, perhaps with a certain amount of extra effort, but without excessive overtime.

Finally, if the financial system is computerized, is correct information being generated without an unusually large number of manual corrections having to be made? Mistakes will creep into almost any system, but the computerized reports should be basically correct most of the time. Exercise 9.1 is designed to help you evaluate your reporting system.

EXERCISE 9.1 ■■■■■■■■■■■■■■■■■■■■■■■

Your Current Financial Reporting System

1. Have you asked the users of the reporting system for their comments and suggestions?

_____

_____

2. Can you determine instances where the reporting system has helped you become a better manager?

_____

3. Do you and other managers look forward to receiving the reports?

_____

_____

4. Do you read the reports when received or are they stacked on your credenza to be examined later when you "have time"?

_____

_____

5. Can new people in the firm quickly understand and use the reports?

_____

_____

6. Do people have the information they need to manage without being overloaded with information?

_____

_____

7. List five strengths of your current financial reporting system.

1. _____
2. _____
3. _____
4. _____
5. _____

8. List five weaknesses of your current reporting system.

1. _____
2. _____
3. _____
4. _____
5. _____

9. List the five ways you could improve your financial reporting system.

1. _____

2. _____

3. _____

4. _____

5. _____

9.2 ELEMENTS OF A GOOD FINANCIAL OPERATING SYSTEM

For a system to meet the needs of management, it must have credibility. A system gains credibility as follows:

1. **It must be accurate.** This does not mean that the numbers must just add up, but rather that any mistakes in the system must be corrected in the next reporting period. There is nothing more discouraging to project managers and department heads than to have mistakes go uncorrected after they are reported to the financial manager. If they persist, the people using the system will just ignore the reports.

2. **The reports must be timely** in order to be useful. How timely the reports are depends on how the firm is organized and how much it is willing to spend. Some of the largest companies gather data from all over the world and have their financial reports within a few days after the close of the month. Of course, these companies spend large sums of money on their reporting systems. The typical architectural or engineering firm should not have to wait longer than two weeks after the close of the accounting period to receive financial statements. As it is, this is halfway into the next reporting period, and any longer wait means that virtually nothing can be done to make corrections on what the statements reveal. Any firm having to wait longer than two weeks should consult with its independent auditors to see what can be done to speed up the accounting process.

3. **The reports should be fair.** By fair it is meant that cost

allocations to the various profit centers should be made on an equitable basis. Overhead must be distributed in such a manner that those receiving a portion of it understand the basis of allocation, and while they may not like it, they should recognize that there is no fairer way possible to distribute the burden. Generally, direct labor is the basis for distributing overhead costs, but this may not always be the best way if, for example, one profit center manager uses outside contract labor while another uses in-house staff.

4. The reports should be clear, which means that they must be quickly and easily understood. The reports should not require further analysis or additional calculations on the reader's part. One of the best ways of presenting clear reports is through charts and graphs. This type of visual presentation is easier to read than columns of figures, and graphics keep people interested in the presentation.

The sample reports shown in Exhibits 9.1–9.15, and discussed in more detail below, have all been used in presentations to management. While the data are fictitious, the charts can be used to develop a firm's own reporting presentations. Graphics look more attractive if they are presented in color, but color charts take longer to produce and, in presenting the latest financial information, there is often not enough time to prepare color charts.

How to Choose a Computerized Financial Operating System

1. *Identify One or Two Systems that Seem to Meet Your Needs.* There is no one "best" financial management system. Each design firm is unique, and each available system offers different capabilities and features. Choosing the right financial management system is a matter of finding the one that meets your needs the best.

2. *Make or Confirm Your Choice After a Hands-On Demonstration.* Choosing a system is an important decision, and you should see what you are buying before you buy it. Don't settle for watching someone else. Sit at the computer, make selections from the menus, enter data, and print reports yourself. Loading a demonstra-

GROSS AND NET FEES EARNED OVER A 10-YEAR PERIOD

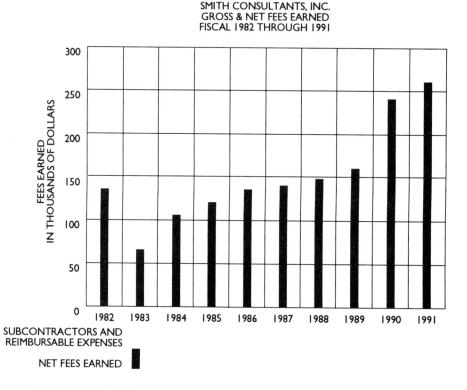

SMITH CONSULTANTS, INC.
GROSS & NET FEES EARNED
FISCAL 1982 THROUGH 1991

SUBCONTRACTORS AND
REIMBURSABLE EXPENSES

NET FEES EARNED

Exhibit 9.1 This chart shows a steady growth rate in revenues after recovery from the 1982–1991 recession. Note the sharply higher revenues in the last two years.

tion version onto your computer will provide you the most ability to "play" with it, and most of today's demo packages are full software systems loaded only with a time bomb if you don't pay.

3. *Buy the System and Install It.* Read the manuals before you start. The decisions you make when you install your new system will determine how well it meets your needs. Some choices are extremely difficult to change later, so be sure you understand the decisions you are making.

Types of Graphics Used in Reports

Exhibit 9.1 is a bar graph showing revenues over a ten-year period. At first, a simple presentation such as this may appear

BREAKDOWN OF REVENUE BY CLIENT TYPE

SMITH CONSULTANTS, INC.
BREAKDOWN OF REVENUES BY CLIENT TYPE

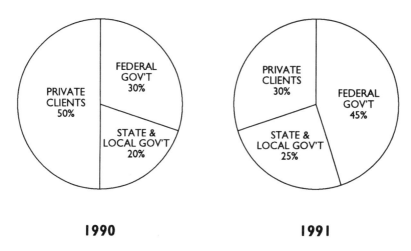

Exhibit 9.2 This chart shows the distribution of revenue by client
type for the last two years. Note the sharp, higher dependency on
the federal government for revenue.

not to have enough information to justify the chart. However,
the more information displayed in a chart, the more difficult
it is to read and comprehend. Therefore, in this case, rather
than showing a detailed breakdown of revenue by type on the
one chart, it is more effective to substitute another, such as
the pie chart shown in Exhibit 9.2. Exhibit 9.3 is another bar
chart showing a ten-year history of operating profit. Exhibit
9.4 illustrates a ratio, in this case percentages of profit to net
fees earned over a ten-year period. The ratio is compared
with a profit goal of 25%. Whenever ratios are portrayed in
graphic form, it is important to compare them with some
base or goal; otherwise the ratio has little meaning except for
historical purposes. Exhibit 9.5 is a graphic portrayal of
productivity factors, or the percent of direct labor to total labor by office or profit center. In this case, the actual productivity factors are compared with the factors needed to meet
budget.

Exhibit 9.6 is a line graph comparing cumulative fees
earned during a fiscal year with the budget. Note how quickly

OPERATING PROFIT OVER A 10-YEAR PERIOD

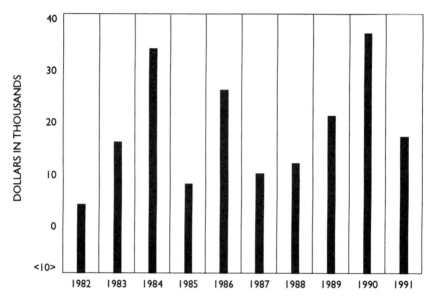

SMITH CONSULTANTS, INC.
OPERATING PROFIT (PRETAX AND PREBONUS/PROFIT SHARING)
FISCAL 1982 THROUGH 1991 (IN THOUSANDS)

Exhibit 9.3   A 10-year history of operating profit is likely to fluctuate in this manner in a professional service firm, particularly a smaller one.

the comparison between actual and budget figures can be made without studying a large number of figures and making mental calculations.

Exhibit 9.7 is a similar chart showing the same comparisons for pretax profit. The people who can most appreciate these charts are chief executive officers and managing principals, who have little time to spend analyzing data. These people must be able to glean the status of a situation quickly in order to make decisions.

EXERCISE 9.2 ■■■■■■■■■■■■■■■■

Analyzing Operating Systems

Multiple Choice

1. An important feature of an operating system is
   a. accuracy of calculations.

PERCENTAGE OF PROFIT TO NET FEES EARNED

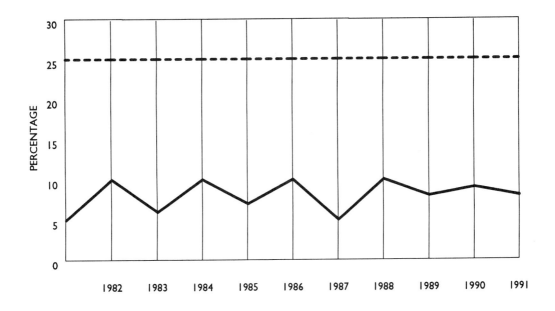

SMITH CONSULTANTS, INC.
PERCENTAGE OF PROFIT TO NET FEES EARNED.
FISCAL 1982 THROUGH 1991

PROFIT GOAL ━ ━ ━ ━ ━

Exhibit 9.4   The firm has set a high profit goal that it has not come close to achieving. Perhaps the goal is unrealistic.

    b. mistake correction capability.
    c. accuracy of printed reports.
    d. none of the above.

2. Financial reports are useful only if
    a. they are prepared each month.
    b. they are prepared every Monday.
    c. they are timely.
    d. a and b only.

3. A "fair report" means
    a. direct labor is accurate.
    b. costs are distributed equally.
    c. indirect costs are fair.
    d. cost allocations to profit centers are made on an equitable basis.

PRODUCTIVITY FACTORS

SMITH CONSULTANTS, INC.
PRODUCTIVITY FACTOR (% DIRECT LABOR TO TOTAL LABOR)
FISCAL 1991

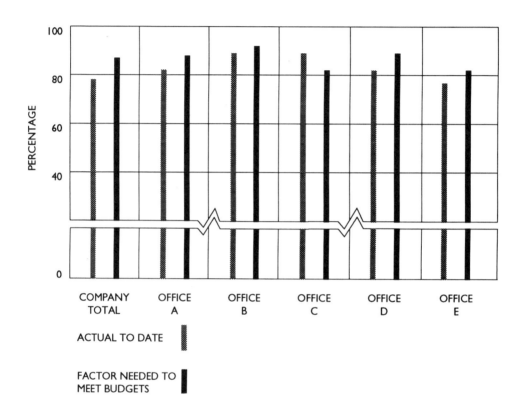

ACTUAL TO DATE

FACTOR NEEDED TO
MEET BUDGETS

Exhibit 9.5 With the exception of Office C, none of the other offices has achieved a sufficiently high productivity factor to meet budget. The budgets may have to be revised.

4. A financial report is not helpful if
   a. it is unclear.
   b. important data do not stand out.
   c. it has no graphs or charts.
   d. all of the above.
   e. a and c only.

5. When choosing a financial operating system
   a. listen to the sales person.
   b. sit at the computer and use it yourself.

COMPARISION OF CUMULATIVE FEES EARNED VERSUS BUDGET

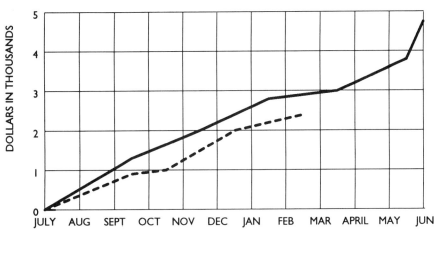

SMITH CONSULTANTS, INC.
COMPARISION OF CUMULATIVE NET FEES EARNED VERSUS BUDGET
JULY 1990 TO JUNE 1991

F/Y 1990 BUDGET ━━━━
F/Y 1991 ACTUAL ━ ━ ━

Exhibit 9.6 Actual net fees have remained under budget since the first of the year. With higher revenues budgeted for the latter part of the year, it appears to be unlikely that the budget will be met.

    c. rely on published reports only for analysis.
    d. none of the above.

6. You should be closely involved in the system installation because
    a. you need to make choices in the beginning that are difficult to change later.
    b. you need to control its use.
    c. no one else is capable.
    d. a and b only.
    e. b and c only.

COMPARISION OF CUMULATIVE PRETAX PROFIT VERSUS BUDGET

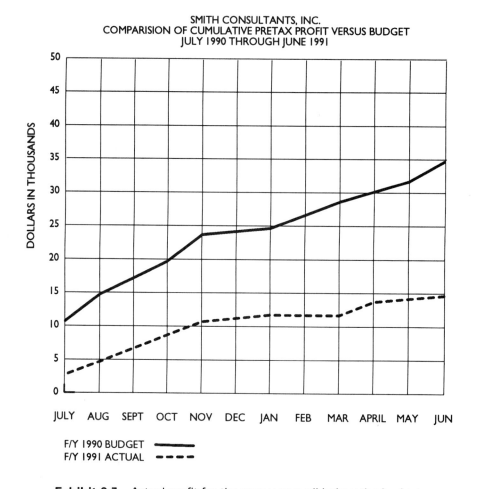

Exhibit 9.7 Actual profit for the year was well below the budget. This requires an explanation.

9.3 OTHER METHODS OF PRESENTING UNDERSTANDABLE REPORTS

Limiting Account Breakdowns

There are other ways besides the use of graphics to present clear and useful reports. One method is to limit the number of account breakdowns as reports are submitted on top management. For example, Exhibit 9.8 is a detailed presentation of a profit and loss statement that is useful for a profit center manager in a larger firm. It shows in detail the various

PROFIT AND LOSS STATEMENT FOR LARGE FIRM

Smith Consultants, Inc. (Large Firm)
Office A Income Statement
Feb. 1993

	Current Month	Year to Date
Revenue		
Project revenue	$304,830	$2,434,640
Other income	29,820	250,560
Total Revenue	$334,650	$2,685,200
Operating Expenses		
Salaries: Direct	$121,725	$ 981,800
Indirect	28,392	343,241
Payroll taxes	4,653	37,224
Vacations	6,489	51,912
Sick leave	7,048	56,384
Holidays	9,355	74,840
Group health insurance	1,100	8,800
Severance pay	801	6,408
Consultants	3,658	29,264
Data processing	1,791	14,328
Legal and accounting	2,743	21,944
Temporary secretarial	2,330	18,640
Travel	7,580	60,640
Promotion	6,001	48,008
Rental of space	22,104	196,832
Supplies	6,703	53,624
Furniture and equipment lease	2,292	18,336
Depreciation	3,800	30,400
Insurance and bonding	1,605	12,840
Printing and reproduction	8,200	65,600
Repairs and maintenance	9,097	72,776
Dues and subscriptions	4,032	32,256
Employee procurement	1,698	13,584
Telephone	4,302	14,416
Postage and freight	9,642	77,136
Interest	5,618	44,944
Conferences	2,491	19,928
Miscellaneous	2,892	23,136
Other direct expenses	9,968	79,744
Total Operating Expenses	$298,110	$2,488,985
Net Profit Before Taxes	$ 36,540	$ 196,215

Exhibit 9.8 A large design firm needs many account breakdowns in order to control costs. In this case merging accounts would create large balances that would require further breakdowns in order to be analyzed properly.

PROFIT AND LOSS STATEMENT FOR A SMALLER FIRM

Smith Consultants, Inc. (Small Firm)
Income Statement
Feb. 1993

	Current Month	Year to Date
Revenue		
Project revenue	$29,423	$102,980
Other income	1,542	5,397
Total Revenue	$30,965	$108,377
Operating Expenses		
Salaries: Direct	$10,121	$ 35,423
Indirect	4,732	16,562
Payroll taxes	1,527	5,344
Vacations, holidays, sick leave	951	3,329
Group insurance	89	312
Data processing	284	994
Legal and accounting	580	2,030
Promotion	3,131	10,958
Rental of space	4,297	15,040
Supplies	147	515
Furniture and equipment lease	289	1,011
Depreciation	816	2,856
Liability insurance	115	403
Printing and reproduction	680	2,380
Dues and subscriptions	1,412	4,942
Telephone	115	403
Miscellaneous	100	350
Other direct expenses	1,012	3,542
Total Operating Expenses	$30,398	$106,394
Net Profit Before Tax	$ 567	$ 1,983

Exhibit 9.9 Fewer account breakdowns are needed in a smaller firm.

charges to his or her profit center. Exhibit 9.9 is a profit and loss statement for a smaller firm. The item labelled "miscellaneous" is kept to a minimum to eliminate questions about this account. By contrast, Exhibit 9.10 is a financial report to senior management in a larger firm. It eliminates detailed

FINANCIAL REPORT FOR TOP MANAGEMENT

Smith Consultants, Inc.
Office A Income Statement (in Thousands)
Feb. 1993

	Current Month		Year to Date	
	Actual	**Forecast**	**Actual**	**Forecast**
Revenue				
Project revenue	$305	$300	$2,435	$2,650
Other income	30	40	250	250
Total Revenue	$335	$340	$2,685	$2,900
Operating Expenses				
Project expenses	$132	$140	$1,062	$1,120
General overhead	166	160	1,427	1,570
Total Expenses	$298	$300	$2,489	$2,690
Net Profit Before Tax	$ 37	$ 40	$ 196	$ 210

Exhibit 9.10 Note how easy it is to grasp the meaning of a report that contains a few key numbers.

breakdowns and concentrates instead on comparisons with forecasted results. The practice of limiting account break-downs presented to higher levels of management is generally effective. However, it should be recognized that there are some profit center managers who are simply not interested in knowing the details and some senior management personnel who insist on detailed reports. Therefore, the first rule is to know the audience for the reports and to give them what they need and want.

Exception Reporting

Another effective way of presenting financial reports is through exception reporting. Exception reporting operates on the premise that managers are usually flooded with too much information and therefore have difficulty recognizing the important material that they should know. By highlighting information that is out of the ordinary and not reporting certain information that is within established parameters, the manager can concentrate on what is important. Exhibit 9.11

PROJECTS IN TROUBLE

Smith Consultants, Inc.
Projects Exceeding Budgets by 10%
Feb. 1993

	Project Revenue ($)	**Profit/Loss ($)**
Office A		
Project C	$ 7,489	($121)
Project E	129,834	26
Project F	60,234	19
Project H	9,834	(14)
Office B		
Project K	$ 19,334	($ 42)
Project M	12,468	4

Exhibit 9.11 This exception report listing projects in difficulty would be very useful for managing principals with little time to read reports. Figures in parentheses in the last column represent the dollar value of losses on projects.

is a report listing projects "in trouble," that is, projects that have exceeded budgets by 10% or more. A manager need only scan this list to know which projects need attention. One problem with a listing like this is that once a project makes the list, it is not likely to be removed until completed, so the list becomes increasingly lengthy. Exception reporting can be readily adapted to computerized reports, since pertinent information can be asterisked or highlighted in some way. In a manual reporting system, red circles can be drawn around the information to be highlighted.

People should only receive reports on which they can take action. This means that reports "for information only" should be minimized in the interest of reducing the information glut. For example, project managers need to have detailed information on the projects they control, but they do not generally need information on other managers' projects. Routine status reports should be examined and eliminated after they have served their purpose. A good illustration is a crisis report generated to meet a specific need. For example, the principals of the firm may need to monitor cash on a daily basis when there is a severe cash shortage. But once the situation has passed, only the financial manager may need to monitor cash daily. Therefore, a daily cash report to the principals is no longer necessary.

Comparative Reporting

Another effective way of reporting financial information is through comparative data. Comparative data are presented in the form of variance reports where data are compared with a budget or historical period. Comparisons are easy to grasp, but it is important to have a method for highlighting the significant variances. One method, as shown in Exhibit 9.12, is to bracket the unfavorable information. That is, where revenues are lower than budget, which is unfavorable, the difference is bracketed. Where expenses are higher than budget, which is also unfavorable, the difference is bracketed. Where profit is lower than budget, which is unfavorable, the difference is bracketed. The reader of the report then need only scan the variance column for the larger bracketed amounts, and he or she understands the significance of the report in a very short period of time. He or she can then concentrate on finding the reasons for the variances, which is the important matter.

Highlighting Important Information

Still another method of presenting effective financial reports is shown in Exhibit 9.13, where the current information, which is the most important information, is highlighted by shading the comparative data. This method helps focus the reader's attention and is quite effective when presenting a large number of figures. Rounding to the nearest meaningful dollar amounts, whether hundreds or thousands, also enhances the readability of the reports.

Use of Ratios

Ratio analysis is another technique often used to present financial information. Ratios present key indicators of performance, such as average collection period and sales per employee, and they are particularly useful when compared with averages of other similar firms. Exhibits 9.14 and 9.15 are examples of such comparisons. Each year since 1979 PSMJ has published its annual Professional Services Management Jour-

VARIANCE REPORT

Smith Consultants, Inc.
Office A Income Statement/Variance Report (in Thousands)
Feb. 1993

	Actual	Budget	Variance
Revenue			
Project revenue	$305	$315	[$10]
Other income	29	28	
Total Revenue	$334	$343	[$9]
Operating Expenses			
Salaries: Direct	$121	$116	[$5]
Indirect	29	26	[3]
Payroll taxes	5	5	—
Vacations	6	6	—
Sick leave	7	7	—
Holidays	9	10	1
Group insurance	1	1	—
Severance pay	1	1	—
Consultants	3	3	—
Data processing	2	3	1
Legal and accounting	2	2	—
Temporary secretarial	2	4	2
Travel	8	10	2
Promotion	7	6	[1]
Rental of space	22	22	—
Supplies	7	3	[4]
Furniture and equipment lease	2	2	—
Depreciation	3	3	—
Insurance and bonding	1	1	—
Printing and reproduction	9	11	2
Repairs and maintenance	9	9	—
Dues and subscriptions	5	4	[1]
Employee procurement	2	3	1
Telephone/Fax	5	6	1
Postage and freight	9	11	2
Interest	6	1	[5]
Conference	2	2	—
Miscellaneous	3	3	—
Other direct expenses	10	10	—
Total Operating Expenses	$298	$291	[$7]
Net Profit Before Tax	$ 36	$ 52	[$16]

Exhibit 9.12 Note how easy it is to grasp the meaning of this report by looking for the large bracketed numbers in the last column.

INCOME STATEMENT WITH CURRENT INFORMATION HIGHLIGHTED

SMITH CONSULTANTS, INC.
OFFICE A INCOME STATEMENT (IN THOUSANDS)
FEBRUARY, 1993

	CURRENT MONTH			YEAR TO DATE		
REVENUE	Last Year	Actual	Forecast	Last Year	Actual	Forecast
Project Revenue	$291	$305	$300	$2,105	$2,435	$2,650
Other Income	22	30	40	190	250	250
Total Revenue	$313	$335	$340	$2,295	$2,685	$2,900
OPERATING EXPENSES						
Project Expenses	$121	$132	$140	$998	$1,062	$1,120
General Overhead	158	166	160	1,302	1,427	1,570
Total Expense	$279	$298	$300	$2,300	$2,486	$2,690
Net Profit Before Tax	$34	$37	$40	($5)	$196	$210

Exhibit 9.13

nal Financial Statistics Survey, which highlights hundreds of statistical ratios specifically for design firms.

EXERCISE 9.3 ▋

Presenting Understandable Reports

1. One way to present clear and useful reports is to limit the number of

_____

2. Exception reports assume that managers are

_____

3. One problem with an exception report listing is that once a project makes the list,

_____

_____

4. People should only receive reports on which

_____

_____

COMPARISON OF SELECTED RATIOS

Smith Consultants, Inc.
Comparison of Selected Ratios
Fiscal 1993

	Upper Quartile	Median	Lower Quartile	Smith Consultants, Inc.
Return on sales (%)	8.7	4.11	2.03	3.5
Return on net worth (%)	47.4	26.4	16.6	13.6
Sales per employee ($)	52,680	29,920	23,220	22,614
Collection period (days)	91	61	33	158
Sales (in thousands of $)	4,370	2,110	1,460	9,836
Net working capital to sales (%)	20.3	11.0	5.0	16.9

Exhibit 9.14 This report is useful for comparing your firm's experience with averages in the industry.

5. Variance reports present data that are compared with

_____

Making Changes in Your Firm

1. When was the last time you updated your financial reporting system?

_____

2. Could you benefit from a review of your system?

_____

3. How long would it take to analyze the effectiveness of your financial reports?

_____

9.4 USING FINANCIAL REPORTS

The most important factor in presenting financial reports is to know your audience and to present them with the information they need and want in order to manage effectively. Generally, readers want summaries and conclusions. The financial manager should try to anticipate any questions that might be asked about the reports. He or she should be prepared to explain the reasons for any unfavorable results.

Reports should be directed to the people who can take ac-

BALANCE SHEET ACCOUNTS AS PERCENTAGE OF NET SALES

Smith Consultants, Inc.
Balance Sheet Accounts as Percentage of Net Sales
Fiscal 1983

	(Median, %)	Smith Consultants, Inc. (%)
Cash	2.5	1.8
Accounts receivable	17.0	43.2
Inventory	4.5	
Note Receivable	1.5	
Other current assets	4.0	0.2
Total current assets	18.0	45.2
Futures and equipment	6.0	4.3
Real estate	4.0	3.2
Other noncurrent assets	2.0	2.3
Total assets	25.0	54.9
Accounts payable	2.0	3.3
Bank loans	5.0	5.1
Notes payable	2.0	
Other current liabilities	7.0	19.9
Total current liabilities	8.0	28.3
Long-term liabilities	6.0	0.5
Stock/net worth	19.0	26.1
Total liabilities and capital	30.5	54.9

Exhibit 9.15 The reader of this report should highlight the amounts with significant variances and ask the financial manager for possible explanation.

tion and achieve results. These people need a minimum of key information that tells them what they should know quickly and succinctly. They should not be overwhelmed with a lot of reports and data. Reports that emphasize the profit and loss approach are generally the most effective when comparing results of a single project, a profit center, or the firm as a whole. Ratios are also very effective in conveying a lot of information with very few numbers, but to be really effective, for meaningful comparisons to be drawn, the ratios must be compared with a base or with results from other firms.

Reports should present the latest financial information available, which means that meetings should be scheduled when reports are issued. At the meeting the financial information should not be read aloud line by line; only the significant items should be mentioned and comparisons drawn. Then, as questions are raised, the financial manager can discuss whatever additional detail is required.

After the meeting it is well to follow up on the reports by requesting suggestions for improvement. It is possible that the financial manager may still be providing more information than is necessary or required, and you will discover this by asking for suggestions. The financial manager should also examine what other firms are doing by discussing reporting techniques with counterparts in other firms.

Reporting as a Basis for Decision Making

How financial reports are prepared and presented is important and, to a certain degree, influences whether they are read and used. Reports to the principals of the firm should be typed on standard size paper and bound into a folder with dividers or colored tabs for ease in reading and carrying in a briefcase. Do not present reports on lined accounting paper; they are difficult to read. The reports should have a summary narrative on top for the benefit of those who are unable to attend the summary meeting.

In presenting the reports, the financial manager should point out highlights and interpret the results. The financial manager must be prepared to answer questions. If he or she does not have an answer, it should be obtained later and reported back to the questioner. The entire focus of the presentation should be on the future and what the figures mean in terms of future results. There is nothing anyone can do to change what has already happened, but the past gives us the best indication of what is likely to happen in the future.

When presenting financial information that will be the basis for significant policy decisions, such as opening or closing an office or deciding to enter a new market, it is most important that the financial manager clearly present options and alternatives and discuss their pros and cons. However, the financial manager should not make a recommendation unless asked. Generally, three options should be presented, if possible, and the effects of each described.

If a recommendation is requested, the financial manager should present it and make it clear that this is an opinion. Of course, it is necessary to support the conclusions, and the financial manager should be prepared to answer questions that may arise. If there is any controversy or disagreement with the numbers, it is most important that it be settled beforehand. Nothing can demoralize a meeting or lead to ineffective decision-making more than having two people disagree over numbers while the rest of the participants do not know whose numbers to believe. Since the financial manager is generally the one to give the presentation, there should be an arrangement beforehand to get clarification and agreement, particularly if the financial manager has cause to believe that someone at the meeting will take exception to the figures. There may still be disagreement, but if everyone understands the reason for it and why the numbers are different, then they can at least make an intelligent decision.

EXERCISE 9.4

Using Reports to the Best Advantage

Multiple Choice

1. When preparing a financial report, readers generally
    a. read the entire report.
    b. do not read anything beyond the first page.
    c. want summaries and conclusions.
    d. none of the above.

2. Financial reports should be distributed to
    a. the CEO.
    b. those who take action and achieve results.
    c. the project manager.
    d. the accountants.

3. Reports are most effective if they focus on
    a. profit/loss.
    b. ratios.
    c. the firm as a whole.
    d. all of the above.
    e. none of the above.

4. Reports should provide
    a. last week's results.
    b. last month's results.
    c. yesterday's results.
    d. the latest financial information available.

5. After presentation of a financial report, it is best to
   a. gather up all reports and keep them.
   b. request suggestions for improvement.
   c. examine their future.
   d. none of the above.

6. When presenting a financial report, it is important to
   a. summarize all losses.
   b. summarize all gains.
   c. summarize the report highlights.
   d. none of the above.

7. Nothing can be more demoralizing in a meeting than
   a. two people arguing.
   b. two people disagreeing over numbers and the rest confused as to who is right.
   c. two people thinking the same way.
   d. none of the above.

8. Prior to the presentation, the financial manager should be sure to
   a. clarify the numbers.
   b. head off disputes by getting everyone's opinion.
   c. stay away from "hot" subjects.
   d. none of the above.

9.5 REPORTING IN SMALLER DESIGN FIRMS

The principals in a small firm do not have time to review voluminous reports, any more than their large-firm counterparts. Therefore it is just as important that they have a system that meets their needs. In some cases an outside consultant may have to be hired to review the system and design the necessary reports in the proper format. When this has been set up, the bookkeeper can be shown how to follow the system and produce future reports.

Graphics systems are now available on some of the smaller computers, and they can be very effective in producing charts and graphs from accounting data, similar to those shown in Exhibits 9.1–9.7. Not only are the computer graphics more accurate than hand-drawn charts, but the system can be set up to produce these reports on a routine basis. As technology improves and the cost of this equipment comes within reach of smaller firms, reporting systems can be effective and meaningful to firms of all sizes.

Certain key reports listed in Exhibits 9.8–9.15 can and should be adapted for use in smaller firms. For example, Exhibit 9.10 shows how a smaller firm should combine accounts in the income statement so as to present a more readable report with significant numbers for comparison. The principle of exception reporting should be used by firms of all sizes, and therefore the report showing profits exceeding budgets in Exhibit 9.11 is applicable to smaller firms as well. Variance reporting is another technique that is useful to the smaller firm, and the principals will appreciate a report such as that shown in Exhibit 9.12, which they can quickly scan to find significant deviations from the budget. The use of ratios for comparison purposes is also helpful to firms of all sizes. In this case, if the survey data are broken down by size of firm it will be particularly helpful to the smaller firm.

EXERCISE 9.5

Discussion Problem

Background. The President of Smith Architects is in his late sixties and has been thinking about retirement for several years. However, he has been overwhelmed with the day-to-day task of running the firm for so many years that he has not devoted any time to finding a prospective buyer or thinking about any other aspects of ownership transition.

One day he receives a call from the senior vice-president of a larger firm on the East Coast, whom he had met casually a while back. The senior vice-president was frank in stating that his firm was looking to acquire an architectural firm of about the size of Smith Architects, and he was holding very preliminary discussions with several candidates at the moment. The president said he would be willing to explore the possibilities unofficially, with the stipulation that these talks be held in strictest confidence. Since the senior vice-president was going to be in town, dinner was arranged and the senior vice-president stressed that they would be spending only a little time on financial details at these preliminary discussions and suggested that the president put together some data in a highly visual form that they could review together.

WORK IN PROGRESS/AGED RECEIVABLES

Smith Architects, Inc.
Work in Progress/Aged Receivables
As of 12/31/93

Client	Total ($)	Work in Progress ($)	Current ($)	Accounts Receivable 30 Days ($)	60 Days ($)	90 Days and Over ($)
Bailey Builders	$ 15,500	$10,000	$ 5,500			
Joe McDermott	42,520	6,520	16,000	15,000		5,000
First Federal	10,000	1,500	8,500			
Tom Jackson	19,000	6,500			12,500	
Demontrond	5,123	2,560	2,563			
Cy-Fair Schools	12,350	4,500	4,850	3,000		
Harris County	4,600	3,600	1,000			
Montgomery County	4,511	1,200	750	2,561		
City of Humble	4,486	1,890	2,596			
Totals	$118,090	$38,270	$41,759	$ 20,561	$12,500	$ 5,000

Exhibit 9.16 Listing of unbilled work in progress and accounts receivable by client is broken down according to the number of days that accounts receivable are outstanding.

Assignment. Exhibits 9.16–9.20 are examples of the reports prepared by Smith Architects. Review each one to determine whether it is pertinent for discussion at the meeting. If so, sketch a rough outline of how it might be presented in graphic format. What other kinds of graphic presentations would be effective?

_____

_____

_____

_____

_____

_____

_____

_____

_____

_____

_____

INCOME STATEMENTS

Smith Architects, Inc.
Income Statements 1990–1993 (est.)

	1990	1991	1992	1993 (est.)
Income				
Fees earned	$233,880	$280,734	$325,481	$470,000
Reimbursable expenses	2,975	9,514	11,123	20,000
Other income	812	612	1,012	5,000
Total Income	237,667	290,860	337,616	495,000
Direct Expenses				
Direct salaries: Principals	$ 17,089	$ 19,225	$ 20,441	$ 25,000
Employees	61,916	74,235	88,040	100,000
Total Direct Salaries	$ 79,005	$ 93,460	$108,481	$125,000
Outside services	$ 15,901	$ 10,009	$ 11,049	$ 10,000
Other direct expenses	5,311	12,618	12,808	5,000
Total Direct Expenses	$100,217	$116,087	$132,338	$140,000
Indirect Expenses				
Administrative salaries: Principals	$ 16,327	$ 22,225	$ 30,462	$ 28,000
Employees	18,714	20,234	32,564	33,000
Temporary employees	6,021	5,618	2,618	2,000
Vacation/holiday/sick time	10,427	11,812	13,002	14,000
Payroll related expenses	7,227	8,002	9,382	10,000
Office expenses	22,536	26,018	28,888	30,000
Legal and accounting	2,601	3,101	4,014	3,000
Automobile expenses	4,228	5,600	6,437	6,000
Depreciation	916	1,114	1,445	2,000
Business development	2,806	3,418	4,055	5,000
Other indirect expenses	8,302	14,718	28,061	27,000
Total Indirect Expenses	100,105	121,860	160,928	160,000
Total Expenses	200,322	237,947	293,266	300,000
Profit/Loss Before Taxes	$ 37,345	$ 52,913	$ 44,350	$ 55,000

Exhibit 9.17 Summary listing of most recent income statements includes estimates for the current year.

FINAL EXAMINATION—CHAPTER 9

Multiple Choice

1. The main purpose of financial reporting is
   a. to report past results.
   b. to indicate where the firm is heading.

INCOME STATEMENTS AND BALANCE SHEETS

Smith Architects, Inc.
Pro-Forma Income Statements and Balance Sheets 1994–1995

	1994 ($)	1995 ($)
Income Statements		
Project revenue	$500,000	$550,000
Other income		
Total Revenue	$500,000	$550,000
Operating expenses		
Project expenses	$200,000	$225,000
General overhead	248,000	270,000
Total Expenses	$448,000	$495,000
Net Profit Before Taxes	$ 52,000	$ 55,000
Balance Sheets		
Assets		
Cash	$ 48,000	$ 33,000
Accounts receivable	120,300	135,300
Work in progress	78,200	98,200
Other current assets	25,600	25,600
Fixed assets	85,000	85,000
Total assets	$357,100	$377,100
Liabilities and equity		
Liabilities		
Accounts payable	$ 75,000	$ 57,000
Notes payable	25,000	20,000
Other liabilities	42,000	30,000
Total Liabilities	$142,000	$107,000
Equity	$215,100	$270,100
Total Liability and Equity	$357,100	$377,100

Exhibit 9.18 Here are balance sheets projected for the current year and estimated for the following year.

    c. to present analysis.
    d. none of the above.

2. A report with overhead cost allocations distributed equally to all projects is known as
    a. an accounts receivable report.
    b. a cash flow report.
    c. a fair report.
    d. none of the above.

PROJECTED REVENUE BY CLIENT TYPE

Smith Architects, Inc.
1992, 1993 (Est.), 1994 (Est.)

	1993 ($)	1994 ($)	1995 ($)
Private Sector Clients			
Bailey Builders	$ 25,500.00	$ 15,000.00	$ 35,000.00
Joe McDermott	85,200.00	40,000.00	65,000.00
First Federal	47,500.00	50,000.00	70,000.00
Tom Jackson	80,300.00	80,000.00	90,000.00
Demontrond	60,250.00	20,000.00	40,000.00
Subtotal	$298,750.00	$205,000.00	$300,000.00
Projected sales			
City bank		$ 45,000.00	$ 35,000.00
Office plaza		20,000.00	25,000.00
Subtotal		65,000.00	60,000.00
Total		$270,000.00	$360,000.00
State/Local Government			
Cy-Fair Schools	$ 45,000.00	$ 15,000.00	$ 30,000.00
Harris County	26,300.00	20,000.00	30,000.00
Montgomery County	24,600.00	30,000.00	15,000.00
City of Humble	99,850.00	20,000.00	20,000.00
Subtotal	$196,250.00	$ 85,000.00	$ 95,000.00
Projected revenue			
Hobby Airport		$100,000.00	$ 70,000.00
Houston Port Authority		45,000.00	25,000.00
Subtotal		145,000.00	95,000.00
Total		$230,000.00	$190,000.00
Grand Total	$495,000.00	$500,000.00	$550,000.00

Exhibit 9.19 Actual and estimated revenue earned on major projects, listed according to type of client.

3. When choosing a computerized financial reporting system for your firm
   a. be sure to hire a consultant.
   b. be involved in each and every step.
   c. be alert to cost savings.
   d. all of the above.
   e. none of the above.

4. Once a project makes it to an exception report
   a. it is in trouble.

DEPRECIATION EXPENSE BY EQUIPMENT TYPE

Smith Architects, Inc.
Depreciation Schedule as of 12/31/98

	Date Purchased	Original Cost ($)	Depreciation ($)	Net 1300k Value ($)
Furniture and Fixtures				
4 executive desks	06/18/96	$ 8	$ 6	$ 2
4 executive chairs	06/18/96	2	2	0
4 side chairs	06/18/96	2	2	0
4 credenzas	06/18/96	4	3	
4 secretarial desks	06/18/96	4	3	
4 secretarial chairs	06/18/96	1	1	0
4 side chairs	06/18/96	1	1	0
15 standard wood desks	07/20/96	12	10	2
Etc.				
Total furniture and fixtures		$ 432	$ 205	$ 227
Leasehold Improvements				
Telephone installation	03/21/95	$ 12	$ 12	$ 0
Security system	04/03/96	7	7	0
Etc.				
Total Leasehold Improvements		$ 668	$ 26	$ 342
Transportation Equipment				
3 Lexus sedans	02/28/98	$ 30	$ 30	$ 0
Etc.				
Total transportation equipment		$ 412	$ 80	$ 332

(In Thousands)

Exhibit 9.20 This schedule of fixed assets by type of equipment is necessary to determine depreciation expense.

    b. it doesn't come off the report.
    c. it is hopeless.
    d. b and c only.
    e. a and b only.

5. The most effective reports show
    a. profit/loss
    b. only key information.
    c. summaries.
    d. all of the above.
    e. none of the above.

6. Readers needs to see financial information
   a. they can use right away to make a difference.
   b. they can analyze later.
   c. in reports with many pages.
   d. none of the above.

7. When presenting a financial report, it is best to
   a. point out only the problems.
   b. talk about positive results.
   c. summarize the highlights verbally.
   d. all of the above.

8. Small firm principals generally
   a. put off financial reporting.
   b. have too much to analyze.
   c. have an outside consultant to review their reporting system.
   d. none of the above.

9. Financial reports are only useful if they are
   a. complex.
   b. involved.
   c. lengthy.
   d. clear and concise.

10. An exception report is
    a. not useful for small firms.
    b. most useful for large firms.
    c. a and b only.
    d. b and c only.

10 PURCHASING

Chapter Summary

- Establishing a design firm purchasing service
- Profitable purchasing for clients
- Purchases from funds in an escrow account
- Markup on furniture purchases
- Deposits required on furnishings
- Drawbacks to establishing a purchasing function
- The financial manager's role

The Importance of Purchasing

The basic principles of purchasing that apply to smaller interior design firms apply to any kind of purchasing arrangement. The design firm that offers clients a purchasing service presents a whole new set of problems to the financial manager. These firms go beyond specifying furniture and furnishings to be provided by ordering the materials and arranging for their installation. This function is often handled by an expediter in the interiors firm or a separate department may be necessary, depending on the size and volume of orders. The expediter is responsible for working with the designers to select manufacturers, place purchase orders, expedite deliveries, and arrange for supervision of the installation crews. This is a large and important responsibility that many interior design firms are not equipped to handle. For that reason many firms, particularly the smaller ones, only perform this service for a few clients or on smaller projects. On larger projects, the client may be referred to a company that specializes in large-scale purchasing.

10.1 PURCHASING FORMS AND PROCEDURES

Following are some sample forms and procedures used in the purchasing function:

SUMMARY BID FORM

Proposal for Furniture, Furnishings, and Equipment
Dollar Bank
First Floor of Smith Building

FROM: _____

	Amount
Section 1 Gilbert	_____
Section 2 Gunlocke	_____
Section 3 Howe	_____
Section 4 IIL	_____
Section 5 JG	_____
Section 6 Modern Mode	_____
Section 7 Stendig	_____
Section 8 Stow Davis	_____
Total Dealer Net	_____
Plus _____ % profit	_____
Subtotal "A"	_____
Plus _____ % overhead, freight, delivery, and installation	_____
Subtotal "B"	_____
Plus sales tax (where applicable) on subtotal "A"	_____
Plus net packing charges	_____
Grand Total	_____
_____ % Discount for immediate payment within 15 days of invoice	_____
Total	_____

Submitted by: _____ _____

Authorized Signature   *Date*

Exhibit 10.1 The summary bid form allows the interior designer and the client to compare the various bids.

Summary Bid Form

Comparison of bids is facilitated when a summary bid document is prepared, such as that shown for an interiors firm in Exhibit 10.1. This summary permits the firm and client to prepare a spreadsheet analysis of the various bids. It also quickly isolates those dealers who are unable to bid on all items.

Preparing the summary in this fashion enables the firm and the client to compare discounts offered by the manufacturer to the various dealers. The form also isolates the dealer's add-on costs and profit, and those dealers who do not wish to disclose this information are eliminated from bidding. The

PROJECT PRODUCT LIST

SOLD TO	INSTALLED AT	SHIPPED TO	JOB # 7002
ABC Interiors	Haven Motel	Haven Motel	CUSTOMER ORDER: 1546
CONTACT: J. Glenn	CONTACT: R. Rosen	CONTACT: R. Rosen	

QTY	MFG NUMBER	DESCRIPTION		SHIP DATE	UNIT LIST	INVOICE	RECEIPT TICKET
15	416	Custom Table Lamps	Blue Shades	4/12	$25.00	$375.00	
26	2118	T.V. Sets	Std. Commercial Grade	5/1	$400.00	$10,400.00	181
50	1167	Framed Prints	Seascapes	6/1	$25.00	$1,250.00	.52
40	211	Floor Lamps	Green Shades	4/12	$35.00	$1,400.00	
	Total					$26,000	

Exhibit 10.2 This report is a comprehensive listing of all items purchased.

form also clarifies the application of sales tax only to the furniture portion of the cost.

Project Product List

This form (as shown in Exhibit 10.2) is used to list specific quantities, manufacturers, specifications, and costs for all items purchased through the interiors firm. When the list is completed to the designer's satisfaction and accepted by the client, it is forwarded to the expediter who fills out purchase orders for the items listed.

The project product list is kept by the expediter until all purchase orders have been prepared and signed. The list is then sent back to the designer, who uses it to check purchase orders. After approval, the list is returned to the expediter, who retains it, as no original information is erased when

PURCHASE ORDER .

Able Lighting Mfging Company   SHIP TO   Haven Motel
121 East Street   211 South Avenue
New York, N.Y.   Norfolk, Virginia

DATE	DELIVERY DATE	SHIP VIA	F O B	TERMS	PURCHASE ORDER NO	
2/28	4/2	Smith Transport	Dest.	30 Days Net	1645	
QUANTITY	DESCRIPTION				PRICE	AMOUNT
15	#416 Cust. Table Lamps (Blue Shades)				$25.00	$ 375.00
40	#211 Floor Lamps (Green Shades)				35.00	1,400.00
20	#121 Ceiling Fixtures (Modern)				50.00	1,000.00
	Total					$17,500.00

✗ NOT FOR RESALE   ▢ FOR RESALE   TAX NUMBER _____

_____JGR_____
Authorized Signature

_____TMG_____
Designer

Exhibit 10.3 Purchase orders are standard documents used by most businesses to purchase supplies and equipment.

change orders occur. All additions or subtractions are listed on separate lines.

Purchase Order

Upon receipt of the project product list, the expediter prepares a purchase order, shown in Exhibit 10.3, with six copies as follows:

1. *White*: Original copy to manufacturer.
2. *Blue*: Copy to chief executive.
3. *White*: Copy to job file, expediter.

4. *Yellow*: Copy to master file.

5. *Pink*: Copy to accounting.

6. *Orange*: Copy to unbilled file.

The expediter types purchase orders with the information shown and signs in the appropriate place. The yellow copy is filed immediately in the master file. All other copies, together with the project product list, are sent to the designer for checking and distribution.

The chronological numbering of purchase orders must be maintained by the expediter to ensure that unauthorized purchases are not made. Purchase orders containing errors in typing are marked void and sent to the accounting department for filing. The yellow copy of all purchase orders, including the voided ones, should be kept in a master file. If blank purchase orders are used to replace voided ones, this should be noted on the voided copy.

Purchase Order List

As the expediter generates purchase orders, each one is listed chronologically on the purchase order list shown in Exhibit 10.4 with the date issued, identification of the person taking the purchase order, manufacturer, project number, and amount. As invoices that correspond to project purchase orders are received by the expediter from manufacturers, the expediter posts the amount invoiced on the purchase order list and calculates the open purchase order balance. In the case of repeated invoicing on one purchase order, the amount invoiced and open purchase order balance are erased and updated each time an additional invoice is received. Each week the expediter makes one copy and forwards it to the accounting department for preparation of the cash flow report. The accounting department totals all open purchase order balances and transfers the appropriate number to the cash flow report. The copy of the purchase order list is stapled to the cash flow report for backup support.

PURCHASE ORDER LIST

PURCHASE ORDER	DATE ISSUED	TAKEN BY	MANUFACTURER	PROJECT NUMBER	AMOUNT	AMOUNT INVOICED DATE	OPEN PURCHASE ORDER BALANCE
645	2/28	RMG	Able	7002	$17,500⁰⁰	$375⁰⁰ 4/12	$17,125⁰⁰
1640	3/2	JJR	Baker	7002	$20,000⁰⁰	$20,000 4/16	0
1647	3/5	BRG	Charlie	7002	$15,000⁰⁰		15,000⁰⁰
TOTALS					$415,000⁰⁰	$200,000⁰⁰	$215,000⁰⁰

Exhibit 10.4   This report is useful to show unfilled purchase orders.

EXERCISE 10.1 ■■■■■

Reviewing Purchasing Forms

1. A summary document is prepared in order to analyze

_____

2. The summary bid form isolates both

_____

and _____

3. The project product list is used to list

_____

_____

4. The expediter fills out _____ for the items listed on the project product list.

5. A purchase order must be prepared in _____ copies.

6. A chronological numbering of purchase orders must be maintained to ensure _____ .

7. Each purchase order is listed on the purchase order list as it is _____ and should include

_____

_____

8. The accounting department (or person) totals all open purchase order balances and

_____

_____

10.2 FINANCIAL ASPECTS OF PURCHASING SERVICES

The key to a successful purchasing service is to avoid committing the firm's own money. The profit margins available by marking up furniture purchases by, say, 10%, are simply not sufficient to offset the carrying charges on the money outstanding with manufacturers. That is the reason why many firms do not provide purchasing services.

One method of resolving this problem is to request a deposit from the client of from one-third to one-half of the total amount of the furnishings to be ordered. This money is placed in an escrow account and not deposited with the firm's funds. As individual orders are placed with the manufacturers, a portion of the money is withdrawn to pay the deposits required by certain manufacturers to begin production. Particularly in the case of large custom orders, the manufacturers may want from one-third to one-half as a deposit. In other cases manufacturers will want full payment before delivery.

Other manufacturers with whom the interiors firm has dealt in the past will ship the merchandise on open account. This generally means payment in 30 days, with perhaps a discount for payment in 10 days. If there are sufficient funds in the escrow account, the interiors firm may be able to pay in 10 days, in which case it may get to keep the discount, depending on the terms of the agreement with the client. In any event, the interiors firm should immediately invoice the client for any furnishings that have been shipped. The interiors firm expects to be paid in full on these shipments and not out of the escrow account. These terms need to be carefully explained to clients so they understand the purpose of the escrow account. It is only to take care of advance deposits that may be required, and eventually it is credited against the last shipment of furnishings.

On smaller projects the interiors firm can sometimes ask for and obtain a deposit of 100% of the furnishings costs. These instances are rare, but when they occur the interiors firm is in a much better position to take advantage of all discounts for prompt payment offered by manufacturers. The purchasing service then becomes profitable enough to make it attractive.

Disadvantages of Purchasing

There are several drawbacks to providing a purchasing service to clients. In the case of damaged merchandise, the expediter is required to spend time negotiating with the manufacturer, the freight carrier, and the insurance company. If the merchandise delivered is not as ordered—say it is the wrong model or color—time must be spent straightening out this problem. If a client should suddenly go bankrupt or otherwise be unable to pay for the merchandise, the firm, acting as agent for the client, is likely to be involved in working out a settlement with the manufacturer. This is particularly true if the merchandise was custom ordered. An attorney should therefore be involved in preparing the standard contract used for purchasing services.

Coordination with Financial Manager

It is very important in running a purchasing service that the expediter work closely with the financial manager. The purchasing service requires large sums of money, and it must be carefully controlled so that the clients' deposits are used most effectively. Escrow accounts also give the financial manager an opportunity to invest these funds so that they earn maximum interest up until the time they are needed.

The financial manager can also monitor the entire purchasing service to evaluate whether it is a profitable endeavor.

Some principals of the firm may wish to provide this service as an accommodation to their clients. If they realize it is not profitable, their attitude toward it may change.

EXERCISE 10.2 ■

Evaluating the Business of Purchasing Services

Multiple Choice

1. The most important aspect of running a profitable purchasing service is
   a. to run it as smoothly as possible.
   b. to avoid payment as long as possible.
   c. to avoid committing the firm's money as long as possible.
   d. none of the above.

2. One way to avoid over-commitment of resources is to
   a. require 100% payment up front.
   b. require the client to pay one-third to one-half of the purchasing cost up front.
   c. a 30-day billing cycle from the manufacturer.
   d. all of the above.

3. Drawbacks to purchasing include
   a. delivery problems.
   b. too much delivered.
   c. damaged items.
   d. a and b only.
   e. a and c only.

4. An attorney needs to be involved in preparing
   a. all purchase orders.
   b. a standard contract for purchasing services.
   c. any litigation involved in delivery.
   d. none of the above.

5. If merchandise is delivered in the wrong color, who is responsible for resolving this problem?
   a. the expediter.
   b. the client.
   c. the manufacturer.
   d. all of the above.
   e. none of the above.

6. An escrow account is favorable because
   a. it lets the client know how much to expect to pay.
   b. the client can expect delivery within 60 days.
   c. the financial manager is appeased.
   d. the financial manager can invest the funds to earn maximum interest.

Discussion Problem

Background. Your ten-person interior design firm has been asked by your largest client to undertake the purchasing function for a chain of small hotels they are opening in the South. Previously, you had done the interior design work for their hotels and your specifications were then given to the client's purchasing department to obtain the furnishings. The client has been unhappy with the turnover in its purchasing department and the problems this has caused its management. As a result, the client has reduced the staff and limited the purchasing department's duties to normal routine purchases of consumable supplies and equipment for the hotels.

You know that if you do not accept this responsibility the client will probably contract with another interiors firm in the city to perform this service. It will then be only a matter of time before the new firm replaces you completely.

The most important question is who will do the purchasing: Can someone within the firm be trained to handle it or must you hire someone from outside? You arrange a meeting with the other principal in your firm to discuss this matter.

Assignment. What considerations should you give to the formation of a purchasing department in your firm? List the advantages and disadvantages, and on balance, what course of action you will take. List the qualifications for the person assuming the purchasing function. Where can you find information on the salary range for this position?

_____

_____

_____

_____

_____

_____

_____

_____

_____

_____

_____

_____

_____

_____

_____

_____

_____

FINAL EXAMINATION—CHAPTER 10

Multiple Choice

1. Some design firms and interiors firms provide purchasing services
   a. to provide as a courtesy to clients.
   b. to make additional profits.
   c. to expedite purchasing.
   d. none of the above.

2. The summary bid form is used for
   a. financial purposes.
   b. sales tax.
   c. comparison of subcontractor bids.
   d. none of the above.

3. The project product list helps to
   a. expedite the process.
   b. organize all purchase items.
   c. as a check against purchase orders.
   d. all of the above.
   e. none of the above.

4. A purchase order is used by
   a. the client.
   b. the design professional.
   c. the expediter.
   d. none of the above.

5. The purchase order list is
   a. not really necessary.
   b. stapled to the cash flow report for backup.
   c. critical to the design.
   d. all of the above.

6. Clients should pay
   a. none of the inventory costs until project completion.
   b. one-third to one-half of inventory in advance.
   c. for full service consulting.
   d. all of the above.

7. On smaller projects, clients often pay
   a. nothing up front.
   b. 50% up front.
   c. 100% up front.
   d. none of the above.

8. An attorney should provide
   a. project management advice.
   b. the name of a good accountant.
   c. a standard contract for purchasing services.
   d. no services.

9. Escrow accounts are most useful if they are
   a. applied right away.
   b. invested to gain interest.
   c. profitable.
   d. left alone.

10. If you refuse to provide purchasing services, you may
    a. lose business to another firm.
    b. avoid an unprofitable service.
    c. hire an outside expediter.
    d. all of the above.
    e. none of the above.

11

CAPITAL EQUIPMENT ACQUISITIONS

Chapter Summary

- The advantages and disadvantages of outright purchase
- The difference between leasing and renting
- The risks of a third-party lease
- Why a leasing company can sometimes make an offer even more attractive than a bank loan (even though the leasing company must borrow its funds at a bank and still make a profit)
- How to arrange equipment financing through a leasing company
- Important clauses in a rental contract
- How to prepare a cost analysis to compare purchasing, leasing, and renting costs

Capital Equipment

All professional design firms use capital equipment, and indications are that more and more of this equipment will be used in the future. Word processing equipment, mini and micro computers, and computer-aided drafting and design equipment are commonplace in all offices today. The method of acquiring this equipment will largely be delegated to the financial manager, who must analyze the various options of purchasing, leasing, or renting.

11.1 PURCHASING

The outright purchase of equipment is the easiest and quickest method and, in addition, has the following advantages:

1. Outright purchase is often the least expensive, because you are not paying a leasing company's fee (but this is not always the case, as will be seen later in this chapter).

2. When the equipment is fully depreciated, the owner can operate it at "no charge," which can be a competitive advantage or else give the owner a higher profit margin.

3. The owner has full control over the equipment. That is, the owner can move it, sell it, modify it, rent it, or do anything else, provided it is not pledged against a bank loan that may have restrictive covenants regarding the equipment in the agreement.

4. The initial outlay of cash means that no further outlays will be required, and therefore no further cash planning is involved in this transaction.

The disadvantages of the outright purchase are as follows:

1. It ties up funds that might better be used for working capital purposes.

2. If the firm must borrow additional funds to make the purchase, its limited borrowing capacity is used up.

3. With a purchase the firm takes on the full risk of obsolescence, which can be significant in the case of new equipment coming on the market.

4. The owner must handle the insurance and maintenance costs on the equipment, which may not always be the case with leased or rented equipment.

EXERCISE 11.1

Exploring Purchasing Options

True or False

T F   Outright purchase is always the least expensive alternative.

T F   When equipment is purchased, the owner has full control.

T F   Cash planning is necessary after initial purchase.

T   F   Purchasing monopolizes cash.

T   F   It is well-advised to borrow in order to purchase capital equipment.

T   F   The greatest risk in purchase is obsolescence.

T   F   The equipment owner must handle insurance and maintenance costs of purchased equipment.

11.2   LEASING

Leasing differs from renting in that the former generally includes some provision for eventual ownership of the equipment by the lessee. Leasing combines the advantages of having the equipment available when needed with some of the advantages of owning. Other advantages of leasing are

1. A major advantage is that you do not have to come up with the full amount of cash all at once.
2. The lessor can often buy equipment for less than an individual purchaser because the lessor often buys in quantity.
3. Equipment breakdowns may be the responsibility of the lessor, depending upon how the contract is written. In addition, the lessor assumes responsibility for obsolescence of the equipment. Of course, the lease price takes the factor of obsolescence into account.
4. Upon disposition of the equipment, the lessor can often obtain a higher selling price for the same reason that the lessor can purchase it at a lower price, because of the volume of transactions.

The disadvantages of leasing are as follows:

1. The firm is undertaking a fixed obligation that must be paid in bad times as well as good.
2. The leasing cost includes a profit to the leasing company over and above the cost of equipment and financing.
3. To deal with a leasing company, a firm needs a "track record," similar to what it needs when borrowing from a bank. The leasing company must be assured that the

firm has sufficient financial strength to pay the lease, and this requires that financial information be disclosed to the leasing company.

4. The firm is at the mercy of current interest rates at the time it makes the transaction. The leasing company bases its charges on its own cost of borrowing money, which may be higher than what a bank would charge if the firm went directly to borrow from the bank.

EXERCISE 11.2

Exploring Leasing Opportunities

1. How does leasing differ from renting?

_____

_____

2. Advantages of leasing include:

   1. _____

   2. _____

   3. _____

3. Disadvantages of leasing include:

   1. _____

   2. _____

   3. _____

4. Leasing rates depend on current _____

5. Lease price takes into account the factor of _____

   _____

6. To deal with a leasing company, a firm needs to

   _____

   _____

11.3 RENTING

Renting does not involve any acquisition of ownership of the equipment and is generally considered to be a short-term expedient. The advantages of renting are:

1. You have the equipment when you need it and are not burdened with payments when the need has passed.
2. It enables a firm to try out new equipment or different types of equipment without making a financial commitment.
3. It enables the firm's personnel to get training, particularly on computer equipment.
4. Rental equipment may be able to handle a temporary overload situation.

The disadvantages of renting are as follows:

1. It is generally the most expensive method of acquiring capital equipment.
2. The equipment may not be available when you need it, and it is usually not in new condition.
3. Rental agreements are tightly worded documents written by the equipment owner's attorney. They generally place most of the obligations on the renter and few on the owner.

Important details, like who is responsible for insurance and maintenance and who pays for equipment installation and removal, need to be clearly understood at the time a rental agreement is signed. It is important to know what can be reasonably expected in the way of response time to service calls and what constitutes excessive downtime. If the firm needs to acquire additional liability insurance to protect the equipment, this needs to be known.

Obviously, it is important for the firm's attorney to review a rental agreement. Just because an agreement is printed and is made to appear like a standard contract is no reason to believe it cannot be modified, with clauses added or deleted.

EXERCISE 11.3

Renting Options

Multiple Choice

1. Renting is considered
   a. a standard practice.
   b. a good investment.

    c. a long-term solution.

    d. a short-term expedient.

2. Renting allows you to

    a. get training on computer equipment.

    b. try out new equipment before you buy.

    c. rent as needed.

    d. all of the above.

    e. none of the above.

3. The most expensive method of acquiring capital equipment is

    a. leasing.

    b. purchasing.

    c. selling.

    d. renting.

4. Rental agreements place most of the obligations on

    a. the equipment owner.

    b. the design professional.

    c. the renter.

    d. the insurance carrier.

5. An attorney should read all rental agreements to determine

    a. if additional insurance is required.

    b. if it should be purchased.

    c. the degree of risk involved.

    d. the cost.

11.4 COST ANALYSIS

When a firm decides to acquire capital equipment, the financial manager should prepare a detailed cost analysis listing the various options available. An example of a cost analysis is shown in Exhibit 11.1. If the principals of a smaller firm are not comfortable with making their own analysis, they should ask their accountant to assist them. They should also not hesitate to ask his or her advice regarding the contemplated purchase. Many accountants are involved in acquiring computers for their own practice and they can give advice from personal experience.

While financial considerations are an important element in the final decision, very often nonfinancial reasons, such as better service to clients or competitive pressures, can be the

COST COMPARISON FOR LEASE, PURCHASE, OR RENTAL OF $100,000 EQUIPMENT

Lease[1]		Purchase[2]		Rental[3]	
Total purchase price + interest	$137,500	Total purchase price + interest	$137,500	Total rental price + interest	$111,750
Less: tax savings @ 46% rate (top tax bracket) on $137,000	63,250	Less: Interest	37,500	Less: Tax savings @ 45% tax rate on $111,750	51,405
		Depreciation	95,000		
		Subtotal	$132,500		
Net cost over 5 years	$ 74,250	@ 46% tax rate	$ 60,950	Net cost over 3 years	$ 60,345
		Investment tax credit	10,000		
		Total deductions	70,950		
		Net cost over 5 years	66,550		

[1]Assume straight lease with no pass-through of investment tax credit, and because lessor can purchase equipment at lower price, he or she can finance at same rate as bank (15%) and still make a profit.
[2]Financed by $100,000 bank loan at 15%.
[3]Assume renter of equipment wishes to recover 90% of cost over three-year period of rental agreement at 15%.

Exhibit 11.1   This analysis indicates the least expensive alternative is an outright purchase financed over a five-year period.

overriding consideration in the acquisition of capital equipment.

EXERCISE 11.4 ▪▪▪▪▪▪▪▪▪▪▪▪▪▪

Discussion Problem

Background. Your architectural firm is interested in acquiring CADD equipment because you recognize that it will be important to your future growth and ability to remain competitive. You are presently using a service bureau, but you want to own your own equipment. One equipment manufacturer has offered to train your staff at another architectural firm where he has installed this equipment. The other firm agrees and arrangements are made to hold classes once a week after hours. Members of your firm participate on a voluntary basis.

You examine the alternatives in financing the equipment and decide that leasing is your best alternative. The equipment manufacturer recommends a leasing firm that he uses. Several years ago you leased some furniture from another leasing company, and you decide to ask both firms to submit a proposal.

Assignment. List the advantages and disadvantages of using a leasing company for this transaction. What clauses to protect you should be included in the lease document? What other considerations besides price should be examined when deciding between the two firms?

_____

_____

_____

_____

_____

_____

_____

_____

_____

_____

_____

_____

_____

_____

FINAL EXAMINATION—LESSON 11

True or False

T F   Outright purchase does not always tie up funds.

T F   The owner of purchased equipment receives insurance coverage from the manufacturer.

T F With an outright purchase, there is always a risk of obsolescence.

T F Leasing differs from renting because it includes a provision for sale of the equipment.

T F Leasing is a fixed obligation that must be paid in both good times and bad.

T F A firm is at the mercy of current interest rates when negotiating an equipment lease.

T F The leasing company bases its charges on its own cost of borrowing money.

T F Leasing financing charges are always lower than bank financing charges.

T F Leasing equipment can be less expensive than a one-time, overall purchase because leasing companies buy in quantity.

T F A firm must have a good credit rating to lease equipment.

T F Renting involves some acquisition of ownership.

T F You cannot renege on a rental agreement.

T F Renting is not advisable for temporary overload situations.

T F Equipment may not always be readily available when you decide to rent it.

T F Rental agreements are prepared by accountants.

T F Rental agreements place most of the burden on the equipment owner.

T F Rental of equipment is the least expensive method of acquiring capital equipment.

T F One way to try out equipment without making a commitment is to lease it.

T F The financial manager should prepare a detailed cost analysis listing all options available for capital equipment acquisitions.

T F While financial considerations are important, often better service to clients or competitive pressures may be overriding considerations.

12 INTERNAL FINANCIAL CONTROLS

Chapter Summary

- Internal financial controls and why they are important
- The end of year audit versus proper financial controls
- Small design firm controls
- Fidelity bond coverage
- Splitting financial duties to achieve better financial control

A Precarious Balance

One place where most design firms have a weakness is in the area of internal financial controls. This is an accountant's term and it means assuring that the financial transactions of the firm are carried out in accordance with management's directives. For example, the principals of a firm expect that the payroll checks will reflect each individual's current salary, or the number of hours worked multiplied by the current hourly rate. There should be no fictitious names on the payroll. What proof do the principals have that their wishes are being carried out? In smaller firms the managing principal may sign all checks and is probably familiar enough with the staff and operations to spot any obvious discrepancies. However, as a firm grows, the managing principal does not have time to check everything personally, particularly in the financial area. More and more reliance is placed on others.

12.1 THE IMPORTANCE OF CONTROLS

Fortunately, most people hired are honest and trust in them is not misplaced. Occasionally, however, a dishonest employee will be hired and this person can wreak havoc in an office,

WEEKLY LISTING OF CASH RECEIPTS

DATE __2/28__

| CHECK | | FROM | AMOUNT |
NO.	DATE		
1896	2/24	ABC Development Corp	$15,000
289	2/24	Junction City, Texas	2,489
1602	2/25	Johnstown Independent School District	21,621
143	2/26	General Hospital Corp.	4,000
2962	2/27	Schenectady County Hospital	13,500
TOTAL			$91,028

Exhibit 12.1 In a smaller firm the receptionist can maintain this log of incoming checks as the mail is opened and sorted.

often for long periods of time, before being discovered. Exhibit 12.1 contains a story of how one bookkeeper embezzled from a design firm.

An audit is performed to express an opinion on the financial statements. Auditors are trained to look for discrepancies, of course, and if any are found they will be pursued. However, an audit is designed to test only a sample number of transactions, so it cannot be relied upon to uncover fraud.

Nevertheless, the end of year audit is a good starting point to begin to establish internal controls. The auditor is trained to look for weaknesses in this area during the course of the audit and will report the findings following the completion of the audit. In many cases the auditor will prepare a formal letter to management disclosing the findings, but the principals of the firm should meet with the auditor and discuss possible improvements.

In smaller firms that do not have an end of year audit, it may be worthwhile to ask the outside CPA firm that prepares the tax returns to do a special internal controls review. The one-time charge for this service would be a worthwhile investment if the firm implements the changes that are suggested.

Insurance is available to cover some of the exposure, and it should be purchased as part of a complete liability coverage program. This insurance is called "fidelity bond coverage" and it protects the firm from theft by anyone who handles funds. Premiums are generally inexpensive, and the firm should discuss the amount of coverage it needs with its insurance broker.

EXERCISE 12.1

Your Internal Control System

1. Auditors are trained to look for

_____

2. An audit can test only

_____

3. Smaller firms may hire a CPA to

_____

_____

4. Insurance is available to

_____

5. Fidelity bond insurance covers

_____

_____

12.1 SUGGESTIONS FOR BETTER INTERNAL CONTROLS

Splitting up accounting duties is one of the most effective way to improve internal controls and to remove temptation from otherwise honest people. Why key duties are split, it then requires collusion on the part of two or more people to accomplish the same theft, and thus it becomes more difficult. For example, whoever prepares checks should not have the responsibility for reconciling the monthly bank statements. Otherwise there is no control over what checks can be written. Likewise, checks received in the mail should be logged in by someone other than the bookkeeper who pre-

CASH STATUS REPORT

Month: 2/28
Account name: First Bank of Smithtown/Operating Account   Account number: 1234

Date	Beginning Balance	Deposits	Check		Other Adjustments*	Balance
			Numbers	Amount		
2/7	$ 18,000	$ 26,000	189-215	$14,500	0	$ 29,500
2/14	29,000	9,000	216-235	36,000	+ $18 *	1,982
2/21	1,982	40,000	236-261	29,000	0	12,982
2/28	12,982	14,000	262-280	19,000	0	7,982

TOTAL _____

*Other Adjustments (Explain) __Bank service charge deducted in error in January.__

Prepared By: __J.D.T.__   Date: __2/28__
Approved By: __P.M.H.__   Date: __3/1__

Exhibit 12.2   This form should be prepared by someone other than the person who writes the checks. It should then be reconciled with the books of account.

pares the bank deposit, so that there is a duplicate record of incoming receipts. Exhibit 12.2 is a simple form that can be kept by someone other than the chief accountant or bookkeeper to keep track of cash.

The problem in most smaller design firms is that there isn't a pool of accounting department employes among whom these duties can be split. In that case, someone from outside the accounting department, like the receptionist, could open the mail and record the checks before giving them to the bookkeeper.

No matter what the size of the firm, the managing principal can become part of the internal control procedure by periodically inspecting the financial records and tracing one or two transactions. An obvious starting point is to examine the payroll records of everyone in the accounting department. Another fairly obvious check is to make certain that accounting personnel take their vacations. Beyond this, the managing principal can demonstrate an interest in good financial record keeping and show that he or she does not take these matters lightly. The managing principal can use the checklist shown in Exhibit 12.3 to examine the firm's procedures and make some necessary improvements right away.

EXERCISE 12.2 ■■■■■■■■■■■■■■■■■■■■■■■■■■

Improving Internal Controls

1. Checks received in the mail should be

_____

2. One way to avoid theft is to

_____

3. One problem in most small firms is that there aren't enough people available for

_____

_____

4. The managing principal can become part of the internal control procedure by

_____

_____

Discussion Problem

Background. Your 15-person interior design firm has had the same bookkeeper since shortly after you founded the firm 22 years ago. Mrs. Green has been diligent in her duties since her first day on the job and her attendance record has been outstanding. She has kept books on a manual basis all these years and you have never had a problem in the accounting area that she could not handle. Your firm has never been audited and your outside accountant prepares the tax returns from information supplied by Mrs. Green. You often wonder how you could ever function without her.

You get your opportunity when she is suddenly taken ill and must be confined to the hospital for six weeks. Your outside accountant offers to provide you with one of his bookkeepers to help during this period. After working in your office a few days the new bookkeeper tells you that the accounting records are in poor shape. Bank statements have not been reconciled for three months, there are errors in posting, and

CHECKLIST FOR INTERNAL CONTROL

YES	NO	
		General
☐	☐	Are accounting records kept up to date and balanced monthly?
☐	☐	Are cash projections made?
☐	☐	Does the managing principal take a direct and active interest in the financial affairs and reports that are made available?
☐	☐	Are the personal funds of the principals and their personal income and expenses completely segregated from the firm?
☐	☐	Is the managing principal satisfied that all employees are honest?
☐	☐	Is a chart of accounts used?
☐	☐	Does the managing principal use a budget system for monitoring income and expenses?
☐	☐	Is the bookkeeper required to take an annual vacation?
		Cash Receipts
☐	☐	Are receipts deposited intact daily?
☐	☐	Are employees who handle funds bonded?
☐	☐	Does someone other than the bookkeeper open the mail?
☐	☐	Does someone other than the bookkeeper list mail receipts before turning them over to the bookkeeper?
☐	☐	Is the listing subsequently traced to the cash receipts journal?
☐	☐	Do two different people reconcile the bank records and make out the deposit slip?
		Accounts Receivable and Sales
☐	☐	Are monthly statements sent to all clients?
☐	☐	Does the managing principal review statements before mailing them?
☐	☐	Are account write-offs approved only by the managing principal?
☐	☐	Are invoices prenumbered and controlled?
☐	☐	Are clients' accounts balanced regularly?
		Cash Disbursement
☐	☐	Does the managing principal never sign blank checks?

Exhibit 12.3 This checklist can be used to begin a review of the firm's internal financial controls

YES	NO	
☐	☐	Do different people reconcile the bank records and write the checks?
☐	☐	Are all disbursements made by check?
☐	☐	Does the managing principal sign checks only after they are properly completed?
☐	☐	Are all voided checks retained and accounted for?
☐	☐	Are prenumbered checks used?
☐	☐	Is a controlled, mechanical check protector used?
☐	☐	Is the managing principal's signature required on checks?
☐	☐	Does the managing principal review the bank reconciliation?
☐	☐	Is a petty cash fund used and is it reconciled periodically?

Notes Receivable and Investments

YES	NO	
☐	☐	Does the managing principal have sole access to notes and investment certificates?

Property Assets

YES	NO	
☐	☐	Are there detailed records available of property assets and allowances for depreciation?
☐	☐	Is the managing principal acquainted with property assets owned by the company?
☐	☐	Are retirements of assets approved by the managing principal?

Accounts Payable and Purchases

YES	NO	
☐	☐	Are purchase orders used?
☐	☐	Does someone other than the bookkeeper always do the purchasing?
☐	☐	Are suppliers' monthly statements regularly compared with recorded liabilities?
☐	☐	Are suppliers' monthly statements checked by the managing principal periodically if disbursements are made only from invoice?

Payroll

YES	NO	
☐	☐	Are the employees hired by the managing principal?
☐	☐	Would the managing principal be aware of the absence of any employee?
☐	☐	Does the managing principal approve, sign, and distribute payroll checks?

Exhibit 12.3   Continued.

the general ledger has been out of balance for almost a year. Mrs. Green has been covering up discrepancies since 1985, although there is no evidence of fraud.

Assignment. How do you go about correcting this situation? List the key ingredients in an internal control system in even the smallest of firms. What steps can you take to minimize the likelihood of this situation even happening again?

_____

_____

_____

_____

_____

_____

_____

_____

_____

_____

_____

_____

_____

_____

_____

FINAL EXAMINATION—CHAPTER 12

Multiple Choice

1. Financial controls are necessary to
    a. prevent embezzlement.
    b. prevent theft.
    c. check accuracy.
    d. all of the above.
    e. none of the above.

2. Small firms, in lieu of performing a year-end audit, can
    a. hire an attorney to check staff records.
    b. hire an auditor to perform a complete audit.

    c. hire a CPA to prepare a special internal control review.
    d. none of the above.

3. Fidelity bond insurance protects
    a. auditors from liability.
    b. firm owners from theft.
    c. a firm from theft by anyone that handles funds.
    d. none of the above.

4. One way to improve financial controls is to
    a. divide up duties.
    b. divide up salaries.
    c. divide up office space.
    d. all of the above.

5. The managing principal can participate in internal controls by
    a. periodically inspecting the financial records.
    b. tracing one or two transactions.
    c. setting up controls within the office.
    d. all of the above.

True or False

T **F** A dishonest employee can wreak havoc in an office for long periods of time before being discovered.

T **F** The auditor will review all transactions and uncover all possible discrepancies.

T **F** Fidelity bond coverage cannot be obtained from your regular insurance broker.

T **F** One financial control system is to have one person write the checks and another balance the checkbook.

T **F** Accounting records do not need to be balanced monthly.

T **F** The managing principal should take an active interest in financial affairs.

T **F** Monthly statements need not be sent to all clients.

13
WHO IS THE FINANCIAL MANAGER?

Chapter Summary

- What to look for when hiring a financial manager
- How to find the right person
- Educational background needed for the job
- How to compensate the financial manager
- Duties of the financial manager
- Problems a financial manager encounters in a professional services firm
- Other duties a financial manager performs
- Position description of financial manager

Roles and Responsibilities

The financial manager's expertise is vital to the financial health and overall profitability of the firm. This person should not be simply a "bean counter" who balances the books each month and handles payroll, but rather a financial planner who continually monitors performance, reports results, and is constantly alert to financial warning signals in order to notify others in management in time to take corrective action. If he or she is not performing those functions there are two possible reasons: either the wrong person is in charge of financial activities, or else the firm has not given the right person the opportunity and encouragement to perform this important task.

13.1 FINANCIAL MANAGEMENT ALTERNATIVES

What size does a firm have to be to afford a financial manager? Unfortunately there is no easy answer to this question because it depends on how the firm is organized, whether it is single or multidisciplined, and its requirements for financial information. Smaller firms should utilize the services of an outside accountant to give them the financial advice that is normally obtained from the full-time financial manager in a larger firm. Outside accountants work with a variety of firms, both large and small, and they can often be of considerable help in showing a principal how to prepare a budget, cash forecast, or other useful financial report. The problem is that while accountants have this information, they often are so busy and preoccupied with auditing and tax work that it never occurs to them that their client may need help in other areas as well. The principals of smaller firms should tap this valuable resource.

By combining administrative functions (such as management of clerical staff) with the financial function, it is possible to create the position of business manager in smaller firms. This person handles all business management aspects of the firm, and the job is varied and important enough to attract a capable person. Often there is someone already in the firm who has worked for many years and who is familiar with all aspects of the operations. With additional training it may be possible for that person to grow into the business manager's position.

Another opportunity for the smaller firm to acquire this capability is through an architect or engineer with some business administration training and an aptitude and interest in the business management aspects of the firm. If the person wishes to pursue administrative as well as design activities, an arrangement for splitting these duties might be set up. This is particularly feasible if there is a knowledgeable bookkeeper available to handle the detailed accounting work.

Smaller firms must face the problem of keeping a newly hired financial or business manager productively employed and not bored with the job. This can best be accomplished by giving him or her important extra assignments. For example, every firm needs a plan for ownership succession. Other firms seek to grow by acquiring small firms in the same or other disciplines. They must search out and evaluate these opportunities. The financial manager in smaller firms can be of considerable help if given these added responsibilities.

EXERCISE 13.1 ▬▬▬▬▬▬▬▬▬▬▬▬▬

Determing the Need for a Financial Manager

1. What is the size of your firm? _____

2. Have you ever used an outside accountant? _____

3. Who manages the clerical staff at this time?

   _____

4. Could he or she benefit from financial management training and grow into the role of financial manager or business manager? _____

5. What other duties could you assign to the financial manager?

   1. Ownership transition planning?

      _____

   2. Growth/acquisitions?

      _____

   3. Other?

      _____

13.2 ROLE OF THE FINANCIAL MANAGER

The financial manager is in a unique position: No one else in the firm has a perspective on every financial activity that goes on within the organization. The financial manager sees everything that relates to money and has first-hand knowledge of the latest information on the financial status of projects. From this vantage point he or she probably knows more about what is going on within the firm than anyone else. As a result, the financial manager is an important strategic source of information.

This person can assist project managers with practically any question dealing with the financial aspects of their projects. Everything from time charges to the smallest detail of reimbursable expenses are in the financial manager's control.

In larger firms he or she is an important source of information for department or profit center managers because the financial manager can trace every item of expense charged against their budgets. Detailed knowledge of indirect labor charges is also within the financial manager's field of expertise, so other managers can rely on the financial manager for summary reports and explanations of financial results, as well as analyses of trends and forecasts.

The most difficult problem facing the financial manager in a design firm has nothing to do with the technical aspects of the work. It is simply a matter of communications. Because the financial manager's background and training are generally different from that of the design professional, he or she may have a difficult time communicating with others. It is up to the financial manager to make the necessary changes to improve this communications gap because he or she alone has this background in the organization. It is the financial manager's task to change ways of thinking about accounting problems and technical jargon when mingling with the technical staff. Design professionals need quick information, particularly about projects. The need for absolute accuracy can often be traded away if it means getting approximate information that much sooner. Operating managers often want the financial manager's best guess as to the outcome of the reporting period even before financial statements are complete. Being able to respond to these "unreasonable" requests in an intelligent manner makes the diffference between a financial manager who is accepted as part of the management team and one who remains excluded because the technical staff really does not understand what he or she does.

EXERCISE 13.2

The Financial Manager's Role

1. Why is the financial manager one of the most important positions in the firm?

_____

2. How can the financial manager help the project managers in your firm?

_____

3. Why are communications of paramount importance?

_____

4. In what ways can the financial manager change the thinking about project finances?

5. How important is absolute accuracy?

6. When is a best guess sufficient?

7. How can the financial manager be accepted as part of the team?

13.3   REQUIREMENTS OF A FINANCIAL MANAGER

When looking for a financial manager it is important to have a well-thought-out position description. This is useful for both the firm and prospective employee as it saves the time of both parties. The requirements of the position vary, of course, with the size of the firm and number of people handling financial matters. Exhibit 13.1 is an example of a detailed position description that can serve as a checklist of most duties performed by a financial manager in a larger firm. It can be adapted to the specific requirements of almost any large-to-medium-size firm. Exhibit 13.2 is a position description for a business manager of a smaller firm.

In larger firms this position requires a business administration background with experience in a professional services firm. Financial managers may also have an undergraduate degree in a technical discipline (architecture or engineering) and a graduate degree in business administration. Experience in a service organization rather than in one dealing with products is generally preferable. The financial manager usually reports to the chief executive officer or managing principal of the firm. If the financial manager's duties include such administrative activities as supervision of the support

POSITION DESCRIPTION FOR A MEDIUM TO LARGER FIRM

TITLE

Financial Manager (Chief Financial Officer reporting directly to the President).

RESPONSIBILITIES

Planning

Provide projections of short- and long-term financial objectives, develop and maintain financial plans that guide the firm toward attainment of these objectives, and report financial status on a regular basis to allow for adjustments to plans.

Controlling

Develop, direct, and coordinate budgets and projections to ensure that technical functions are consistently executed in accordance with legal requirements and sound business practice. Co-ordinate audits, provide reports that help all departments perform within the limits of the firm's financial plan, and initiate measures and procedures by which the firm's business is conducted with maximum efficiency and economy.

Financing

Recommend means for providing funds to meet long- and short-term requirements, manage funds in order to meet capital needs of the firm, review current financial position regularly, and note any significant deviations from sound management, and develop and recommend appropriate action.

CAPABILITIES

Education

A bachelor's degree in business administration with primary studies in accounting and finance. An MBA and/or CPA desirable.

Experience

At least * years experience in finance and accounting, of which at least * years should be in a management position of a service firm requiring financial forecasting, planning, and reporting. Computer experience desirable.

Competence

Established competence with acceptable references from supervisors.

Exhibit 13.1 Position descriptions should list in considerable detail the background, experience, and requirements necessary to fill the position successfully.

Characteristics

Disciplined time management and attention to detail balanced with the ability to see the organizational whole while having flexibility in approach. Requires a person skilled at communicating with management personnel and directors of the firm. Integrity, technical competence, openness to new approaches, ability to work with others, and willingness to operate with a small staff are paramount.

DUTIES

1. Recommend overall financial objectives, strategies, and policies of the firm consistent with approved purposes and objectives.
2. Recommend the organization plans and succession plans, both short- and long-range, for those elements of the organization under his or her direction.
3. Through continuing contact with departments, keep abreast of operating plans that affect financial projections including staffing, capital expenditures, and operating programs.
4. Ensure that all appropriate firmwide and departmental objectives, policies, and procedures are communicated and explained to all employees under his or her direction.
5. Advise senior management of impact of legislation and regulations on firm's affairs.
6. Maintain liaison with such governmental agencies as necessary in order to ensure compliance with local, state, and federal regulations.
7. Assure that accounting operations are effectively and efficiently performed.
8. Prepare periodic financial, analytical, and interpretive reports for management, and provide statistical and analytical services to project managers and department heads.
9. Assure that all legal requirements for proper record keeping are met, as well as all recording and reporting requirements for regulatory agencies as required by law.
10. Work closely with senior management in analyzing the firm's long- and short-term capital requirements.
11. Maintain adequate funds to meet current requirements and obligations, and consult with senior management in planning future requirements.
12. Recommend to senior management sources of funds, assist in the negotiation of loans as required, and follow up on the administration and repayment of loans as funds become available and as terms of agreements stipulate.
13. Develop investment program and manage firm's investments.
14. Maintain contact with banking executives and financial officers of other firms in order to exchange information of mutual value and interest.
15. Assure protection of assets through adequate internal controls and develop an insurance program providing protection against insurable risks.
16. Review and approve proposals before submission to clients.
17. Help departments formulate pricing policy and provide data for review and analysis.
18. Prescribe the basic terms and conditions to be used in contracts including but not limited to type of contract, payment terms, and rights granted or obtained.
19. Prepare or supervise preparation and filing of tax returns and oversee all tax matters.

*Mainly depending on salary offered.

Exhibit 13.1 Continued.

POSITION DESCRIPTION FOR A SMALL FIRM

TITLE

Business Manager (reporting to managing partner).

RESPONSIBILITIES

1. Keep books of account; prepare financial statements and project management reports.
2. Prepare budgets, analyze variances, and advise the managing partner so that corrective action can be taken.
3. Prepare workpapers and schedule auditors as needed to prepare audit and tax returns.
4. Supervise billing, collection, and disbursement of funds.
5. Manage the cash position of the firm and prepare cash reports and forecasts for the managing partner.
6. Review liability and employee insurance programs to ensure they are adequate.

CAPABILITIES

A bachelor's degree in business administration. A bachelor's degree in architecture or engineering with MBA highly desirable. Salary based upon experience.

DUTIES

1. Manage the support staff, including secretaries (except partners' secretaries), bookkeeper, librarian, receptionist, and mail room personnel.
2. Take charge of all purchasing activities and be responsible for adequate supplies.
3. Supervise all other office management functions, such as personnel records, insurance claims, central files, and company automobiles.

Exhibit 13.2 Note that this position description lists the other duties to be performed by the candidate in addition to financial duties.

---

staff and purchasing, this should be made clear at the time of hiring.

Salary surveys are available and should be consulted with establishing a salary range for this position. If the firm uses the services of an employment agency or executive recruiting firm, contacts there can often be of considerable help in determining the appropriate salary for the position. Since the position is generally on a level with other officers of the firm, the usual "perks" should be available to the financial manager in a larger firm. Exhibit 13.3 shows the profiles of typical financial/business managers.

The importance that management attributes to the position is a significant factor in determining the kind of person hired and his or her attitude after settling into the job. If it is made clear that this position has been created to help the firm achieve financial goals and improve management, then others in the firm will understand its purpose.

EXERCISE 13.3 ■

Job Requirements for a Financial Manager

1. What background should a financial manager have?

_____

_____

2. What level of experience is necessary?

_____

3. Name several ways in which you could determine the financial manager's salary:

_____

_____

_____

4. Write out the attributes you are looking for in a financial manager:

_____

_____

_____

_____

_____

_____

THREE TYPICAL PROFILES OF A FINANCIAL/BUSINESS MANAGER

1. ALAN BUTTERS

Background

Bachelor's degree in architecture plus masters in business administration. Began work in large (400-person) architectural firm in project management, but after a year transferred over into finance and administration. After four years, moved to a 150-person architectural/interior design firm as business manager handling all business and financial functions with the help of two bookkeepers and one accounting clerk. After six years was recently hired as vice president—finance of 300-person architect firm.

Responsibilities

In charge of all accounting for financial functions and manages a seven-person staff working out of two offices. Reports to president of the firm. His first assignment is to install a fully computerized accounting system in both offices that will take the place of the partially computerized system presently in use. The present system is rapidly becoming outdated and unable to handle the present volume of work.

1993 Salary

$75,000 plus approximately 15% bonus and profit sharing. Company automobile and the usual prerequisites of the other officers in the firm. Currently, owns a 2% stock interest in the firm and has been offered the opportunity to buy more stock.

SANDRA McMAHON

Background

Bachelor's degree in business administration plus Certified Public Accounting. After three years with a public accounting firm she was hired as controller by one of their clients, a freight forwarder. She stayed there one year but did not like the work. Subsequently she was hired by a 70-person consulting engineering firm and land surveyor, where she has been employed for the past three years.

Responsibilities

Her primary responsibilities have been to install a project budgeting system and to supervise a cost-reduction program as a result of a recent downturn in revenues. For economy reasons, the office manager who was in charge of the support staff was let go, and McMahon was put in charge. She now finds it necessary to spend extra hours at the office on weekends to keep up with the increased responsibilities.

1993 Salary

$58,000 plus company automobile. Because of economic circumstances no bonuses were paid last year and none are likely this year. Merit increases have tended to be small and company benefits are limited.

Exhibit 13.3 The wide range of salaries, responsibilities, and backgrounds is typical of the people who fill this position in design firms.

JIM STEVENS

Background

Graduated from a local two-year business college and immediately went to work for a five-person interior design firm as a bookkeeper and general office assistant. Stayed with the firm for 16 years as it grew into a 40-person organization. Stevens is highly skills in the bookkeeping function and thoroughly familiar with the firm.

Responsibilities

His responsibilities have been largely confined to the bookkeeping function while the managing principal handles the broader functions of finance. For example, Stevens had no background or experience in negotiating a bank line of credit that the firm needed. The managing principal had to handle the task himself. The principals are considering the possibility of hiring a manager in charge of finance and administration.

1993 Salary

$45,000 plus approximately 5% bonus. There are no additional benefits other than the usual ones available to all employees.

Exhibit 13.3 Continued.

13.4 COORDINATING WITH OTHER FINANCIAL PROFESSIONALS

The financial manager is the primary contact between the firm and its independent auditor, tax preparer, and management consultant. If the design firm employs an accounting firm to handle these functions, different members of the accounting firm will be involved. The audit and tax work will be handled by specialists in these fields, and if other management services are required, such as, for example, for the installation of a computerized accounting system, other specialists in the accounting firm will handle this task. The financial manager coordinates these activities and sees that they are accomplished on time and in accordance with management's wishes.

Sometimes a smaller design firm will employ the services of an individual accountant or member of a very small accounting firm. In this case one accountant cannot be expected to have expertise in all these areas. The accounting practitioner may handle the tax work and usually no audit is performed. The financial manager of the design firm may then have to look elsewhere for assistance with management services. Consultants who are specialists in the design profession may have to be retained, or the accounting practitioner may recommend assistance from another firm.

EXERCISE 13.4 ████████████████████

COORDINATION

1. How does the financial manager coordinate the various consultants/functions in your firm?

_____

_____

2. In the boxes below, fill in the liaison with other design professionals:

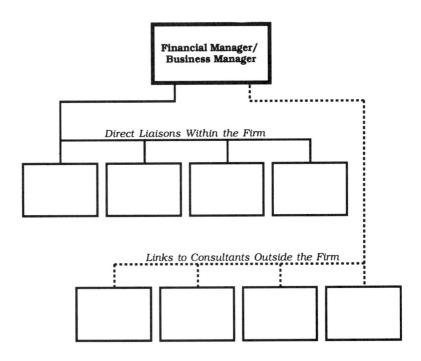

13.5 OVERALL RESPONSIBILITIES

The financial manager, by virtue of the position, fosters accountability throughout the organization. Someone at a high enough level is now studying the records and bringing to management's attention anything that looks out of the ordinary. Rather than just being a watchdog, the financial manager is a planner who should look to the future and help the firm achieve its objectives.

In many instances, funds must be raised for growth and maintenance of operations, and it is the financial manager who negotiates loans for additional working capital. When new assets are obtained, such as computer equipment, special purpose loans or leasing arrangements, the financial manager usually handles these transactions. He or she must also recognize when new equity must be raised and work with the principals to secure additional capital when necessary.

In short, the financial manager's responsibilities extend beyond the day-to-day activities of keeping up with accounting transactions. This person can exert a direct impact on the overall success of the firm.

EXERCISE 13.5

Discussion Problem

Background. You are the managing principal of a 15-person arcitectural firm that recently lost its business manager to a higher paying job. The business manager had been with the firm for ten years and was totally familiar with all its aspects. As a result, the accounting function practically "ran itself," and you had little involvement. You engaged your auditing firm to conduct a search for a suitable candidate, and after three months they have presented you with two candidates: Ed Stanley and Burt Waters. Stanley has ten years experience with a service firm (dry cleaning chain) and suitable education. He is bright and eager and has excellent references from his former employer. Waters had his own accounting/ bookkeeping firm for ten years. For the last five years his largest client was a consulting engineering firm. He also has suitable education and references.

Stanley's experience with a dry cleaning firm will not transfer easily to your firm. Weigh his ability to make changes as distinct from keeping a system operating. For example, did he install a new accounting system for his former employer?

Waters' experience with an engineering firm will allow him to understand your accounting system more easily. It would be interesting to know why he is giving up his accounting/

bookkeeping practice. If you could engage him to handle your work in his accounting/bookkeeping practice for a few months you could try out his services before making a commitment to hire him.

Assignment. List the kinds of questions you would ask each candidate to evaluate which one to hire. Then list advantages and disadvantages of each aspect of both backgrounds as presented.

Questions to ask each candidate:

_____

_____

_____

_____

_____

_____

Stanley		**Waters**	
Advantages	*Disadvantages*	*Advantages*	*Disadvantages*

FINAL EXAMINATION—CHAPTER 13

True or False

T   F   In a small firm, the business manager is too busy to take on extra assignments.

T   F   The financial manager is a "bean counter."

T   F   The financial manager helps the project manager by providing expense reports, detailed labor charges, and summary units.

T F   In a larger firm, the business manager need not have a business degree.

T F   The financial manager typically coordinates the work of auditors and tax preparers.

T F   The financial manager does not foster accountability in the firm.

Multiple Choice

1. The financial manager monitors performance of all aspects of the firm so as to be able to
   a. be alert to financial warning signals.
   b. warn others in management in time to take corrective action.
   c. both.

2. A smaller firm business manager typically
   a. performs other functions such as design work or administrative duties.
   b. may be an architect or engineer.
   c. does not oversee tax preparation.
   d. a and b.
   e. b and c.

3. The need for absolute accounting accuracy can be traded for
   a. project profits.
   b. approximate, quickly prepared project information.
   c. budget analyses.

4. Salary information for financial managers can be determined by:
   a. a best guess.
   b. a salary survey.
   c. an employment agency.
   d. a and c.
   e. b and c.

5. The financial manager oversees the work of
   a. administrative people.
   b. accountant.
   c. tax preparer.
   d. b and c only.
   e. a, b, and c.

6. The financial manager is
   a. a negotiator.
   b. a planner who looks to the future to help the firm achieve its objectives.
   c. a fundraiser for growth and maintenance operations.
   d. all of the above.

INDEX